Vladimir Sorokin's Discourses

A Companion

Companions to Russian Literature

Series Editor
THOMAS SEIFRID (University of Southern California, Los Angeles)

Vladimir Sorokin's Discourses

A Companion

Dirk Uffelmann

Boston
2020

Library of Congress Cataloging-in-Publication Data

Names: Uffelmann, Dirk, author.

Title: Vladimir Sorokin's discourses: a companion / Dirk Uffelmann.

Other titles: Companions to Russian literature.

Description: Boston: Academic Studies Press, 2020. | Series: Companions to Russian literature | Includes bibliographical references and index.

Identifiers: LCCN 2019050253 (print) | LCCN 2019050254 (ebook) | ISBN 9781644692844 (hardback) | ISBN 9781644692851 (paperback) | ISBN 9781644692868 (adobe pdf)

Subjects: LCSH: Sorokin, Vladimir, 1955—Criticism and interpretation. | Sorokin, Vladimir, 1955—Aesthetics. | Russian prose literature—20th century—History and criticism. | Russian prose literature—21st century—History and criticism.

Classification: LCC PG3488.O66 Z94 2020 (print) | LCC PG3488.O66 (ebook) | DDC 891.73/5—dc23

LC record available at https://lccn.loc.gov/2019050253
LC ebook record available at https://lccn.loc.gov/2019050254

Copyright © Academic Studies Press, 2020
ISBN 9781644692844 (hardcover)
ISBN 9781644692851 (paperback)
ISBN9781644692868 (electronic, Adobe PDF)

Academic Studies Press
1577 Beacon Street
Brookline, MA 02446, USA
press@academicstudiespress.com
www.academicstudiespress.com

Book design by Kryon Publishing Services, Inc.
kryonpublishing.com
Cover artwork by Vladimir Sorokin, reproduced by the author's permission.

Table of Contents

Acknowledgments

The idea for this book came from Thomas Seifrid, who invited me to contribute this volume to his series of *Companions to Russian Literature* and gave supportive advice on improving the manuscript. Stehn Aztlan Mortensen read the entire draft and greatly contributed to polishing my arguments. The anonymous reviewer provided further useful hints to improve my manuscript. I also owe many helpful suggestions to my indefatigable native editor Melissa Favara. Monika Hilbert and Valentina Fëdorova diligently cross-checked the quotes, the hyperlinks, and the bibliographical information and compiled the word list for the index. Roy Chan nicely lent his double competence in both Russian and Mandarin to correct the Romanization of Sorokin's occasional Cyrillic transcription of Chinese.

Special thanks go to Vladimir Sorokin, who proposed his painting "Tolstoi and Potato" ["Tolstoi i kartofel'"] as a cover illustration for both the multidiscursive thread of the book and its parallel reading of Sorokin and Tolstoi (esp. chapter Eleven), making this book about Sorokin, the writer, to a certain degree also a book by Sorokin, the painter.

I dedicate *Vladimir Sorokin's Discourses: A Companion* to my revered academic teacher Igor´ Pavlovich Smirnov, who first brought me into contact with Sorokin's—then still unpublished—works in the form of typewritten manuscripts. Without his inspiration and selfless support for my first independent academic steps I would never have evolved to the point of writing this book.

A Note on Transliteration, Translation, and Referencing

*V*ladimir Sorokin's Discourses: A Companion consistently uses the Library of Congress transliteration style for Russian and other languages with Cyrillic alphabets (Dostoevskii, not Dostoevsky; El´tsin, not Yeltsin); the only exception is spellings of names in quotes and book titles, which are given according to the original source. Where published translations from Russian or other languages are available, they are quoted, but accompanied with a reference to the original (for example, when quoting Sorokin's *The Queue* [*Ochered'*]: Eng. Sorokin 1988a; Russ. 1986b). Unless otherwise noted or implied in a reference to an English-language publication, all translations are my own.

Because of Sorokin's heightened sensitivity to diverse registers of language, quotes from his fictional texts, but also from his journalistic essays and his interviews, are provided in both English translation and the Russian original to help readers who want to base their own writing about Sorokin on this Companion. Sorokin scholarship from all accessible Slavic, Germanic, and Romance languages is quoted, except for crucial terms, in English translation only.

The references in brackets in the main text follow the name-year scheme, referring to the four-part bibliography at the end of the book, which starts with English publications of Sorokin's works, followed by the Russian originals, selected translations into other languages, and research and other literature. Where there is more than one publication by Sorokin or scholars per year, the entries are distinguished by adding letters to the years (for example, Sorokin 2004a, 2004b, and so on). The multilingual research bibliography, the most comprehensive in Sorokin scholarship so far, includes English translations in order to facilitate further research. Fostering further investigations is also the purpose for which the existing scholarship on Sorokin, which has been drastically increasing since 2000, is amply referenced in this Companion's interpretations of example texts, allowing to situate them in the general tendencies that prevail in the study and canonization of Sorokin.

Chapters Three and Ten of this Companion include parts of an earlier article devoted to *The Norm* and *Day of the Oprichnik* (Uffelmann 2009). Chapter Nine contains a few paragraphs reworked from my paper on periodization of Sorokin's works (Uffelmann 2006), while chapter Twelve comprises ideas from an article on *Telluria* and Eurasianism (Uffelmann 2017). Chapter Eight uses fragments of a conference-volume contribution on *Blue Lard* (Uffelmann 2013b), while chapters Four and Eleven draw on German-language investigations of *Marina's Thirtieth Love* (Uffelmann 2003) and *The Blizzard* (Uffelmann 2012a).

DISCLAIMER

Vladimir Sorokin's works are (in)famous for plots containing violence, sex, and the consumption of disgusting materials. Although it would be a misunderstanding to take these scenes at face value—they should rather be interpreted as materializations of metaphors from Russian vulgar language (see chapter Three), laying bare the hidden violence in political or cultural practices (see chapter Five)—a researcher writing a *Companion to Sorokin* is left with no choice but to quote both Sorokin's reimaginations of political and cultural violence and indecency as well as the metaphors from Russian vulgar language that he materializes in his plots. There is, therefore, likely no way for the unprepared reader to avoid being momentarily taken aback by this linguistic register, but the interpreter refuses any responsibility for this side-effect of his analytical task.

CHAPTER 1

Introduction: Late Soviet Culture and Moscow's Artistic Underground

When the Soviet dictator Iosif Stalin died on March 5, 1953, tens of thousands of Soviet citizens cried in a fit of mass hysteria and lined up to see his coffin (cf. Sorokin 2008a, 258). This paradoxical reaction, however, subsequently gave way to a feeling of relief caused by the softening of terror and repression (Clark 2000, 210–1). Under Stalin's successors, the Stalinist total-itarian mobilization, which compelled every single citizen to eagerly follow ubiquitous ideological prescriptions (Firsov 2008, 46), was eased into authori-tarian rule, which aimed mainly at the regime's self-preservation while conced-ing a considerable "privatization of Soviet society" (Shlapentokh 1989, 153). Whereas in the 1960s and 70s the ideology of Marxism-Leninism remained unquestionable, it sufficed if the citizens routinely performed the political rituals inherited from the Stalinist mobilized society (such as May parades) and reproduced standardized speech acts (like self-criticism at a work-brigade meeting) in public (Yurchak 2006, 25).

In the Thaw period (1953–1964) and the stagnation (1964–1982) that followed, those who—unlike a tiny group of political dissidents—did not publicly protest against the Soviet order but displayed a "civil inattention" to politics, could expect to be left alone by the state (Klepikova 2018, 42) in the private sphere that they carved out (cf. Boym 1994, 94). While public expres-sion of "dissident thinking" [*inakomyslie*] remained punishable, non-public "deviant thinking" [*raznomyslie*] was now tolerated (Firsov 2008). This implied the concession of semi-private settings—kitchen talks, apartment exhibitions (see Glanc 2017, 239–40), self-organized excursions "out of the city," infor-mal cafés—to which the population's relative freedom of expression was con-fined (Ritter 2008, 142–54). The colloquial word "get-together" [*tusovka*] described the various social practices of seclusion of an "informal public" (Zdravomyslova, Voronkov 2002, 57) and a "semi-private" sphere partly cut off from ideological officialdom. One such secluded semi-private site was the studio of painter and installation artist Il'ia Kabakov (cf. Jackson 2010, 108, 178). The second youngest among the performance artists, poets, and prose writers who gathered there was Vladimir Georgievich Sorokin.

Vladimir Sorokin was born in Bykovo, a small town close to the Soviet capital city of Moscow, into a family of intelligentsia on August 7, 1955; his father, Georgii Sorokin, was a professor of metallurgy. The parents supported the musical, literary, and visual-art interests of their son Volodia, who was taking painting courses at the Pushkin Museum (see Orens 2007, 703). His various artistic interests, including theatrical imitation, for example of the Secretary General of the Communist Party, Leonid Brezhnev, helped him to cope with his stuttering (Sorokin, V.B. 2004). Literature especially served for him as a "shield" ["щит"] behind which he could hide. Tellingly, his first attempt at writing at the age of thirteen was also camouflaged as a translation from English and not presented as his own achievement (Sorokin, Genis, Vail' 1992, 139).

Information about the future writer's early years until roughly 1985 (see 24smi 2017) is scarce because the early (Soviet-time) Sorokin made a sharp distinction between his semi-public appearance as a writer and his private life. His writings were utterly un-autobiographical, or, as later described by critics, of an "impersonal" type (Skoropanova 2002, 211). When biographers expressed interest in the beginnings of his artistic impulses, he appeared rather amused by these psycho-biographical interpretations (see Chitnis 2005, 123) as illustrated in his contribution to an Austrian-German academic volume on *Psychopoetics* [*Psychopoetik*] (Hansen-Löve 1992), in which Sorokin playfully reduces the complex factors leading up to his artistic activity to a little incident in the family's flat: as a child he fell from a heater, landing with his neck on the heater's dowel (Sorokin 1992b, 566). Biographers who take this and other elements of Sorokin's distanced psychoanalytical auto-fiction (see Sorokin, Shapoval 1998, 18; cf. Stelleman 2016, 520), such as stammering because of a castration threat (Sorokin 1992b, 568; Sorokin, Laird 1999, 156), for biographical truth (Weststeijn 1995, 39; Kustanovich 2004, 302–3; Kasper 2007, 472) underestimate Sorokin's interest in standardized narrative scripts at the expense of any "unique biography" (Alaniz 2013, 214–5; cf. Sasse 2003, 222–3).

More convincing are Sorokin's descriptions of his early confrontations with violence in Soviet society: in a 1995 interview with Serafima Roll, Sorokin recalled witnessing violence in Crimea during his childhood

(Eng. Sorokin, Roll 1998, 79–80; Russ. 1996, 124), which the biographer Konstantin Kustanovich (2004, 303) again readily linked with the fictional rape of a ten-year-old girl by her father in Sorokin's novel *Marina's Thirtieth Love* [*Tridtsataia liubov' Mariny*].

Having attended various schools in the Moscow region, Sorokin graduated from the Gubkin Russian State University of Oil and Gas [then *Moskovskii institut neftianoi i gazovoi promyshlennosti imeni Gubkina*] as a mechanical engineer in 1977. During his studies he had a first inauspicious publication in the company magazine *For the Workers in the Petroleum Industry* [*Za kadry neftianikov*]. Sorokin also began designing amateur book illustrations. Both activities point to the fact that his decision to attend the Gubkin Institute was motivated rather by the intention to avoid serving in the Soviet Army than by a proper interest in engineering (24smi 2017). If we are to believe this to be his primary motivation, it is perhaps not so surprising that he decided to work in the broader context of literature after his graduation. He started out as an editor for the magazine *Shift* [*Smena*], from which he was fired for his non-membership in the Soviet youth organization *Komsomol*. Due to this moderate anti-Soviet attitude he found himself designing and illustrating books in the 1970s and 80s to make a living. For some time Sorokin continued with his own painting (with small exhibitions in Moscow in the late 1980s), but then gave that up in order to reembark on his literary journey (Sorokin, Shapoval 1998, 7) at the age of twenty-three or twenty-four (Sorokin, Khvors 2008; Sorokin, Tetzlaff 2009); he returned to painting only in November 2014 and showed that work when he participated in the 2015 Venice Biennale and held an exhibition in Berlin and Tallinn.

Sorokin appeared in Moscow's conceptualist circle in the mid-1970s (cf. Sorokin, Ahrest-Korotkova 2010) as a very cultured, good-looking, yet reluctant young man, accompanied by his pretty wife Irina, a teacher of music, whom he married in the year of his graduation in 1977. The charming family picture was complete when Irina gave birth to their twin daughters Anna and Mariia in 1980. Fellow conceptualists such as Iosif Bakshtein and Pavel Peppershtein later recalled the amazement caused by the fact that this reserved young man made his entrance in the circle with unprecedentedly brutal violations of the still officially binding Soviet aesthetic norms (Danilkin 2002).

After the First Congress of Soviet writers from 1934, officially published literature had to adhere to the imperatives of Socialist Realism, a newly forged doctrine which coordinated all the previous divergent aesthetics—from avant-garde to post-symbolism—and literary groups into one binding paradigm rigorously controlled by various Soviet state institutions for censoring, editing, publishing, promoting, and teaching literature. Socialist Realism with its normative postulates—partiality, reflection, typicity, revolutionary romanticism, positive heroes, and folksiness (Günther 1984, 18–54), all together amounting to the imaginative production of a Socialist order and moral code as it *should* be (Eng. Siniavskii 1960, 76; Russ. Siniavskii 1967, 434; cf. Dobrenko 2011, 108–12)—turned into a ritual for dissimulating the actual deficits of Soviet society. Socialist-Realist novels performed the pedagogical phantasma of disciplining an insubordinate young individual into a self-sacrificing member of the collective under the guidance of an older mentor (see Clark 2000, 167–9). Confronting the positive young hero(es) with negative representatives of the old order, it created a dichotomy of pro- and anti-Soviet activities. In its rigid moralistic normativity, however, Socialist Realism only served to perpetuate an older tradition that posited Russian writers as a source of moral authority.

The enforced unification of Soviet literature reached its apex in the years before Stalin's death, the detrimental Zhdanov era (1948–1953; see Clark 2000, 191–4). The liberalization thereafter, culminating in Nikita Khrushchev's 1956 speech in which Stalin's successor reduced all the terrorizing features of Stalinism to Stalin's own "cult of personality" [*kul´t lichnosti*], also issued a critique of what came to be known as the varnishing of reality [*lakirovka*] in Socialist Realism (cf. Günther 1984, 34–6). Khrushchev went as far as personally supporting the publication of Aleksandr Solzhenitsyn's story about the hitherto tabooed Soviet work camps *One Day in the Life of Ivan Denisovich* [*Odin den´ Ivana Denisovicha*] in the November issue of the thick journal *Novyi mir* in 1962.

Having been himself socialized into the Stalinist bureaucracy with its traditionalist (realist and moralistic) aesthetics, however, Khrushchev reacted with anger to an exhibition of avant-garde paintings in the Manezh in the center of Moscow on December 1 of the same year. The public appearance of the avant-garde remained banned. After Khrushchev was toppled from his post of Secretary General in 1964, Socialist Realism was reinstalled as an aesthetic norm with the political goal of bridging the blatant gap between the revolutionary ideals of communism and the reality of state socialism. Brezhnev shared Khrushchev's lack of understanding for avant-garde art. In 1974 the devastation of the so-called Bulldozer exhibition caused fear among unofficial artists (cf. Jackson 2010, 54) and forced one of the organizers, Oskar Rabin, into emigration. In 1978 the editors of an uncensored almanac of avant-garde literature, *Metropol* [*Metropol´*], were prosecuted.

The hostile aesthetic climate of the late Soviet Union accelerated the retreat of non-conformist artists into the periphery, either on a permanent basis as with Rabin's Lianozovo group based in wooden barracks roughly 100 kilometers from the city center of Moscow, or on particular occasions, as in the case of the performance group *Collective Actions* [*Kollektivnye deistviia*] around Andrei Monastyrskii, who from 1976 on organized excursions "out of town" [*za gorod*] to conduct their performances.

The forced marginalization of unofficial art contributed to the group consciousness of the Moscow Conceptualists as well (Tupitsyn 1998, 50). For their unofficial art, there was no alternative to conspiracy and going underground. The semi-private spaces of retreat used by the Moscow Conceptual Group were not as marginal as those of the Lianozovo-group, however. In contrast to their predecessors, the conceptualists regularly met in the members' flats in downtown Moscow, which were usually very small, so people were seated very close to each other. This produced a cozy atmosphere, as fondly reflected upon by Kabakov, for example, in his *Kitchen Series* [*Kukhonnaia seriia*] (1982). With the relocation to studios at Festival'naia Street in 1975 the regular gatherings transformed into a form of constant living and working together. The artists appropriated the communal way of living that led Viktor Tupitsyn to the formulation of "'contractual' communality" (Tupitsyn 1998, 54).

The communal reality of the underground allowed its members to concentrate their intellectual and emotional energy within a narrow sphere. Comparable to literary cafés such as *Derzanie* or *Saigon* (Zdravomyslova 2003) that popped up in the 1960s and 70s, this circle functioned as one of the varieties of "internal emigration" that constituted late Soviet everyday life (Yurchak 2006, 132). It was not a dissident circle that aimed at reaching out to a broader public with anti-Soviet political ideas, but an a-political community of people interested in "private art" (see Degot' 1991, 17; Eşanu 2013, 58–60). The artistic underground was one of the milieus which "created a kind of 'deterritorialized' reality that did not fit the binary categories of either support or opposition to the state" (Yurchak 2006, 34). This third space beyond the markers of pro- and anti-Soviet was their way of "being inside and outside at the same time," as Alexei Yurchak pointed out in his seminal monograph from 2006 about the last Soviet generation (Yurchak 2006, 132).

The group that gathered in the Festival'naia studios and in private apartments on a regular basis consisted of painters such as Erik Bulatov (b. 1933), Viktor Pivovarov (b. 1937), and Il'ia Kabakov (b. 1933), performance artists-cum-writers such as Dmitrii Aleksandrovich Prigov (1940–2007) and Andrei Monastyrskii (b. 1949), theoreticians such as Boris Groys (b. 1947), and writers such as Lev Rubinshtein (b. 1947), Vladimir Sorokin (b. 1955), and Pivovarov's son Pavel Peppershtein (b. 1966). Rather than distinguishing among themselves as belonging to this or that generation, which was uncommon in the Moscow Conceptualist circle (Sorokin, Shapoval 1998, 7–8), they differentiated a core group from the closer associations with affiliated members not concerned with conceptual art themselves, such as the philosopher Mikhail Ryklin (b. 1948; see Groys 1997, 413), about forty people in all (Sorokin, Shapoval 1998, 14). Yet, all were perceived as part of "one's own circle" [*svoi krug*]. The group displayed strong intellectual intimacy with their own internal mechanisms of self-canonization and a recognizable (pseudo-)terminology (Kabakov, in: Groys, Kabakov 1993, 26; cf. Barabanov 2011, 66–9) as collected in their "glossary" by Andrei Monastyrskii (1999, abridged English translation in Eşanu 2013, 295–327), which betrays an undeniable fun factor; for example, Monastyrskii lists Sorokin as co-author of the concept "Rotten Pinocchios" [*Gnilye Buratino*] (Monastyrskii 1999, 35).

When the members of the Moscow conceptualist circle were not communicating exclusively among themselves in closed and—in the case of literature—oral presentations in kitchens and studios (Glanc 2017, 242), limiting themselves to producing texts "for the drawer," they turned to unofficial means of publication, called self-publishing [*samizdat*]. Samizdat mostly relied on a typewriter, on which one could type a text, producing several copies at once with the help of carbon paper, or a mimeograph (Glanc 2017, 242–4). The idea was that no censor would ever come across something that was produced this way, giving rise to an alternative, uncensored [*nepodtsenzurnaia*] Soviet literature.

Hand-typed uncensored manuscripts were exactly the form in which fellow conceptualists would first read Sorokin's short stories. On rarer occasions his texts made it into samizdat journals abroad as was the case with the short stories "The Tobacco Pouch" ["Kiset"], "The Road Accident" ["Dorozhnoe proisshestvie"], and "The Ditch" ["Zemlianka"], published in Prague in *Mitin zhurnal* (Sorokin 1986b; 1986c; 1987a; 1987b). A year earlier six stories appeared in the so-called *tamizdat* (publication "there," that is, in the West), in the Paris-based "unofficial Russian art revue" *A–Ya* (Sorokin 1985a). The biggest achievement in terms of gaining recognition was the publication of Sorokin's first book, *The Queue* [*Ochered'*], released by the émigré publishing house Sintaksis in Paris in 1985 (Sorokin 1985b). For his *tamizdat* publications Sorokin was questioned by the Soviet Intelligence Service, the KGB, but due to the organization's declining professionalism this experience of personal repression proved not too traumatic (Sorokin, Shapoval 1998, 8). Given the continuous threat of the KGB confiscating manuscripts and samizdat editions, underground writers would seek out a "fridge" [*kholodil'nik*], a person who would save their manuscripts while remaining either unsuspected of collaborating with underground artists, or otherwise out of the reach of the KGB. In the case of Sorokin the émigré scholar Igor´ P. Smirnov's flats in Munich fulfilled this function. I personally vividly recall my first contact with Sorokin's texts at the University of Konstanz in 1993 via photocopies of typewritten manuscripts of Sorokin's early works stemming from the "Smirnov fridge."

This illustrates the fact that the group of Moscow Conceptualists was surrounded by émigré scholars such as Igor´ Smirnov and Mikhail Epstein (Atlanta, GA), Western Slavists (Sabine Hänsgen, Georg Witte), and a few interested Western diplomats. These were also the target audience of *ёps* or Erofeev-Prigov-Sorokin, a trio which started in Viktor Erofeev's (b. 1947) private apartment in 1982 (Erofeev, Prigov, Sorokin 2002, 9) and continued with the three reading their texts to hand-picked listeners in other informal public locations. The troika stylized itself as the "first circle of the underground" ["первый круг подполья"] (Erofeev, Prigov, Sorokin 2002, 10), and was hence founded on a kind of initiation for interested outsiders. Their reading performances were subsequently extended and outsiders like American diplomats and KGB officers managed to mix with the audience. Given the way in which Erofeev, in his introduction to the anthology *ёps* (the acronym made from the initials of the three second names sounds vulgar to the Russian ear) of 2002 exhibits his pride in the fact that the group seemed to draw in female students (Erofeev, Prigov, Sorokin 2002, 20–2), the gradual opening-up of the group for an urban, intellectual, alternative public was clearly intentional.

Even if within the Moscow Conceptualist group a distinction on the basis of age or even generations was uncommon, the artistic practice and underlying understanding of conceptualism underwent a clear development. The group understood itself as treading in the footsteps of international artists linked to Western Concept Art like the Fluxus group (Kabakov, in: Groys, Kabakov 1993, 26) or Joseph Kossuth, whom Sorokin indirectly quoted in 1992: "in conceptualism not the object is relevant, but the relationship to the object. Conceptualism is a distanced relationship both toward the work of art, and to culture in general" ["в концептуализме актуальна не вещь, а отношение к этой вещи. Концептуализм—это дистанционное отношение и к произведению, и к культуре в целом"] (Sorokin, Rasskazova 1992, 120). In what appears as the manifesto of "Moscow Romantic Conceptualism" ["Moskovskii romanticheskii kontseptualizm"], published bilingually in *A–Ya* in 1979, the group's theoretician, Boris Groys, also drew on American Concept Art (Groys 1979, 4), but strove for a distinction by adding the epithet "Romantic" which was skipped later (Groys 2010, 4–8; Smith 2012, 62). Against the backdrop of this half-exclusion and half-inclusion of the Russian variety into the international context (Hillings 2011, 264) Groys defines conceptualism as a meta-reflection on the conditions under and the way in which art is produced and received:

> [...] it may be interpreted more broadly, by referring to any attempt to withdraw from considering art works as material objects intended for contemplation and aesthetic evaluation. Instead, it should incourage [sic] solicitation and formation of the conditions that determine the viewer's perception of the work of art, the process of its inception by the artist, its relation to factors in the environment, and its temporal status. (Eng. and Russ. Groys 1979, 3, trans. Keith Hammond)

Groys's first Russian example is Lev Rubinshtein's file cards. Lev Rubinshtein took the genre inspiration from his work as a librarian: over many years he wrote his series on file cards, reflecting the way bureaucratic texts are built and drawing attention to the external conditions of text production rather than to their content. A significant example is Rubinshtein's *The Next Program* [*Ocherednaia programma*] (1975):

Number one	Номер первый,
which speaks for itself;	говорящий сам за себя;
Number two	Номер второй,
which outlines the basic terms;	намечающий основные понятия;
Number three	Номер третий,
which continues outlining the	продолжающий намечать
basic terms;	основные понятия;
Number four	Номер четвертый,
which continues outlining the	продолжающий намечать
basic terms;	основные понятия;
Number five	Номер пятый,

where the outlining of the basic terms is continued;	где продолжают намечаться основные понятия;
Number six	Номер шестой,
which finally starts using some of the basic terms;	уже оперирующий некоторыми из основных понятий;
Number seven	Номер седьмой,
marked by the sudden recognition bias [...]	отмеченный внезапный[м] эффектом узнавания [...]
(trans. Valentina Fëdorova, unpublished)	(Rubinshtein 1995, 7)

Devoid of any local Russian, let alone Soviet ideological context, Rubinshtein's series reflects on the way in which a text is construed. This kind of literature acquires literariness from its reflection on textuality.

Having come initially more from visual art than from literature, Sorokin saw himself as influenced by the painter Erik Bulatov (Glanc 1995, 9; Orens 2007, 702–3). In Bulatov we find a semiotic reflection on language as a means of constructing meaning. His painting "Seva's Blueness" ["Sevina sineva"] (reproduced in Tamruchi 1995, 41) from 1979 arranges the Cyrillic letters for "blueness" and the similar sounding possessive adjective "Seva's," in two opposed cones (one bottom-up in dark blue, one top-down in white) against the backdrop of a blue sky with white clouds. Like René Magritte's painted pipe which is declared not to be a pipe at all (1929), Bulatov's painting problematizes the interrelation between words and pictures representing something beyond themselves, in Bulatov's case the color blue and a clouded sky covered partially not only by clouds, but also by the letters in the foreground. Like with Rubinshtein's postcards, apart from the Cyrillic letters, nothing points to any Russian, let alone Soviet contexts, but to the sky seen from any point on the earth and the relationship of signifiers and signified in general.

In other works, where Bulatov deals with Soviet slogans, he questions the Soviet order without confronting it in a dissident, anti-Soviet way. This is less the case with the abstract, meta-semiotic conceptualism as illustrated above, and more evident in the second-variety approach, which explores less the conditions of art and reception in general, but rather particular modes of cultural production such as Socialist Realism. I propose to call the latter the "intertextual" and "sots-art" tendency in Moscow Conceptualism.

The history of the "intertextual" period of Moscow Conceptualism begins in the early 1970s with a kind of "social turn" that Kabakov locates in Bulatov's work of 1972 (Kabakov 1999, 79), thus ending his own early ("metaphysical," "abstract") strivings for "whiteness" and "emptiness" (cf. Kabakov 1999, 72; Eşanu 2013, 74–7). An example from the trend born out of the "social turn" is Erik Bulatov's *Unanimous* [*Edinoglasno*] (1987; reproduced in Kholmogorova 1994, 36), a canvas painting in the traditional style of Socialist Realism, depicting the members of the Supreme Soviet whose only role in the fictitious Soviet democracy was to applaud—unanimously—the decisions of the inner circle of power, the Central Committee. Although this political reference seems to have a polemical vector, Bulatov's work lacks any overt mockery, and the device of faithfully emulating the style of realist canvas painting and Soviet slogans becomes obvious. It is only the exaggerated combination of both genres which subverts the apparent affirmation of the dominating ideology and the compulsory style of its representation.

The same strange combination of affirmation and exaggerated obedience is evident in Dmitrii Aleksandrovich Prigov's famous poem "When here stands watch Miliciaman" ["Kogda zdes´ na postu stoit Militsaner…"] (1978).

When here stands watch Miliciaman	Когда здесь на посту стоит Милицанер
He can see far and wide to Vnukovo	Ему до Внуково простор весь открывается
To West and East looks Miliciaman	На Запад и Восток глядит Милицанер
And emptiness opens beyond them	И пустота за ними открывается
The center where Miliciaman stands—	И центр, где стоит Милицанер —
The view of him opens from anywhere	Взгляд на него отовсюду открывается
From anywhere one can see Militiaman	Отовсюду виден Милиционер
From East one can see Militiaman	С Востока виден Милиционер
From South one can see Militiaman	И с Юга виден Милиционер
From sea one can see Militiaman	И с моря виден Милиционер
From sky one can see Militiaman	И с неба виден Милиционер
From underground…	И с-под земли...
Nor does he keep out of sight	Да он и не скрывается
(trans. Valentina Fëdorova, unpublished)	(Prigov 2003, 43)

This text addresses the totalitarian project of total control over the society, alluding to the heroic Soviet myth of the Cheka, the political police. Despite the rhetoric of repetition and the centering of the whole world around one policeman (in the Soviet context: a militiaman), this poem would be misunderstood if read as mockery pure and simple. As an aesthetic category, the Soviet myth of the *militsaner*— exactly in vulgarized pronunciation as reproduced in Prigov's orthography— continues to function as a legend which is re-performed in the poem.

The vector of potential political criticism is even less pronounced in Kabakov's albums and paintings reflecting the reality of Soviet housing departments. These administrative units served as transmitters of social control and fulfilled an additional function as a field for the dilettantish artistic activity of the inhabitants. An illustrative example is a meticulously handwritten plan for emptying the dust bin in a communal flat, *Schedule for Emptying the Wastebin* [*Raspisanie vynosa pomoinogo vedra*] (1980, reproduced in Tamruchi 1995, 7), which was prepared with naïve care (in Kabakov's meta-naïve reproduction).

Something similar can be said about Vladimir Sorokin's first "mature" short story (cf. Sokolov 2005, 137), "The Swim" ["Zaplyv"], which was received with reservation by other Soviet prose writers, but highly appreciated by his fellow conceptualists (Uznayvse 2018) and served as a kind of calling card for his entry into the circle (Sorokin, Ahrest-Korotkova 2010). It was reworked between 1979 and 1988 (Sorokin 2008c, 23; cf. Zolotonosov 2008), before being included in the novel *Blue Lard* [*Goluboe salo*] in 1991 (Sorokin 1999, 137–44), the collection *Morning of a Sniper* [*Utro snaipera*] in 2002 (Sorokin 2002c, 7–16), and the eponymous 2008 collection *The Swim* [*Zaplyv*] (Sorokin 2008c, 13–23). Brian James Baer included his English translation in his anthology of Russian short stories from 2017 (Sorokin 2017a). The story is situated on the border between visual art and literature. It reminds the reader of early silent film in which textual information is given in the form of letters—especially monumental films from the totalitarian periods of Soviet and German history.

"The Swim" is about a brigade of military swimmers who, while holding torches in their right hands, form quotations, performing a ritualistic genre called "motivational swims" [*agitatsionnye zaplyvy*] (Eng. Sorokin 2017a, 180, trans. Brian James Baer; Russ. Sorokin 2002c, 8). The protagonist Ivan is part of quote number 26, which goes as follows:

ONE OF THE MOST IMPORTANT ISSUES IN MODERN SPECIAL
PURPOSE BOROUGH CONSTRUCTION WAS, IS AND WILL BE
THE ISSUE OF THE TIMELY INTENSIFICATION OF CONTRAST.

ОДНИМ ИЗ ВАЖНЕЙШИХ ВОПРОСОВ СОВРЕМЕННОГО ЦЕЛЕВОГО СТРОИТЕЛЬСТВА БОРО ЯВЛЯЛСЯ, ЯВЛЯЕТСЯ И БУДЕТ ЯВЛЯТЬСЯ ВОПРОС СВОЕВРЕМЕННОГО УСИЛЕНИЯ КОНТРАСТА. (Eng. Sorokin 2017a, 180; Russ. Sorokin 2002c, 8)

This is clearly an ideological slogan, referring to communist slogans on posters during parades, but with the enigmatic central signifier "BOROUGH" ["БОРО"] instead of "communism." Ivan's inner monologue first reflects the pride of the swimmer who does not question the ideological content, but feels privileged by his task of performing the comma between "WAS" and "IS" and by having been awarded the "State Swimming Medal" ["медаль «Государственный пловец»"] (Eng. Sorokin 2017a, 182; Russ. Sorokin 2002c, 9). Ivan does not complain about the military discipline imposed on the swimmers, but silently performs his part in the squadron:

> Ivan knew exactly where his place was—six meters from the left-most head; and he was swimming at a calm, measured pace, controlling his breath. He mustn't stray either to the left or to the right [...]

> Иван точно знал своё место – шесть метров от левой крайней головы [—]и плыл со спокойной размеренностью, сдерживая дыхание. Нельзя отклоняться ни влево, ни вправо [...] (Eng. Sorokin 2017a, 184; Russ. Sorokin 2002c, 10)

However, holding up his torch for five hours for the 1018th time (Eng. Sorokin 2017a, 188; Russ. Sorokin 2002c, 11–2), all the while only with his right hand, has physiological repercussions. Ivan's right arm becomes deformed, twice as heavily muscled as the left arm, and each of the 1018 times brings a continuous tremor, increasing pain, and eventually temporary paralysis of the entire arm. The mass ovations from the bridges above help him suppress the pain, and when he squeezes the torch, it eases the pain for a second. During his 1018th swim, however, this causes the petroleum to trickle down on him, and he dies, burning to death. The ovations from above do not stop with the disappearance of Ivan (the comma) but increase when whole letters formed by other swimmers, who obviously also burn to death, disappear, leaving only semi-vulgar parts of words such as "ETSIA" ["ЕТСЯ"] (Eng. Sorokin 2017a, 194; Russ. Sorokin 2002c, 15).

The self-sacrifice of the parade swimmers for the sake of perform-ing (enigmatic) ideological messages is ignored or even welcomed by the cheering masses. The individual's fate drowns in the mass spectacle, which might be read as an empathic statement about the alienation of man in socialism or in modernity more generally (Dreyer 2011, 199–200). The story ends with a pun that can be interpreted in this direction: when the second half of the ideological message number 26 disappears and the comma (Ivan) drowns, a new meaning emerges—the erasure of the individual:

ONE OF THE MOST IMPORTANT ISSUES OF MODERN BOR-OUGH CONSTRUCTION WAS [I].

ОДНИМ ИЗ ВАЖНЕЙШИХ ВОПРОСОВ СОВРЕМЕННОГО ЦЕЛЕВОГО СТРОИТЕЛЬСТВА БОРО ЯВЛЯЛСЯ Я. (Eng. Sorokin 2017a, 194; Russ. Sorokin 2002c, 16)

As the "The Swim" illustrates, in the second, "intertextual" tendency in Moscow Conceptualism conceptual reflection on the conditions of art in general is only one aspect among many—and for this second tendency, not the most characteristic one. Insofar as this book is concerned with Vladimir Sorokin, who entered the scene of Moscow Conceptualism in the mid-1970s, the intertextual play with and stylization of entire discourses such as classical Russian literature or Soviet Sots-Realism are of greater relevance here. Lev Danilkin and Peter Deutschmann call this "meta-discursivity" [*metadiskurs*; Metadiskursivität] (Danilkin 1996; Deutschmann 1998), pointing to the fact that Moscow Conceptualist art refers rather to collective stereotypes than to one single, identifiable intertext. In Mikhail Epstein's words from his 1995 pioneering monograph *After the Future: The Paradoxes of Postmodernism and Contemporary Russian Culture*:

> The structures and stereotypes that are singled out do not belong to any one concrete consciousness, but rather to consciousness in general—the author's as much as the character's. For this reason conceptualist works cannot be placed in the category of humorous or ironic pieces, in which the author maintains a certain distance between himself (or, which is the same thing, the realm of the ideal) and the reality that he is mocking. (Epstein 1995, 33, trans. Anesa Miller-Pogacar)

In most cases, the main background and intertext for Moscow Conceptualism of the 1970s and early 80s is Socialist Realism, as Aleksandr Genis sums up with his quasi-mathematical formula "Russian postmodernism = avant-garde + *sots-realism*" (Genis 1999, 206). The "reproduction" of the clichés of Sots-Realism makes Moscow Conceptualism the nearest relative of Sots-Art as developed by Vitalii Komar (b. 1943) and Aleksandr Melamid (b. 1945), who by the late 1970s had already emigrated to the United States (Groys 1997, 414; on the overlapping use of the two terms, see Akinsha 2011). Since Sorokin was inspired by both (Bogdanova 1995, 17), I propose to distinguish two sub-branches of conceptualist inspirations for his oeuvre—"sots-art conceptualism" and "white conceptualism."

To be sure, the reference to official Soviet discourses in Moscow Conceptualism is less antagonistically polemical than in Sots-Art; in the conceptualists' take on Soviet officialdom the undermining potential is encapsulated in an estranging emulation, commonly described as "subversive affirmation": "[...] subversive affirmation means 'living in the discourses, in the language of the discourses,' which flows into a concept of a—now poetical—totalization. Each way of writing can be simulated, everything can be [...] said" (Sasse, Schramm 1997, 317).

What does a reproduction of a foreign discourse in a "subversive-affirmative" manner, which avoids any direct assertion (Epshtein 1989, 230), do to the artist's authorship? According to a broad consensus in scholarly literature (cf. Sasse 2003, 206–7), the conceptualist artist appears in a detached position, as a "medium" (Ryklin 1998), whose "reenactment" (Witte 1989, 152) of foreign modes of writing passes the responsibility to the "recycled clichés of earlier literary genres" (Vladiv-Glover 1999b, 24). The intermediary instance of an "author-character" [*personazhnyi avtor*] (Gundlakh 1985, 76) manages to preserve the factual author's "innocence" (Smirnov 1995, 140) by resorting to a "pseudonymic" kind of writing (Groys 2000a, 246), a "merely graphical copying" (Ryklin 1992, 207) which eventually "imitates imitation itself" (Sasse 2003, 202).

With such a detached emulation of Soviet discourses the conceptualists capture the performative nature of late Soviet ritualized speech, writing, and visual art by performing it again artistically. Thus it is also true for them what Alexei Yurchak argues against dissident accusations of life under state socialism as a "lie" (Havel) or "dissimulation" (Kharkhordin 1999, 357; see Yurchak 2006, 17). While ritual quotidian performance had only a hidden subversive potential and functioned ambiguously as a half-affirmative and half-emptying performance of official Soviet culture, the conceptualist "subversive affirmation" laid bare this general tendency in its exaggerated and estranged artistic emulations of Socialist Realism and Soviet monumental style.

With the end of the Soviet Union the all-encompassing context of Soviet discourses gave way to a broader picture. Did this mean the end of a poetics of detached performance and subversive affirmation for the representatives of Moscow Conceptualism in general and Sorokin in particular? This is what most of the existing scholarship suggests (esp. Kuz´min 2001; Smirnov 2004). This book does not aim to trace all representatives of the Moscow Conceptualist group since 1992, but zooms in on Sorokin. For him this Companion provides the opposite answer: after the breakdown of his Soviet reference point, Sorokin turned—as this book intends to demonstrate as its central thesis—to non- and especially post-Soviet cultural production as the references for his meta-exploration, which nevertheless preserved many of the techniques of conceptualization. It is my purpose to demonstrate that his oeuvre since 1992 can be read as a continuous meta-discursive (and thus subversive-affirmative) approach to changing dominant discourses.

This basic assumption motivates the structure of the chapters, which follow in chronological order. Apart from chapter Seven, which provides the background for Sorokin's new media strategy and civic position in post-Soviet Russia, thus continuing the biographical sketch above beyond the 1990s, every chapter is centered around one of Sorokin's longer prose texts. These key texts are used as examples illustrating Sorokin's references to a specific external discourse, different in each chapter. Other texts by Sorokin that fall into the same discursive segment are clustered around this centerpiece of each chapter.

While all chapters contain ample references to international Sorokin research that can offer guidance for further reading, the conclusion (chapter Thirteen) points to niches in existing scholarship inviting future research. It systematizes this Companion's findings concerning the changes in the reference discourses evoked by Sorokin in the different phases of his prose writing and the continuous meta-discursive distance applied.

CHAPTER 2

The Queue and
Collective Speech

In 1985 Sorokin became visible beyond the narrow circle of like-minded Moscow Conceptualists—but exclusively outside of the Soviet Union, where only his first low-profile foray into writing had appeared in the company magazine *For the Workers in the Petroleum Industry* during his studies. Now, Sorokin's earliest serious literary publications appeared in the West. His first tamizdat publication was an excerpt of the Russian original of *The Queue* [*Ochered'*], printed in the Paris-based émigré journal *A–Ya* (Sorokin 1985g) together with five of his stories (Sorokin 1985b, 1985c, 1985d, 1985e, 1985f, see chapter Three). Toward the end of 1985 the complete original of *The Queue* came out, released by the Russian émigré publishing house Sintaksis, also in Paris. Before Polish and English translations of *The Queue* followed in 1988, another Russian-language periodical abroad, Dmitrii Vol´chek's *Mitin zhurnal* in Prague, brought out the Russian originals of the short stories "The Tobacco Pouch" ["Kiset"] and "The Road Accident" ["Dorozhnoe proisshestvie"] in 1986 (Sorokin 1986b, 1986c) and the plays "The Ditch" ["Zemlianka"] and "Pelmeni" ["Pel´meni"] in 1987 (Sorokin 1987a, 1987b). Even though the Russian original of *The Queue* from 1985 came with the genre-designating subtitle "A Novel" ["Roman"], the text itself in its makeup comes closer to Sorokin's plays than to his short stories; indeed, it surpasses them in its dialogical, or rather polylogical, nature.

A book-length publication in tamizdat in Paris in the year 1985, when Gorbachëv's perestroika in the Soviet Union was only beginning, was quite a success for an underground writer. It would take six more years, until the end of 1991, until a small excerpt of *The Queue* was eventually published in the Soviet Union (Sorokin 1991c). This happened just a few weeks before the Union's official dissolution, but in the highly visible popular journal *Ogonek*.

Every contemporary reader from a socialist country recognized the ubiquitous phenomenon to which the title referred: the queue. In the Soviet Union, the worst repercussions of post-war famine were slowly overcome under Stalin's successors as Secretary General of the Communist Party, Nikita Khrushchev (1953–1964) and Leonid Brezhnev (1964–1982), at least for the populations in Moscow and Leningrad. But deficits were still a daily reality in late-Soviet society. The deficit economy had one direct and two indirect effects: the direct effect was the lines in which people waited for the deficit commodities; more indirect effects included, on the one hand, the introduction of restricted shops for the privileged party elite of *nomenklatura* where the offerings were much broader and, on the other, the emergence of informal channels for obtaining that which was difficult to obtain (see Ledeneva 1998, 104–38). While the first effect amounted to a veritable queue culture, the third evolved into a black market that had an even bigger impact on the entire Soviet economy than the initial deficit (see Trotman 2017, 77, 85).

The queue economy underwent three paradigms, as Vladimir Sorokin outlined in his retrospective "Afterword: Farewell to the Queue" to the American re-issue of *The Queue* in 2008: people lined up for "butter and sugar" in the Soviet Union up to the 1960s; they queued for prestigious imported goods in the Brezhnev era of stagnation:

> American Lees and Levi Strauss jeans, Camel and Marlboro cigarettes, "spike" heel and platform shoes, "stocking" boots, cervelat sausage and salami, Sony and Grundig tape recorders, French perfume, Turkish sheepskin coats, muskrat hats, and Bohemian crystal (Sorokin 2008a, 253, trans. Jamey Gambrell);

and with the economic collapse of state socialism, it again came to lining up for "sausage and butter" in the transformational crisis of perestroika during the late 80s and early 90s. In all three periods, people would stand in line not necessarily for exactly what they needed, but for everything they potentially might later exchange for the item they did in fact need, obtained by somebody else for the same purpose of barter (Belovinskii 2017, 561).

Since the economic recession contradicted the official promise of wealth for all living under communism, censored genres such as film and regularly published literature could only indirectly hint at this taboo (see Witte 1989, 156–8; Porter 2017, 514). The main site where the discourse about the economic problems took place was the queue itself with its never-ending anecdotes and jokes about the economic misery. This oral discourse is exactly what Sorokin investigates in his *Queue* (cf. Sorokin, Rasskazova 1992, 121): in this fictional text Sorokin throws his reader directly into a polylogue of nameless Russian speakers which a reader with a socialist background will recognize as highly typical:

> — Comrade, who's last in the queue?
> — I am, I think, but there was a woman in a blue coat after me.
> — So I'm after her?
> — Yes, she'll be back in a moment. You stand behind me in the meantime.
> — You're staying here then, are you?
> — Yes.
> — I just wanted to nip off for a moment—I'll literally be a minute.

> — Товарищ, кто последний?
> — Наверно я, но за мной еще женщина в синем пальто.
> — Значит я за ней?
> — Да. Она щас придет. Становитесь за мной пока.
> — А вы будете стоять?
> — Да.
> — Я на минуту отойти хотел, буквально на минуту … (Eng. Sorokin 1988a, 7, here and further trans. Sally Laird; Russ. 1985a, 5)

The queue is self-organized as people come and go, but secure their place "behind somebody" by informing this person when they will be back. This communicative pattern was performed billions of times in the quotidian deficit culture of socialism. No less characteristic is Sorokin's imagination of how passersby become interested in a queue in a kind of "Pavlovian construct" (Trotman 2017, 87): people do not come to obtain any particular goods, but take the opportunity presented by a randomly assembled queue and get in the line without exactly knowing what they are queuing for. Since queuing, leaving, and coming back can take hours or days—in Sorokin's "novel" the reader acoustically witnesses two days in a row without the characters ever getting a never-finally-determined non-food commodity (see Blair 2009)—the situation becomes reminiscent of Beckett's absurdist play *Waiting for Godot* [*En attendant Godot*] (1949).

The boredom of waiting is eased by multilateral communication with those standing nearby. Sorokin's dialogues warn the reader when somebody new is included in a conversation by adding impersonal addresses such as "citizen" [*grazhdanin* or *grazhdanka*], "miss" [*devushka*], "mate" [*paren'*], "young man" [*molodoi chelovek*], "madam" [*zhenshchina*], "mister" [*muzhchina*], "pops" [*otets*], "gramps" [*ded*], etc.—none of which are polite terms, but common in colloquial Russian (cf. Goehrke 2003–2005, III 370). The only term which has Soviet ideological implications is the typical (official) Soviet address in the plural: "comrades" [*tovarishchi*].

As the addresses display no individuality, the content of communication in Sorokin's *The Queue* consists of collective topoi and stereotypes, for the most part derived from the economic context: "how many each" "they" will be giving at the particular shop; where somebody got something else that s/he wears or carries; what people have heard about other shops. The situation of queuing requires constant social control: everybody is worried about new people pushing their way into the crowd. In Sorokin's take, the social mechanism of constructing and defending an in-group of legitimate queue members leads to the identification of others as people from "out of town" ["приезжие"] (Eng. Sorokin 1988a, 7; Russ. 1985, 5; cf. Belovinskii 2017, 554). In *The Queue* the "out-of-towners" are discriminated against by class as "hillbillies" ["деревня чертова"], contradicting the communist myth of closing the ranks between proletarian industrial workers and the peasants (Eng. Sorokin 1988a, 23; Russ. 1985, 21), or identified with the underprivileged peripheries of the Soviet Union, the Caucasus or Central Asia, subsumed under the racist denominator "Georgians" ["грузины"] (Eng. Sorokin 1988a, 11; Russ. 1985a, 8), thus contradicting another one of socialism's myths: that of internationalism.

Even more remarkable in *The Queue* than the interchangeable social clichés is Sorokin's predilection for direct speech. In this respect *The Queue* continues his playful imitation of foreign voices when a child, and later, the thread of his dramas and film scripts, all focused on direct speech, which Sorokin stylizes (Lichina 2000, 162–3). The American reviewer Tom Swick rightly pointed out Sorokin's "remarkable ear for dialogue" (1998; cf. also Ermolin 2003, 409). The alleged "novel" *The Queue* lacks not only a narrator, but also the names of its speakers—most of the voices remain anonymous— as well as any kind of stage directions. Apart from the paratexts (title, subtitle, author's name, publisher's name and address, and year—the 1985 edition has no ISBN), the text consists of one hundred percent direct speech, graphically introduced by initial em-dashes. The reader is presented with the puzzle of identifying the speakers, with connecting several replies to one particular speaker, and with attributing at least some features, such as gender and age, to each voice.

This confusing task is complicated by a huge amount of redundant information in the text: salespeople for kvass and in a canteen spend pages returning change to their customers (Eng. Sorokin 1988a, 31–4, 94–5; Russ. 1985a,

28–32); people collectively guess crosswords (Eng. Sorokin 1988a, 79–82; Russ. 1985a, 81–4) and read to each other private sale announcements (Eng. Sorokin 1988a, 83–5; Russ. 1985a, 86–8). Even more uniform is the representation of roll calls—on the first evening it consists of the numbers from 1226 to 1263, interrupted by the family names of the persons who were previously assigned one of these numbers; in the morning, those from 1228 to 1268 (Eng. Sorokin 1988a, 47–50, 65–8; Russ. 1985a, 44–7, 68–70). The most demanding part for a reader trying to remain attentive is the third roll call with an endless list of names, interrupted only by a "Yes!" ["Я"], causing even the most attentive reader to momentarily lose focus (Eng. Sorokin 1988a, 113–29; Russ. 1985a, 115–44). At this point in the text practically every reader will catch him/herself leafing through and just looking out for parts that stand out as graphically different (not just "Yes!" and last name; cf. Ohme 2003, 159).

The danger of boring the reader and making him/her leaf through the text is countered by the increased hermeneutic challenges in *The Queue*. Since there is not a single stage direction, we never explicitly learn if a person leaves, pushes or hugs another, apart from the verbal reactions to the preceding unnarrated actions. Most often, this concerns the boy Volodia who is ineffectually disciplined by his mother (or grandmother) and who constantly picks up things he ought not to or runs away where he is not supposed to. Often, the verbal reactions give only an approximate idea of what action the fictitious characters might be reacting to. For example, we do not exactly know whether Vadim hugs, touches or harasses Lena in some way (Eng. Sorokin 1988a, 21, 52; Russ. 1985a, 19, 49)—we can only suppose that he did something she found inappropriate for a new acquaintance.

Also, information about the context of the queue can only be retrieved from the replies of the people standing in it. It seems to be a not exactly defined place somewhere in Moscow (cf. Lichina 2000, 158). The action takes place in the summer heat, from which the people in the queue suffer from noon till the early evening; a big soccer event is said to be taking place in Spain, which allows the reader to assume that this is the World Cup of 1982. Additional hints to wars in Lebanon and between Iran and Iraq support this tentative dating of the plot (Eng. Sorokin 1988a, 27, 78–9; Russ. 1985a, 25, 81; cf. Ohme 2003, 163–4 note 8).

Thus, in Sorokin's *The Queue*, we are in the late Soviet context, the same time when Sorokin (between 1979 and 1985) wrote his early texts (in addition to *The Queue*, these include *The Norm* and a bunch of short stories [chapter Four]). The compulsory collectivism of Stalinism, where every individual deviation could lead to arrest, deportation, or disappearance without a trace, has by then been mitigated in Soviet society. The people in Sorokin's queue allow themselves to strive for individuality by purchasing non-standard items from the West (see Kozlov 2018). But in order to achieve this, they spend hours and days limited to a tiny space in-between the other people in line—Russian queues are very dense—in a condition of "waiting that paralyzes actions and decisions" (Witte 1989, 156).

What is more, the late-Soviet normative collectivism (see Kharkhordin 1999, 279–97) and compulsion to conformist behavior is present in the form of the police's megaphone. Its announcements demonstrate that collective conformism is meant only for ordinary people, but that some are actually "more equal"; the voice of the state authority intrudes into the collective polylogue in capital letters:

CITIZENS! [...] CAN YOU PLEASE BE QUIET! THESE COMRADES HAVE THE RIGHT TO RECEIVE GOODS WITHOUT QUEUING! SO PLEASE KEEP QUIET AND STAY CALM!

ГРАЖДАНЕ! [...] ПРОСЬБА НЕ ШУМЕТЬ! ЭТИ ТОВАРИЩИ ИМЕЮТ ПРАВО ПОЛУЧИТЬ ТОВАР ВНЕ ОЧЕРЕДИ. ТАК ЧТО, НЕ ШУМИТЕ, СТОЙТЕ СПОКОЙНО! (Eng. Sorokin 1988a, 24; Russ. 1985a, 22)

This capitalization opens a long chapter in Sorokin's dealing with typography—not only through capital letters, but also italics, Latin script in a Cyrillic text (see Paulsen 2013; Uffelmann 2013b, 182–4), not to mention blank spaces or entirely empty pages.

Apart from the megaphone's commands, in *The Queue* the socialist state's ideology is only remotely evoked in the queue's conversations (cinema "Stakhanovite"; Eng. Sorokin 1988a, 21; Russ. 1985a, 19). What we read in this fictional text is rather the colloquial critique of the official discourse. The speakers allow themselves to be ironic about empty ideological stereotypes ("I am learning, just as Lenin commanded" / "Учусь, как Ленин завещал"; Eng. 1988a, 75; Russ. 1985a, 77). In late-Soviet discourses, just as Sorokin emulates them in *The Queue*, the expression of discontent is widespread. It includes criticism of industrial mass-apartment buildings (Eng. Sorokin 1988a, 89; Russ. 1985a, 91); anger over tacit privileges for the *nomenklatura*; intercultural stereotypes about the US (Eng. Sorokin 1998a, 150; Russ.

1985a, 173); laments about the corrupt police in particular or "the system" ["система"] in general (Eng. Sorokin 1988a, 91; Russ. 1985a, 93); disillusionment about alienated work (refuting the Marxian ambition to erase this in a socialist society; Eng. Sorokin 1988a, 68; Russ. 1985a, 71); or a critique of the present regime encapsulated in the form of nostalgia for the alleged greater order under Stalin:

— Never used to happen in Stalin's day, though, did it.
— Law and order there was in those days.
— Law and order. And people had a conscience, they really worked.
— That's right. Exceeded the norms.

— А при Сталине разве творилось такое?
— Порядок был.
— Порядок. И работали все на совесть.
— Еще как. Нормы перекрывали. (Eng. Sorokin 1988a, 91; Russ. 1985a, 93)

All of these discursive units are rendered through various anonymous mouths. It would be highly misleading to assume the writer's own political opinion behind this, as with the xenophobia and class discrimination against inhabitants of Russia's provinces mentioned above. The author does not bear responsibility for any political or ethical message (Glanc 2003, 7, 9); it is left to the reader to decide whether s/he wants to stress rather the xenophobic, conflictual, and egoistic facets of the behavior of people in a queue or the altruistic and emotional dimensions.

The same can be said for the characters' ethical or unethical patterns of behavior that transpire from their verbal interactions. Conflict about one's place in the line is the thing that will most frequently precipitate a conversation. Secondly, contact between the genders tends to lead to outspoken conflicts—between Vadim and a male rival over the issue of who can talk to Lena, which quickly escalates into rude behavior with vulgar language ("they talked shit" / "попиздели"; Eng. 1988a, 69 corrected; Russ. 1985a, 71). The colloquial discourse of *The Queue* is, however, hardly gendered itself: Lena reacts no less aggressively later. The interchangeability of aggression in her conversation with a foreign man was not caught by Sally Laird in the English translation ("Хам—хамка—хам," "дура—дурак—дура"; Eng. Sorokin 1988a, 82–3; Russ. 1985a, 85). The rigid self-organization of the queue through numbers, from which those missing during the roll calls in the middle of the night or in the early morning are excluded (Eng. Sorokin 1988a, 65; Russ. 1985a, 68), does not preclude the potential for conflict; it only channels the aggression into mathematics—into the numbers that all people in the queue are assigned (see Sorokin 2008a, 257).

Yet, the voices in Sorokin's queue occasionally also express friendly requests and circumscribe altruistic behavior. The most common altruistic action is holding a place for somebody else who leaves the queue for a few minutes or even hours to take care of other business—or for another queue—and keeping it for him/her during the roll calls. Rarer events include bringing somebody else ice cream, sharing a newspaper, helping out with a cigarette or providing a few spare coins. Volodia's mother even witnesses economic altruism when somebody queuing behind her in the canteen warns her that she just dropped her purse (Eng. Sorokin 1988a, 94; Russ. 1985a, 96).

While these singular actions remain anonymous, individualization of the fictitious characters in Sorokin's *The Queue* requires attributing a name to a voice through somebody else addressing her or him. With little Volodia this happens forty-three times throughout the text, almost exclusively in the form of prohibitions or admonitions. The hyperactive boy Volodia (who shares his diminutive with the author) constantly eludes all attempts to discipline him, thus refuting the pedagogical illusions of Socialist Realism.

The first thread of communications which produces individualization of two people begins when a "girl" and a young man engage in a dialogue, quickly introducing themselves to each other by first names as Lena and Vadim, beginning to flirt (Vadim keeps paying unoriginal compliments to her hair; for example, see Eng. Sorokin 1988a, 28; Russ. 1985a, 26), and switching to the Russian intimate *ty* (Eng. Sorokin 1988a, 12, 14; Russ. 1985a, 10, 12).

Lena keeps reacting icily to Vadim's advances and disappears after a privileged writer who has access to commodities without queues chats with her in the canteen and invites her to the Pushkin Museum, as Vadim is getting tea for her (Eng. Sorokin 1988a, 99–100, 109–10; Russ. 1985a, 101–3, 112). While still hoping for Lena's return, Vadim becomes the main prism of the text (its ear focus). However, this "Soviet Everyman" (Trotman 2017, 76) lacks any outstanding individual, let alone tragic features. His solidary drinking vodka with other men (Eng. Sorokin 1988a, 130–4; Russ. 1985a, 144–9) sheds a rather dubious light on him, but Sorokin gifts him with a happy ending. On the second late afternoon of Vadim's queuing, a thunderstorm starts with heavy rain. Liuda, who has not appeared individually yet but later turns out to be one of the salespeople in the shop the queue is for, suddenly takes care of the drenched Vadim, who was surprised by the rain while asleep on a bench after half a bottle of vodka. She takes him to her apartment in a Stalinist building next to the queue (Eng. Sorokin 1988a, 158; Russ. 1985a, 181), offers to dry and iron his wet shirt, and feeds him fried potatoes. The private space of Liuda's apartment seems to form a total contrast to the public realm of the largely anonymous line—the little paradise of late Soviet life (see Laird 2008, ix–x). Liuda's unexpected altruism prompts Vadim to pronounce a pathetic compliment: "a lady of rare hospitality" ["человек редкой гостеприимности"] (Eng. Sorokin 1988a, 163, corrected; Russ. 1985a, 185). Vadim's subsequent no-less-pathetic toast to Liuda should hardly be read as the text's *fabula docet* either, due to its formulaic nature and the munching that follows:

— All set... everything's wonderful, Lyuda. I tell you what, why don't we drink to the joy of unexpected meetings? There aren't so many joys in life, after all.... So, long may it last... To our meeting....

— Alright then ... to our meeting...

— ....

— .... mm, tasty ....

— Все. Все чудесно. Знаете, Люда, давайте выпьем за радость неожиданных встреч. У нас ведь радостей не так уж много. Так вот, пусть эта всегда будет. За встречу.

— Ну что ж ... за встречу...

— ....

— .... вкусный .... (Eng. Sorokin 1988a, 167; Russ. 1985a, 189)

The reader's increasing suspicion of a naïve ethical reading is supported by the fact that the two lie to each other: Vadim about his being drunk in the afternoon and alleged queuing for a friend, Liuda about her job, pretending to work as an economist instead of a salesperson. Vadim receives a double happy ending—both a private one, as he is invited by an unknown woman for dinner and sex, and an economic one, a promise of privileged access to deficit goods and liberation from the collective compulsion of queuing. However, this leaves the reader with an impression of over-motivation. Combining two happy endings devaluates both of them to stereotypical cultural phantasmas, to a "pseudo-salvation" (Sorokin, Laird 1999, 148).

Also telling is the observation that Vadim uses the same worn-out pickup line on Liuda as the writer uses on Lena, telling Liuda that she reminds him of somebody he once knew, challenging her ambition to be unique (Eng. Sorokin 1988a, 169; Russ. 1985a, 191). Finally, Vadim's unforeseen rendezvous with Liuda turns instrumental when—after having spent the night with her—he jumps up to return to the queue in order to avoid losing his place and learns that she works as a manager in the shop in front of which he was queuing (Eng. Sorokin 1988a, 195–6; Russ. 1985a, 236). Against the backdrop of the deficit economy illustrated in *The Queue*, this is a very influential position (see Ledeneva 1998, 130). Liuda promises to provide him with the desired Western import goods without his having to return to the line of up to 2,000 people for another two days.

It is an open question whether this number exaggerates the dimensions of queues if viewed against the economic reality of the late 1970s and early 80s (Witte 1989, 159; cf. Sorokin, Laird 1999, 150–1)—the food deficits became catastrophically bad only during the economic transformation in the wake of perestroika in the late 1980s and early 1990s. In contrast to many later texts by Sorokin, *The Queue* tempts the reader into reading it referentially: was this really the case? The answer can be postponed because what counts in Sorokin's meta-discursive work of art is the mundane discourse surrounding enormous queues, not the actual length of historical queues in any particular year. The discursive nightmare about apocalyptic queues is the flipside of a no-less-hyperbolic discursive desire for obtaining Western items in Sorokin's *The Queue*: not only an unreachable Mercedes, but also a modest Swedish lighter (Eng. Sorokin 1988a, 38, 42; Russ. 1985a, 36, 40) or some other undetermined "blue-gray" commodity from America.

The "referential temptation" which *The Queue* exerts on its readers—that this describes a historical economic and social reality and not more narrowly a collective discourse about reality (cf. Lunde 2009, 11–2)—is both supported and disturbed by the neo-avant-gardist form of the alleged "novel." *The Queue* is everything but a novel in the traditional sense, presupposing that a novel typically includes the voice of a narrator. There is no narrator who would describe fictional objects; they emerge in front of the reader's eyes only as an effect of their anonymous mentioning by (mostly) anonymous speakers, and thus through their discursive (in this case, oral) rendering.

The need to guess what objects the voices are talking about requires enhanced cognitive activity from the reader. No narrator or stage directions ever indicate whether a fictional character is eating, drinking, or kissing. Only the silence of the voices standing in line consisting of three or more dots when characters eat or drink (Eng. Sorokin 1988a, 96–7, 101; Russ. 1985a, 98–100, 103) represents this invisible corporeal activity. A bit more explanatory language can be found in the kissing scene between Vadim and Liuda:

— You know…I reckon this is the loveliest evening I've had for the last five years.
— Really?
— Mmm.
— Why?
— Because…because…
— Vadim…Vadim…
— My darling…you're gorgeous…
— Vadim…Vadim…
— ………you're love….ly…
— …Vadim…why…ah….
— ………

— Ты знаешь … наверно за последние пять лет это у меня самый чудесный вечер.
— Правда?
— Да…
— А почему?
— Потому что … потому что …
— Вадим … Вадим …
— Прелесть моя … очарование …
— Вадим … Вадим …
— ……… пре … лесть …
— … Вадим … ну зачем … а …
— ……… (Eng. Sorokin 1988a, 174; Russ. 1985a, 196)

No articulated words but interjections come in when somebody chews, sighs, or while Liuda and Vadim are having sex. Here a visual element illustrates mutuality: during their intercourse, the left line of interjections (Liuda's) is mirrored by another one on the right of the page with letters bottom-up (Vadim's; Eng. Sorokin 1988a, 176; Russ. 1985a, 198). Whether this illustrates a certain sexual practice, as Ohme suggests, is as "open to debate" (2003, 160) as with the part where we hear only Vadim moaning "I am not worthy" while Liuda's parts consist of silent lines full of dots (Eng. Sorokin 1988a, 186–7; Russ. 1985a, 208–9). The reduction of acoustic signals culminates in several dozen empty pages in *The Queue*, signaling that somebody is asleep (white in Eng. Sorokin 1988a, 50–66; filled with fuzzy black shreds in Russ. 1985a, 53–64), and further pointing the reader to the "mediality-per-se" [*medial'nost' v sebe*] of empty book paper (Smirnov 1995, 141).

If there was any doubt before, the blank pages make Sorokin's *The Queue* a highly experimental form of literature. Its ambition is not to depict anything special, but rather the opposite: in this early text the writer is interested in the most mundane utterances. The phrases he captures may be repeated thousands of times every day everywhere in Russia (only a small part is specific to the late Soviet Union). Their topics are the weather, soccer, popular songs, TV shows, cats, and, of course, continuous conjectures about the queue.

Conversations about highbrow culture such as classical music (Eng. Sorokin 1988a, 149; Russ. 1985a, 172) or contemporary poetry (Eng. Sorokin 1988a, 164–5; Russ. 1985a, 187–8) in the rapprochement between Vadim and Liuda appear not as signals of literariness, but rather as fake intellectuality. The vast majority of utterances hardly possess any information of value to the reader (Ohme 2003, 157). Accordingly, the conversations in *The Queue* do not amount to a purified standard language; they are instead full of vulgar language, anacolutha, and phonetically reduced forms such as the ungrammatical, but orally common Russian vocative without ending ("Лен" for "Lena"; Russ. Sorokin 1985a, 40; not correspondingly rendered in Eng. 1988a, 42). Sorokin's queue dialogues would perfectly fit in a textbook for learning colloquial Russian, superior to most university manuals of oral conversation.

Thus the content of collective and dialogical conversation is not relevant and all voices in the queue are similar (Witte 1989, 165). What is in the focus of this experimental piece of literature is rather the attempt at a "hyperreal" phonetic transcript of reality (Vishnevskaia 1985, 176) without any subsidiary means of information such as a narrator's voice or stage directions. Sorokin draws the readers' attention to their own hermeneutics: the readers supplement the (invisible, because unnarrated) interactions merely out of their— linguistic and somatic—sonic repercussions.

The ear of the reader is better informed than that of the characters, so the reader would know that Lena will not return, because s/he "witnessed" the privileged writer's invitation to Lena, which Vadim did not hear, resulting in his continuing to wonder what else she might be doing (Eng. Sorokin 1988a, 145; Russ. 1985a, 168). This rather classical device of novelistic writing inserts Sorokin's *The Queue* in a long tradition of dialogical texts in Russian literature, especially the legacy of Fëdor Dostoevskii's dialogic novels as described by Mikhail Bakhtin in his canonical *Problems of Dostoevskii's*

Poetics [*Problemy poetiki Dostoevskogo*] (1963). What is more, Sorokin's focus on collective speech can be legitimately read as a kind of meta-commentary to Bakhtin's theory of the carnival.

While Dostoevskii and Bakhtin are still interested in the content of a dialogic or carnivalesque communication and the semantic effects this form of communication has, Sorokin is not. In *The Queue*, this text of "Mozartian simplicity" (Laird 2008, viii), his interest is much more abstract: the writer conceptualizes the way in which language, here a transcript of everyday speech, represents social interaction and how the reader makes sense out of sounds. This very general semiotic interest makes *The Queue* an organic part of the first, meta-semiotic tendency in Moscow Conceptualism (chapter One). This phonetic polylogue comes closer to the early (white) Bulatov (see Glanc 2003, 6) than to the references of Sots-Art to official Soviet ideology. In Sorokin's early text the replies, which constitute the polylogue of a queue, iconically represent the line of a queue, forming a "textual queue" (Ohme 2003, 162). This meta-interest in representation per se will change at the latest with Sorokin's *The Norm* (chapter Three), which is centered around official Soviet speech. *The Queue*, this highly original masterpiece that marked his appearance on the international literary scene in 1985, is thus Sorokin's "white-most" conceptualist text.

CHAPTER 3

The Norm and Socialist Realism

Sorokin had started working on his second full-length prose book to be published, *The Norm* [*Norma*], in 1979, before writing *The Queue*, but finished the former only in 1984. Given that *The Norm* was released in post-Soviet Russia only in August 1994, nine years after *The Queue* came out in Paris, the difference between the time of the writing of the manuscript and its wider reception is most drastic here. Only the section "The Cattle Plague" ["Padëzh"], the second half of part three of *The Norm* (Sorokin 1994a, 122–46), had already appeared separately in the literary magazine *Volga* in Saratov in 1991 (Sorokin 1991d). Ten years after the Russian original became available in the Russian Federation, selected fragments of part one (Sorokin 1994a, 10–12, 15, 21, 30–1, 37–8, 72–4) were translated into English by Keith Gessen (Sorokin 2004a).

The 256-page-long Russian 1994 edition by the publishers Obscuri Viri and Tri Kita was issued in an initial print run of 5,000 copies of poor print and paper quality, typical of non-mainstream publications in the first post-socialist years. With *The Norm*, the harsh impression is additionally enhanced by avoidable typographical imperfections such as page numbers on title pages (for example, p. 75) and empty pages (p. 218) where they are omitted in professional book design.

The first look at the print appearance of this book offers information about the heterogeneity of the material, which prevents a quick plot summary. Instead, it invites a description of the graphic appearance: the book opens with three pages of a frame narrative in italics (Sorokin 1994a, 3–6). The fourth page looks like the title page of a book but contains only the title "THE NORM" ["HOPMA"] in capital letters (in contrast to the actual title page on p. 3 of this book, giving no author's name, publisher or year of publication). Capital letters on a separate page are also used to introduce each new section of the book, from "PART ONE" ["ЧАСТЬ ПЕРВАЯ"] to "PART EIGHT"

["ЧАСТЬ ВОСЬМАЯ"] (Sorokin 1994a, 9, 245). This combination of capital letters with generous use of paper recurs throughout all of part six (Sorokin 1994a, 189–217), with its twenty-eight slogan-like short sentences containing the noun "NORM" ["НОРМА"].

Part four comes closer to common book design (Sorokin 1994a, 147–60) with its twelve poems. Each is printed on a separate page as is usual in poetry collections. However, in contrast to the typographical practice, Sorokin's poems are aligned not only centrally from left to right, but also from top to bottom, inserting an additional visual-artistic dimension into book design (cf. Gillespie 2000, 307–8). The left alignment typical of poetry is also used in part two, which looks like a continuous poem on twenty-three pages (Sorokin 1994a, 76–98), but the fundamental expectation of variation in poems (as in literature in general) is violated: each line consists of uniform combinations of the adjective "normal" with a noun in the nominative. This deviation lies on the border of visual presentation and semantics (or the reduction of semantics).

Parts one, three, five, and eight display a stark contrast to the relatively white pages of parts two, four, and seven. They come with prose text in block alignment, a very small font, and unusually narrow margins (less than 1 centimeter from the top, 1.5 from the outer margin, 1.8 from the bottom and—most significantly—less than 1 centimeter from the inner margin). In these prose sections the only astonishing thing is that quite a bit of space is "wasted" between paragraphs. The blank space does not look drastic between the letters to Martin Alekseich in part five (Sorokin 1994a, 162–88), but in part one the majority of the one- or two-pages-long vignettes begin on a new page, leaving the bottom of the previous page empty (pp. 12, 42, 56, and 62 are half-filled, pp. 14, 58, and 64 a third full, pp. 47 and 60 only a sixth full).

Many of these typographical inconsistencies look deliberate and signal meta-reflection on the use of paper in printed books and the relationship between letters and white areas (what typographers call the "gray-scale value"). While the intense use of space and the high gray-scale value in the prose sections may well be read as an allusion to the scarcity of paper for unofficial literary production during Soviet times, the almost empty title pages and the single slogans on each page of part seven on the opposite end remind the reader of the "white" period of Moscow Conceptualism. This allows the assumption that *The Norm*, with its internal typographical heterogeneity, partially offers up a general reflection on text production, literariness, and a reader's view of book pages. Additionally, some parts of this text invite a more content-related reading with reference to Soviet culture.

In part two, the reader's automatic attempt at a referential reading is challenged by the salient redundancy in the 1,562 combinations of the adjective "normal" (in Russian nominative slightly varied due to the different endings of the three genera in the singular plus the plural). The block starts with the only capital letter of the section in the first word of the phrase "Normal birth" ["Нормальные роды"]. Given the collocation with related words from the semantic field centered around a childbirth, the beginning creates a rudimentary narrative: the birth from line one seems to be given to a "normal boy" ["нормальный мальчик"] in line two, who is attributed a "normal cry" ["нормальный крик"], and a "normal umbilical cord" ["нормальная пуповина"] by an assumed adult speaker, possibly a nurse or doctor (Sorokin 1994a, 76). The baby meets the "normal" expectations also in terms of eating and digestion:

normal sucking	нормальное сосание
normal urine	нормальная моча
normal feces	нормальный кал
normal diaper	нормальный подгузник
normal nappy	нормальная пеленка
	(Sorokin 1994a, 76)

As the enumeration continues, the boy seems to have left the hospital and started growing up ("normal crawling" / "нормальное ползание," Sorokin 1994a, 76; "normal kindergarten" / "нормальный детсад," 78; "normal handwriting" / "нормальное чистописание," "normal goal" / "нормальный гол," 79; "normal girls" / "нормальные девки," 80). The section amounts to the entire life story of the anonymous male in 1,562 combinations of "normal" with a noun. His adolescence is not devoid of vulgarisms such as "normal fuck" ["нормальная ебля"] (Sorokin 1994a, 82), whereas his early adulthood is filled with Soviet political ideologemes:

normal political instruction [...]	нормальные политзанятия [...]
normal heroism	нормальный героизм
normal responsibility	нормальная самоотверженность
normal dedication	нормальная самоотдача
normal self-discipline	нормальная самодисциплина
	(Sorokin 1994a, 84)

The reemergence of medical terms toward the end, such as "normal concussion" ["нормальная контузия"], accompanied by Soviet-style abbreviations ("normal VTEK" / "нормальный ВТЕК"; Sorokin 1994a, 97) introduces a lethal illness, which ends in an operation with severe complications: "normal coma [...] normal death" ["нормальная кома [...] нормальная смерть"] (98).

In section two, both vulgarisms and Soviet jargon pass without special attention; ideology is viewed as a "normal" ingredient of life. Everything in Soviet people's life is interpreted as complying with the norm. The individual story of joy and suffering is "normalized" and de-individualized by the all-encompassing epithet *normal´nyi*. The enumeration of "normalcies" can be closely connected to Soviet-Russian phraseology; as Juri Talvet correctly observes, the adverb "normally" [*normal´no*] served as a "commonplace in everyday Soviet Russian parlance" (2003). The English equivalent is a laconic colloquial reply (not "acceptably well" [Talvet 2003], but rather something like "eh, well enough"), the standard answer to questions like "how are you?", "how was your day?" Like the American ritual greeting "how are you?," which is not meant as the start of a serious conversation, the Russian *normal´no* is viewed by non-native speakers as too formulaic, uninformative, uncreative, and something not indicative of a continued conversation. For Russian speakers outside the Russian Federation it even bears the burden of Soviet imperialism.

Since Russian *normal´no* rather ends a conversation or at least a thread in a conversation, a life epitomized in all its details as "normal" appears as the result of an utterly schizoid presentation. This can be interpreted either with regard to Soviet political culture—*homo sovieticus* hides her/his private feelings behind formulaic "normalcy"—or made plausible also as a general anthropological feature.

The focus is again—like in *The Queue*—not on anything individual or extraordinary, but on language. The second part of *The Norm* is a linguistic variation about common usage of language in the sense of Eugenio Coseriu. If approached from inside the tradition of Moscow Conceptualism, it shares an interest in colloquial seriality with Rubinshtein's file-card poems.

The "most white" part, section six with its capital-letters-only slogans, reminds the reader of the megaphone instructions from *The Queue*. The first four are grammatical variations of the central expectation of state-planned socialist economy that "norms [in the sense of quantitatively defined quotas] must be fulfilled":

I FULFILLED MY QUOTA!
WE FULFILLED OUR QUOTA!
THEY FULFILLED THEIR QUOTA!
HAVE YOU FULFILLED YOUR QUOTA OR NOT?

Я СВОЮ НОРМУ ВЫПОЛНИЛ!
МЫ СВОЮ НОРМУ ВЫПОЛНИЛИ!
ОНИ СВОЮ НОРМУ ВЫПОЛНИЛИ!
ТЫ СВОЮ НОРМУ ВЫПОЛНИЛ? (Sorokin 1994a, 190–3)

The shift of grammatical person and number is less significant than that from the exclamation point to the question mark: it marks a shift from normative (albeit not necessarily true) affirmation to a threatening question.

The political implications recede in the following colloquial sayings. A different "normality" is meant in "WITH VASIA AND LENA EVERYTHING IS GOING NORMALLY" ["У ВАСИ С ЛЕНОЙ ВСЕ В НОРМЕ"] (literally: "within the norm") and in three analogous constructions with other names (Sorokin 1994a, 194–7). More typically Russian (but not exclusively Soviet) is the cultural acceptance of heavy abuse of vodka in the utterance "ONE LITER, THAT'S DIMA'S NORM" ["ЛИТР—ДИМКИНА НОРМА"] (Sorokin 1994a, 213). With four pages of the pattern "THE ARIA FOR NORMA IS MASTERFUL!" ["АРИЯ НОРМЫ ВИРТУОЗНА!"] (Sorokin 1994a, 198–201) a totally different, historical "Norma" comes into play—the female character from Vincenzo Bellini's opera *Norma* (premiered in 1831). A proper name is also tied to the Georgian tea "Norma" on pp. 206–9 and settlements and buildings on pp. 214–7. Thus the "norms" in this part share only the Russian signifier and appear as an exercise in pragmatic lexicography. Like the second part, this section does not create a fictional world, let alone constitute recognizable characters or even refer to historical persons. The two sections scrutinize the pragmatic rules for the usage of the Russian signifiers *norma* and *normal' no* and give the impression of variations or exercises on a given topic.

The more literary part four has an additional (sub-)title page, "TIMES OF THE YEAR" ["ВРЕМЕНА ГОДА"] (Sorokin 1994a, 148) and thus does not further develop the semantic field around the root *norm-*, but engages with a referential topic—the months of the year—in twelve poems whose first word is always the name of a month in calendric order. Each poem is written in a different, recognizable, yet worn-out style: April proletarianizes a well-known poem by Boris Pasternak ("February. Get ink, shed tears!" / "Fevral'. Dostat' chernil i plakat´!"), July banalizes Evgenii Evtushenko ("USSR—FRG 1955" / "SSSR—FRG 1995 g."), September sexualizes Aleksandr Pushkin (*Eugene Onegin / Evgenii Onegin* II, 32), and so on. The verses in part four are clearly not meant to be aesthetic in themselves; the serial presentation of different modes of writing poems makes this part a meta-poetic exercise in various "normalcies" of lyrical expression.

The letters to Martin Alekseich which form the fifth part of *The Norm* are written by an anonymous, rather unskilled letter writer, an ordinary veteran who apparently looks after Martin Alekseich's dacha in the countryside. The addressee seems to hold a higher position in the hierarchy than the author of the letters, which gives them, as Ol´ga Bogdanova observes, "the form of a steward reporting […] to his landowner" (Bogdanova 2005, 27). The hierarchical difference in this one-sided correspondence and the patronym Alekseevich echoes Dostoevskii's *Poor Folk* [*Bednye liudi*] (1846, cf. Gillespie 2000, 304) and thus a pre-Soviet setting. As gradually becomes clear, the veteran resents Martin Alekseich's lack of acknowledgement of his letters, for which he overcompensates with epistolary graphomania (cf. Tchouboukov-Pianca 1995, 114–5). As he does not receive a single answer from Martin Alekseevich, his letters become increasingly permeated with interjections and words taken from the Russian vulgar language known as *mat*, ending up in ungrammatical sentences and non-lexical swearing:

> Dear Martin Alekseich,
> You think I should slave here and you partake of strawberries there, eat with milk and tell lots of fucking anecdotes on the terrace and we slave away for you here. So I slave there and I not society enlighten you and I shat on you so you not take a dump on me and we I mean peat and for shit! Oh no we also shit for not letting the kulaks and I don't take a dump on and that's it. I fuckwaste for shit and fucked you to let you not slave away and we vermin have fucked you over. I fucked you vermin […] I yourmin fucked caned give up and that's it. I yourmin furned givemin up canit.

> Здравствуйте Мартин Алексеевич!
> Вы думаете я тут значит паши а вы там клубничку приедите с молочком поедите и на тераске анекдотики-хуетики разные а мы тут паши за вас. Значит кто так вот паши а я не общественность просветить вас и я тебя срал чтобы ты не гадить мне а мы значит торф и срать чтобы! Нет уж мы тоже срать чтобы не кулаки и я не гадить на вот и все. Я хуесор

чтобы срал а я ебал тебя чтобы ты не паши а мы гады ебал вас. Я тебя ебал гад. […] Я тега ебал могол сдать и все. Я тега егал сдаты мого. (Sorokin 1994a, 181)

Viacheslav Kuritsyn describes this progressive running off the rails as the "usual device" of Sorokin's prose (Kuritsyn 2001, 96), which often starts with the simulation of a foreign discourse and subsequently its destruction. The last four pages of this fifth part of *The Norm* contain uniform lines consisting of the interjection: "aaaaaaaaaaaa […]" (Sorokin 1994a, 185–8). While the boring epistolography at the beginning is of no interest, the increasing aggression and deformation of language into unarticulated screaming forms the conceptual experiment of this part. Apart from deconstructing social hierarchy as a source of hidden aggression (cf. Bakshtein 1993, 64), it reflects on letters and paper again. What is conceptually interesting in the end becomes a waste of paper as the sheer quantity of the letter "a" alone is what adds to the semantics of this long cry.

The first and largest part of *The Norm* is as serial an exercise as the twelve poems of part four. It consists of thirty short stories, each with entirely new protagonists. In a certain sense, the signifier "norm" functions here as the central thing symbol [Dingsymbol], around which the action of a novella revolves according to Paul Heyse's falcon theory from 1871; the social panorama of Soviet society revolves around this catalyst for psychological and sociological dynamics. The "protagonists," who have individual names but hardly any history, are characterized almost exclusively in terms of their communications, given in phonetic notation (if not as exclusively as in *The Queue*). The short passages of narrator's discourse do not inform the reader what kind of food goes by the product name "Norma," preserving the hermetic impression of a community that does not question any social practice. The unprepared reader only gradually begins to realize what "Norma" might be. Any doubts are dispelled in the eleventh short story, a dialogue between a boy and his mother who diligently fulfills her duty of eating "Norma":

"Mum, why do you eat doo-doo?"
"It's not doo-doo. Don't talk nonsense. How many times do I need to tell you?"
"But why?"
"Because." The spoon quickly coped with the pliant mash.
"Mom, tell me! It doesn't taste good. I tried. And it smells like doo-doo."
"What did I tell you! Cut it out!"

— Мам, а зачем ты какашки ешь?

— Это не какашка. Не говори глупости. Сколько раз я тебе говорила?

— Нет, ну а зачем?

— Затем,—ложечка быстро управлялась с податливым месивом.

— Ну, мам, скажи! Ведь не вкусно. Я ж пробовал. И пахнет какашкой.

— Я кому говорю! Не смей! (Eng. Sorokin 2004a, 86; Russ. 1994a, 32–3; trans. Keith Gessen)

Here the reader is confronted with what can be called a classical Lacanian scene: a child who is not yet subjugated to the symbolic order is still objective enough to recognize dried excrement as excrement (cf. Deutschmann 1999, 49). Continuing in the spirit of Jacques Lacan's theory of the inevitable subordination of young people under the norms of the symbolic order, the short story informs us that "Norma" is meant only for adults (Sorokin 1994a, 33). The symbolic order demands that people do exactly what is excluded from the civilizing process: eat excrement. The child's legitimate question concerning the reason for this internal flaw in civilization remains unanswered. In *The Norm*, the counter-civilized norm of shit-eating is fulfilled without being questioned.

In the first part of *The Norm*, the norm of eating "Norma" is imposed through Soviet state power. This makes the reader speculate about an allegorical interpretation of the counter-civilized norm: is it "the shit of propaganda," which Soviet people must swallow on a daily basis? However, as Maksim Marusenkov points out, the narrator avoids mentioning Soviet ideology (2012, 157), thus leaving space for the interpretation of swallowing feces as the "existential absurdity of being as such" (Marusenkov 2012, 160, emphasis in the original), relying on existentialist generalizations in the author's interviews (158–9). The temporal differentiation in *The Norm* suggesting that in Stalin's time the portions (of shit) were bigger, however, speaks in favor of a political reading: the more totalitarian an order becomes, the more "shit the citizens have to swallow" (see Marusenkov 2012, 158). If this is the case, swallowing counter-civilized norms is presented as constitutive of Soviet reality, but dependent on the degree of repression.

The obligatory compliance with this norm leads to a relatively homogeneous society of people who have become accustomed to everything, have learned to go along with everything imposed from above (see Ryklin 1998, 737). Civilized and rational abhorrence are countermanded by "presenting the absurd and unnatural as something commonplace, something self-evident which cannot be avoided", as Irina Skoropanova (1999, 268) points out. Paradoxically, the trite redundancy of swallowing shit only tries the patience of the reader, but hardly any of the obedient eaters.

Parts three, seven, and eight of *The Norm* reinforce this metaliterary tendency. Compared to parts one and five, they are only partially intended for reading. Many readers will merely leaf through some of them once they have grasped the device of redundancy (Bogdanova 2005, 24). In these parts the topic of *The Norm* turns out to be literature and its norms: "[…] the 'main hero' of the work is Soviet literature, whose main codes of genre and style are reproduced in *The Norm*, compounding a kind of anthology of its characteristic patterns" (Skoropanova 1999, 267).

The third part consists of several pieces in different styles of realistic prose. Whereas the initial horse motif is reminiscent of Tolstoi's "Strider" ["Kholstomer"] (1886), the narrative style alternates between Turgenev, Chekhov, and Bunin (Skoropanova 1999, 270), and the rural mood evokes late Soviet village prose with its "'patriotic' ethos" (Gillespie 1997, 164). Back in his native village, the intellectual Anton remembers his rural childhood in the 1930s or 40s in idyllic colors. Anton reads a letter by the nineteenth-century poet Fëdor Tiutchev and understands that Tiutchev was his grandfather; then he finds the handwritten copy of Tiutchev's most frequently quoted—and at the same time most anti-rational—poem, "Russia cannot be grasped with the mind" ["Umom Rossiiu ne poniat'"] (Sorokin 1994a, 111). As the choice of this most stereotypical Tiutchev poem shows, originality is not the goal. On the contrary, knowledge about traditional Russian realism appears to be standardized to such a degree that the two new characters who suddenly discuss this piece of realistic prose about the protagonist Anton and its Tiutchev montage evaluate it as a "normal" ["нормальный рассказ"] (Sorokin 1994a, 121) but somehow "boring" ["скучновато"] story, the latter because of the predictability of the Tiutchev poem (Sorokin 1994a, 122).

Back in the Anton plot, Anton digs up a second chest in which he finds a manuscript entitled "The Cattle Plague"—the segment pre-published in 1991 (Sorokin 1991d)—and begins to read again. This piece, dated May 7–29, 1948, belongs to the poetics of Socialist Realism but destroys its clichés. The description of collectivized agriculture, in which people die like cattle, can be connected to Mikhail Sholokhov's *Virgin Soil Upturned* [*Podniataia tselina*] (1932, 1959; cf. Gillespie 2000, 303) or Andrei Platonov's subversion of the Socialist-Realist production novel *The Foundation Pit* [*Kotlovan*] (1930; see Gillespie 1997, 164). The fact that, at the outset, two supervisors seek to impose justice on the Kolkhoz director for not fulfilling the centrally planned quota seems to correspond to the postulates of Socialist Realism. But the brutality with which they burn the director alive is a clear over-implementation of Socialist norms (cf. Deutschmann 1999, 45–6). This, however, means nothing to the two persons evaluating this story; they review it with the standard topos of non-expert conversations about literature from part two of *The Norm*: "normal" ["нормальный"] (Sorokin 1994a, 145). Nevertheless, the interlocutors decide to bury the manuscript again, obviously afraid of the norm-violating literal depiction of Stalinist violence.

The structure of the seventh part follows the principle of seriality again. Here, thirty-two prose texts are introduced by a "Transcript of the main prosecutor's remarks" ["Стенограмма речи главного обвинителя"] (Sorokin 1994a, 220). The prosecutor accuses somebody of violating aesthetic norms. For the sake of metaliterary incrimination he mentions such prominent figures of the art scene as Marcel Duchamp and Sorokin's fellow conceptualist Dmitrii Prigov (Sorokin 1994a, 222). The following thirty-two examples of incriminating texts range from a third of a page to as much as two pages in length.

Reaffirming rather than negotiating the literary norms imposed by the Soviet cultural bureaucracy is also the context of the eighth and last part of *The Norm*. It describes an editorial meeting at which the participants present submitted manuscripts that they have evaluated for this assembly. In their presentations and discussions, they adopt the deformed words of the text: "'I liked the first material *V kungeda po obomoro*. There we have simply and convincingly *pogor mogaram doschasa proboromo Geniamros Normorok*" ["Первый материал—«В кунгеда по обоморо»—мне понравился. В нем просто и убедительно погор могарам досчаса проборомо Гениамрос Норморок"] (Sorokin 1994a, 247). The dwindling difference between the language of the object and editorial metalanguage illustrates the inescapable power of the normative ideological discourse of Soviet literary criticism. It has influenced literature to such a degree that it has ceased to be literature.

Apart from the sections that display redundant patterns with reduced literariness, the book also possesses one indisputably narrative device: the framework plot. It connects a sociological aspect with a metaliterary one. When a certain Boris Gusev is arrested on March 15, 1983—the year Sorokin finished the manuscript of *The Norm*—the secret service confiscates a manuscript of supposedly anti-Soviet literature (Sorokin 1994b, 3; cf. Marusenkov 2012, 150). In the search protocol the responsible officer describes the samizdat-style manuscript in a surprisingly meta-literary manner: "[…] a gray cardboard box … contains … 372 typewritten pages. Title: *The Norm*. No author given" ["(…) папка серого картона. Содержит … 372 машинописных листа. Название «Норма». Автор не указан"] (Sorokin 1994a, 4). In contrast to the inner experimental, "exercise" parts, the framework plot of arrest and confiscation follows the "normal" (anti-)Soviet pattern. The only unusual element is the detail that the expert who is charged with evaluating the manuscript of supposedly "anti-Soviet" literature is a thirteen-year-old boy (Sorokin 1994a, 6). At the end of the framework plot (and the end of the book *The Norm*) the boy finishes his reading and evaluates the manuscript as "four" (Sorokin 1994a, 255). This terse designation has consequences within the KGB hierarchy that controls the correct imposition of Socialist-Realist literary norms in the Soviet Union.

The narrative interdependence of the various levels and framings defies any logical order. It remains unclear which part of the story frames which. Peter Deutschmann interprets this vagueness as a metaliterary message: "*The Norm* is built like an open system of frames that reflects the historical relativity of literary assertions" (Deutschmann 1999, 39). The anti-genealogic quality of norms which becomes especially evident in part eight is a constitutive feature of all of the kinds of norms and quotas with which people in Sorokin's *The Norm* struggle. The unquestioned normality generates a pure being. All connections to a rationale behind these norms or quotas to a reality to which they refer have disappeared long before the various snapshots of *The Norm* were taken: "Sorokin is concerned with the persistence of once erected norms which have lost any connection to the process of their negotiation, their validity, and institutionalization" (Sasse 2003, 228).

It is because of this free-floating automatization that one cannot interpret *The Norm* without considering the metaliterary parts. These sections suggest that there was no exit from the seemingly endless Soviet reality (Yurchak 2006), but only the serial reproduction of acts in compliance with the norms. The dominant device of serialization in particular parts and the all-encompassing quality of all parts put together highlight the "diversity of the little norms that constitute the life of ordinary Soviet people" (Epshtein 2018, 329) and confer on the text the status of an "encyclopedia" (Lipovetsky 2000, 178).

Just as an encyclopedia lists the achievements of other people, in *The Norm* Sorokin imitates foreign texts that are integrated into "his" text almost as "ready-made[s]" (Vail' 1995, 4)· Neither the narrator nor his protagonists become individually identifiable. Narrator and protagonists diminish in an overpowering impersonal, normative reality, in the "schizo-reality"

(Genis 1997, 224) or "schizophrenic absurdity as the norm of the Soviet way of life" (Skoropanova 1999, 268), as various scholars have pointed out.

But a literary text that leaves no exit for its protagonists does not necessarily do the same for its readers. The description of a hopeless situation on the level of the plot or even in the structure of the text itself can obviously trigger a counter-movement in its readers, ranging from moral distancing from the textual world (Sorokin, Laird 1999, 144) to laughter (Smirnov 1999, 67, 72; Talvet 2003). While the former sounds too ethical for conceptualist detached reenactment, the latter is supported by the meta-linguistic basis for the diverse "subplots" of *The Norm*: while transferring the reader's attention to a meta-level, Sorokin provides him with a distance which is constitutive for humor. When trying to understand why people in the plot of section one eat dried feces, the scatological metaphor "in order to survive here, one needs to eat one's fill of shit" [*chtoby tut vyzhit', nuzhno der'ma nazhrat'sia*] (Skoropanova 1999, 268; cf. also Lipovetsky 2000, 178; Kukulin 2002, 263; Bogdanova 2005, 24; Pietraś 2007, 140) comes to mind. By materializing this vulgar metaphor in the fictitious plot of his "novel," Sorokin provides meta-linguistic observations that do not leave the reader inside the hopeless world of Soviet norms and quotas, but lay bare Soviet culture's censored "subconscious" (Groys 2000b, 116), presenting the reader with a humorous meta-position and thus a degree of virtual freedom. What the fictitious characters swallow, is eventually "only *recorded* [*nagovorennoe*] matter" (Ryklin 1998, 737, emphasis in the original).

Irrespective of possible indirect political implications of "the shit of propaganda," the realization of metaphors by literal enactment in a fictitious plot is an utterly conceptual device. One might even argue that it performs a very general metalinguistic and thus "white" Conceptualist technique (cf. chapter One), were it not to such a large degree based on vulgar layers of colloquial language, as well as the fact that the "materialization[s] of an automatized common linguistic metaphor" (Kalinin 2013, 137) in Sorokin's texts often entail drastic or appalling violence.

The device of materializing metaphors has deservedly advanced to a major topic in Sorokin research (Genis 1997, 224; Engel 1997, 62; Ryklin 1998, 742; Berg 2000, 108; Lipovetsky 2000; Uffelmann 2006; Kalinin 2013; Lipovetsky 2013) and will receive more attention later on in this Companion. The following chapters will also attempt to differentiate between various sub-techniques. They will investigate whether a violent plot goes back to an already violent metaphor—like "fuck the mind" in *Four Stout Hearts* [*Serdtsa chetyrech*] (Sorokin 1994d, 104; cf. Sorokin, V.B. 2004) or "Khrushchev scolded Stalin" in *Blue Lard* [*Goluboe salo*] (see chapter Eight)—or to rather harmless idioms such as "horsepower" which is rendered into little horses under a car's hood in *The Blizzard* [*Metel'*] (chapter Eleven). I will also discuss whether the materialized metaphor is explicitly quoted in a fictional text before being materialized in the plot, whether the relevant saying already exists in the text in the imperative form (like in *A Novel* [*Roman*] (chapter Five) and need only be literally performed thereafter, or whether the colloquial metaphor remains an implied enigma yet to be deciphered by attentive readers sensitive to Sorokin's meta-literature—which would mean that it could be deliberately misread by adversarial readers (such as in the Walking Together scandalization of *Blue Lard* in 2002, chapter Eight).

"In order to survive here, one needs to eat one's fill of shit" is not the only implied plot-building metaphor behind *The Norm* where it pertains mostly to part one. The story "The Cattle Plague," embedded in part three, reads again as the materialization of a colloquial metaphor. It embodies the idiom "people die like cattle" (cf. Deutschmann 1999, 45–7; Pietraś 2007, 141), which has only indirect Russian equivalents in *liudi sdokhli kak mukhi* or *liudei pererezali kak svinei / baranov*. Like several other of Sorokin's short stories, this "pseudo-Sots-Realist" (Skoropanova 2002, 213) story first performatively reproduces the norms of Socialist Realism to subsequently deconstruct them by pointing to the disdain for human life in Soviet collectivized agriculture.

Similar deconstructions of Socialist-Realist patterns with the help of materialized metaphors can be found in several of Sorokin's early short stories. The first slim collection of seventeen novellas came out in 1992 (Sorokin 1992a). Various rearranged editions followed in the 1990s and 2000s. The largest, with twenty-nine stories, bore the title *The First Volunteer Saturday Workday* [*Pervyi subbotnik*]. It was initially planned for as early as 1992 (and many researchers were tricked into wrongly listing it as published), but appeared for the first time as part of the 1998 two-volume edition (Sorokin 1998, I 407–594) and reprinted separately only in 2001 (Sorokin 2001a). Eighteen tales were republished in *Morning of a Sniper* [*Utro snaipera*] (Sorokin 2002c), and eleven each in *The Swim* [*Zaplyv*] (Sorokin 2008c) and *The Monoclone* [*Monoklon*] (Sorokin 2010b), respectively.

The majority of these short stories have Socialist Realism as their backdrop, and Sorokin explicitly attested his early stories to be of a "Sots-art manner" ["соцартовская манера"] (Sorokin, Rasskazova 1992, 120). "The First Volunteer Saturday Workday" ["Pervyi subbotnik"]—the title being a signal for Soviet official myths—similarly to *The Norm*—breaches the smooth Socialist-Realist surface with a scatological act. In this case, the allegedly volunteer workers who go to the plant for an unpaid extra shift on a Saturday to support the building of a new socialist society eventually salute themselves for their volunteer work by farting (Sorokin 2001a, 71–3). This twist to indecency can be referred to the vulgar negative evaluation of excessive talking with "they stunk around" [*razvonialis´*]. In "Passing By" ["Proezdom"] the visit by a higher-ranking party official, Georgii Ivanovich, to a district committee of the party derails when he climbs on a desk and defecates on the district committee's documents (Sorokin 1992a, 74–5)—thus materializing the vulgar saying "I shit on this" [*Mne na eto nasrat´*].

Here, as with the practice of "swallowing shit" in the first part of *The Norm*, nobody is ever astonished in the hermetic fictitious worlds of Sorokin's stories. This hermeticism may serve as one of the trademarks of Sorokin's poetics; his version of postmodernism does not include explicit meta-reflection; it rather "lowers" the meta-discourse to the level of hermetic plots. Given their meta-semiotic trajectory, Sorokin's hermetic materializing-metaphor-plots appear as the inversion of René Magritte's *This Is not a Pipe* [*Ceci n'est pas une pipe*] (1929). While Magritte's famous painting refutes identity of image / signifier and object / referent, in the fictional world of Sorokin's texts the metaphor *becomes* the plot.

CHAPTER 4

Marina's Thirtieth Love and Dissident Narratives

Vladimir Sorokin's underground works of the late 1970s and 1980s were written in the final stages of the stagnation period and in the reform era of perestroika, beginning in 1985. From the point of view of intellectual contemporaneity, identifying Sorokin with perestroika and the revolutionary changes it brought is somewhat deceptive. Although he was producing literature during this upheaval, in his texts from the same period Sorokin appears strangely non-contemporary and disconnected from the era. His detached, apolitical stance did not change before the early 2000s (chapter Seven).

Taking Aleksei Yurchak's diagnosis about the population's perception of the eternity of the Soviet order (2006) as a point of reference, disconnectedness from one's own time was perfectly characteristic for the late Soviet period, as hardly anybody foresaw the imminent end of the Soviet system or even envisaged the possibility of such an event. The last years of the stagnation period, with three senile Secretaries General, Brezhnev (1906–1982), Andropov (1914–1984), and Chernenko (1911–1985), were characterized by immobility. Publicly protesting dissidents such as Aleksandr Solzhenitsyn, Vladimir Bukovskii, and Andrei Amalrik failed to effect change, and were instead silenced and exiled.

This societal immobility also applies to Sorokin's conceptual take on stagnation in *Marina's Thirtieth Love* [*Tridtsataia liubov' Mariny*], a novel which was written between 1982 and 1984 and published for the first time in French translation in the watershed year of perestroika, 1987, and then in German toward the end of perestroika, in 1991. The novel reached the wider Russian audience only in 1995 (Sorokin 1995) and has yet to be translated into English.

Marina's Thirtieth Love describes a period in the spring of 1983, when the protagonist Marina Ivanovna Alekseeva is thirty years old. Thus, the time frame from Stalin's death (Sorokin 1995b, I 25) to the time of Andropov constitutes the backdrop to Marina's life (see Sorokin 1995b, 82). Flashbacks are used to show her socialization, from a child, who displays sexual precocity through her father's abuse, to a non-conformist young adult, who moves in dissident circles, prostitutes herself in exchange for scarce products, indulges in jargon and vulgar language, succumbs to the joys of consumerism, and deals with Soviet reality playfully—until she finally undergoes an identity crisis during which she meets the Party functionary Rumiantsev and converts into a model shock worker. Eventually she is assimilated by the collective to such an extent that she disappears completely beneath the ideological discourse of the Andropov period.

From the very beginning, the novel zooms in on eroticism. The reader is immediately thrown into a scene of prostitution in which Marina services the pianist Valentin (Sorokin 1995b, 5–11). This opening scene is arguably that piece of Sorokin's prose which—in stark difference from the alleged pornographic Khrushchev-Stalin encounter from *Blue Lard* (cf. ch. 8)—comes closest to soft porn. The sexual attraction which Marina exerts on both men and women permeates essentially all of her social relations, from party functionaries to dissidents. Marina's disgust in the face of unsolicited daily advances in public (Sorokin 1995b, 85) links the eroticism of the counterculture to the hypocritically prudish Soviet life. In both her semi-private prostitution and her private life Marina is as promiscuous as Irina, the heroine of Viktor Erofeev's *Russian Beauty* [*Russkaia krasavitsa*] (1989), a novel that can serve in many respects as a parallel text about the (erotic) interaction between official and unofficial late-Soviet culture (see Rutten 2010, 163). Sorokin's Marina has, however, never been able to find complete fulfillment for her own love desires. At the purely physical level this means that she has never experienced orgasm with a man (Sorokin 1995b, 12). The novel suggests that for the sake of compensation she seeks out a series of lesbian relationships with twenty-nine female lovers, about whom Marina compiles a scrap book (Sorokin 1995b, 104–17).

Homosexuality had been topical in earlier texts by Sorokin, in the surprising, but restrained male homoeroticism of the story "A Business Proposition" ["Delovoe predlozhenie"] (Eng. Sorokin 1991a; Sorokin 1992, 11–6; cf. Vishevsky 1998, 728) and in the physiologically detailed lesbian sex in one of the thirty vignettes of part one of *The Norm*, also featuring a certain Marina (Sorokin 1994a, 42–5). While lesbian sex was confined to a singular episode in *The Norm*, this series of sexual encounters dominates the first half of *Marina's Thirtieth Love*, full of allusions to the most prominent female homoerotic relationship in the history of Russian literature: that which took place between

Marina Tsvetaeva and Sofiia Parnok (cf. Smirnova 2012). The intertextual allusions, however, in no way individualize Marina's female partners. The title's focus on a desired thirtieth love devaluates the twenty-nine preceding attempts as ultimately unsatisfying. As is common in the early Sorokin, serialization serves as a means of de-individualization: the enumeration of twenty-nine female lovers (Sorokin 1995b, 104–17), whose photos are pasted in Marina's album with the English inscription "ROSE LOVE," a Russian jargon word for homosexuality, is full of stereotypical features, including crude biologisms and racist stereotypes (Sorokin 1995b, 104, 108, 110; cf. Janaszek-Ivaničková 2003, 548).

The serial dissatisfaction compels Marina into a crisis which brings her old discontent with Soviet everyday life to a boil (Sorokin 1995b, 94, 101). Her angelic twenty-ninth love, Sashen´ka, can no longer bring any relief. After an orgy with champagne, hashish, and eleven orgasms Marina dreams of the dissident-moralist writer Aleksandr Solzhenitsyn cursing all of her twenty-nine lovers. Hysterical, Marina then breaks it off with Sashen´ka, violently throwing her out, and drowns herself in an obsessive, lonely drinking bout (Sorokin 1995b, 128–33). After this Marina breaks various social bonds with those around her: she terminates contact with the Central-Committee employee Leonid Petrovich (Sorokin 1995b, 149, 161–2) and knocks down the American Slavist Tony—the latter scene being a compulsory reading for every self-reflective Western enthusiast of Russia. She ceases to fetishize Soviet underground culture: neither the punk rocker Govno [literally: Shit], who drinks his own urine, nor Daniil Andreev's esoteric samizdat compilation *Rose of the World* [*Roza mira*] (published only in 1991) can satisfy her thirst for transgression (Sorokin 1995b, 152–9). Her inner struggle pushes her away from protest practices to normative morality, represented by two authorities in a row, first by the dissident writer Solzhenitsyn, then by the party official Rumiantsev.

In Marina's exclusively sexual way of thinking (cf. Poyntner 2005, 113), her vision of the arrival of Solzhenitsyn as a kind of Messiah (Sorokin 1995b, 86) is accompanied by the hope that he will provide her first heterosexual orgasm:

> Marina was sure that with HIM everything would happen as it should. As it was supposed to happen, but alas, not even once had it happened to her with any man. […] HE… HE always remained a secret knowledge, a hidden possibility of true love, the very same that Marina was fervently dreaming of […].

Марина была уверена, что с НИМ все случится как надо. Как положено случаться, но чего, к сожалению, ни разу не произошло у нее ни с одним мужчиной. [...] ОН... ОН всегда оставался тайным знанием, скрытой возможностью настоящей любви, той самой, о которой так мечтала Марина [...]. (Sorokin 1995b, 103)

In this gender arrangement, the idea of a God-given heterosexual order, perpetuated by atheist Socialist Realism, is reinstalled. Female heterosexual submission is reinstituted—in spite of all of Marina's homosexual and dissident actions of protest. Although Marina's first heterosexual experience was the painful abuse at the hands of her father, his death fails to terminate her submission under the "law of the father." Despite her homosexual libertinage, Marina is continuously subject to a string of paternal authorities: dead personifications of Party authority such as Lenin (Sorokin 1995b, 35, 39), remote authorities such as the émigré Solzhenitsyn, and tangible ones such as the Party functionary Rumiantsev. These various men serve merely as paternal authority for Marina—Lenin and Solzhenitsyn in visions, Marina's father and Rumiantsev in rape. The novel's presentation of an entire sequence of "fathers" and super-egos appears as a deliberate "hypertrophy of the oedipal complex" ["Hypertrophierung des Ödipalen"] (Döring-Smirnov 1992, 561), an undermining of the psychoanalytical pattern by the means of serialization (cf. Dobrenko 1990, 175).

The interchangeability of the diverse father-authorities is emphasized when Sergei Rumiantsev, who in the end takes the place of the paternal figure, appears to Marina at first glance to be Solzhenitsyn's "double" (Sorokin 1995b, 163; cf. Brockhoff 1992, 140). This alleged similarity, however, is refuted by details (no beard, no blue eyes, funny tie; Sorokin 1995b, 164). Rumiantsev simply occupies the position left vacant by Marina's father and only imaginatively filled by Solzhenitsyn, while the ideological divergence is presented as negligible. This was already palpable when the narrator presented Marina as formulaically anti-Soviet, inverting the official saying of the imperative to love Soviet power: "More than everything on earth Marina hated the Soviet power" ["Больше всего на свете Марина ненавидела Советскую власть"] (Sorokin 1995b, 83). This is a true syntactical copy of the idiom "More than everything on earth I love..." As a result, contradictory negation reproduces the very patterns that it negates. The novel projects this observation onto the seemingly antagonistic spheres of official Soviet politics and its dissident critics.

Both official and dissident literature advocated a "hyper-moralistic" humanism yet displayed few differences in their aesthetic preferences (Eng. Erofeyev 1995, x–ii; Russ. Erofeev 1997, 10–2): "Soviet and anti-Soviet literature strove to undo each other in a humanistic tug-of-war" (Eng. Erofeyev 1995, xi; Russ. Erofeev 1997, 10). What Serguei Oushakine in a canonical article calls the "mimetic resistance" of dissident literature reproduces the categories of the enemy's discourse (2001, 200): "While being differently positioned, the dominant and dominated draw on the same vocabulary of symbolic means and rhetorical devices" (Oushakine 2001, 207).

Marina's Thirtieth Love artistically confirms Erofeev's and Oushakine's diagnoses by constructing external similarity between the dissident writer Aleksandr Solzhenitsyn and the representative of the communist regime and ideology, the fictitious Sergei Rumiantsev. If approached from Marina's basic fixation on heterosexuality and father figures, the primitive and uneducated Rumiantsev makes use of the full extent of his alleged authority in the name of the Party. When Marina has a crying fit, Rumiantsev justifies his insistence on escorting her home with the ubiquitous responsibilities of the intelligence services: "I like to be in on everything" ["Мне до всего есть дело ..."] (Sorokin 1995b, 167). The visible frontispiece of the invisible Party is a portrait of Lenin over Rumiantsev's workplace in the factory (Sorokin 1995b, 194). The authorities in Marina's story thus constitute a full circle.

The conversion of the former non-conformist Marina to communist values (and of the dissident narrative to Socialist Realism) begins with a kitchen-table talk in Marina's flat late at night, when Rumiantsev gives Marina a rather simple-minded moralistic instruction. First, he asks whether she "loves the Soviet people" ["(...) ты советских людей любишь? (...) ты наших любишь? Наших? Понимаешь?! Наших! Любишь?"] (Sorokin 1995b, 170). It takes quite some time until the maieutic suggestion has an effect and Marina finally repeats after Rumiantsev that she indeed does (Sorokin 1995b, 175). This sets the stage for two simultaneous "demiurgic penetrations" (Brockhoff 1992, 140)—one vaginal and rape-like by Rumiantsev and one ideological entering through Marina's ear. Only the combination of the two elevates what is described in the novel as the worst sex ever—an uninvited, rude, and clumsy penetration (Sorokin 1995b, 180)—into the plot's decisive ideological turning point.

Even though Marina's final transformation occurs at the moment of her first heterosexual orgasm, it is not the sexual prowess of the party functionary that is responsible. Marina experiences this intercourse while fast asleep and anaesthetized (Sorokin 1995b, 181; see Zakhar'in 1999, 175). What counts is the fact that the radio is switched on and at six in the morning starts playing the Soviet anthem (in the 1977 version):

> UNBREAKABLE UNION OF FREEBORN REPUBLICS, GREAT RUSSIA HAS WELDED FOREVER TO STAND! CREATED IN STRUGGLE BY WILL OF THE PEOPLES, UNITED AND MIGHTY, OUR SOVIET LAND:
>
> Marina cries, her heart breaks from a new inexplicable feeling, and the words, the words … these intoxicating, bright, solemn, and joyful words, they become comprehensible like never before and enter Marina's innermost heart:
>
> SING TO OUR MOTHERLAND, FREE AND UNDYING
>
> СОЮЗ НЕРУШИМЫЙ РЕСПУБЛИК СВОБОДНЫХ СПЛОТИЛА НАВЕКИ ВЕЛИКАЯ РУСЬ! ДА ЗДРАВСТВУЕТ СОЗДАННЫЙ ВОЛЕЙ НАРОДОВ ЕДИНЫЙ МОГУЧИЙ СОВЕТСКИЙ СОЮЗ!
>
> Марина плачет, сердце ее разрывается от нового необъяснимого чувства, а слова, слова … опьяняющие, светлые, торжественные и радостные,—они понятны как никогда и входят в самое сердце:
>
> СЛАВЬСЯ, ОТЕЧЕСТВО НАШЕ СВОБОДНОЕ! (Sorokin 1995b, 182, English using the official CPSU translation)

Drawing on the widespread fascination with the Soviet monumental hymn, even in circles hostile to Soviet ideology (up to the present day), Sorokin invents an "ideological orgasm" as the heterosexual-communist cure for his formerly homosexual-dissident heroine. Marina's cathartic weeping after her first orgasm in the company of a man is credited to the resonance of the "words of the wonderful song" ["слова чудесной песни"] (Sorokin 1995b, 184), not to the heterosexual intercourse and definitely not to Rumiantsev, whose semen Marina registers on her body with surprise (Sorokin 1995b, 185). This intercourse "is no longer a private moment" (Brougher 1998, 103) between two individuals, but a means of de-privatization and de-emancipation. Sylvia Sasse playfully continues Sorokin's materialized metaphor of the "ideological orgasm," emphasizing that it is "the Soviet hymn which after the coitus with Rumiantsev remains lying on her instead of the party secretary and drowns her as a character in the novel" (Sasse 1999, 128). Thus Rumiantsev serves not only as the servile mouthpiece of ideology but also as the instrumental penis-piece of the phallus of the Soviet collective conjured in the Soviet hymn. The anthem degrades the penetration by Rumiantsev to an auxiliary function; without the assistance of the party's authority he would be the same "ineffectual bridegroom" (Rutten 2010, 192) as all his male predecessors in Marina's bed. Correspondingly, Marina does not give birth to Rumiantsev's child, but to a Sots-Realist production novel.

While Rumiantsev has his way with her, Marina associates their sexual intercourse with the abuse by her father (Sorokin 1995b, 180)—that is, with the primal scene of patriarchal violence she experienced. Thus, the orgasm she experiences coincides with her resubmission to the control of paternal authorities (cf. Brougher 1998, 102) and regression to passivity. While Sigmund Freud interpreted heterosexual orgasm as the progress of female sexuality to vaginal passivity (away from a little girl's childish clitoral activity; on the analogy to Freud see Zakhar´in 1999, 175), the playful post-Freudian Sorokin does not share this opinion. What he depicts with amusement is a non-conformist's "collapse into happiness" ["Absturz ins Glück"] (Leitner 1999, 100–1). At this point, orgasm itself becomes a matter of renunciation of individuality, of "salvation from individuation" ["спасение от индивидуации"] (Sorokin, Rasskazova 1992, 124). The novel's plot suggests that late Soviet culture, with its lack of prospects for an end to scenarios of submission, expresses itself via the oxymoron of submission with relish, which the novel renders as the key trope of the late stagnation phase.

Marina submits to heterosexual intercourse as she does to authority (Obermayr 1999, 83). Her submitting to the penetration by authority entails auto-aggression, self-disciplining, and self-humiliation of the heroine. Marina, who has again and again experienced male violence, at the moment of upheaval turns external violence against herself and experiences a fit of passivity which lets her regress to a state of suffering from her childhood. This leads to her renouncement of self-determination and de-emancipation (which is debunked and not advocated by Sorokin, as Halina Janaszek-Ivaničková erroneously assumes; 2003, 549–50). Right away, in the early morning after the radio orgasm, Marina behaves in her household as a domestic worker within the patriarchal order: she "obediently" ["послушно"] serves Rumiantsev (Sorokin 1995b, 186).

Patriarchal gender psychology is, however, not the only authority that is made responsible for Marina's final submission under the father authority of the Party. The novel plays on a second tradition of Russian culture that declares humiliation as socially desirable: Christianity (cf. Uffelmann 2010). Even though the non-conformist Marina is not officially a member of the Russian Orthodox Church, she is religious in a vague sort of way (Sorokin 1995b, 16) and amongst other things keeps a bible, a rosary, a Psalter, and a prayer book in her locked desk drawer (Sorokin 1995b, 104). At the time of her moral crisis Marina recites a long prayer of atonement from memory (Sorokin 1995b, 151–2).

In her unfocused search for a way to cross the Soviet vale of tears, Marina makes use of various sources. When she directs her politico-religious yearnings toward the return of the exile Solzhenitsyn for a while, this distorted image of the Messiah echoes 1) Christ, 2) Tolstoy's peasant habits, 3) the tellurian pathos of the late-Slavophile *pochvennichestvo*, 4) Orthodox Easter, and 5) the pagan symbolism of sunrise (which occurs in Soviet topoi as well and was deconstructed by Bulatov as being para-religious; see Groys 1992, 81–4):

> An oval door opens, and in the dark doorway a FACE appears. [...] in the wise, brave eyes—of a great man who has given himself heart and soul to the service of Russia— there are tears.
> HE [...] comes out dressed in the same sheepskin coat and clasps to his breast a little bag with a handful of Russian soil.
> [...] Up there, illuminated by the rays of the rising sun, HE lifts a heavy hand and slowly crosses himself, sweepingly, marking the First Day of Freedom.
> And everybody crosses themselves, kisses each other, wiping away tears."

> Открывается овальная дверь и в темном проеме показывается ЛИЦО.
> [...] в этих мудрых, мужественных глазах великого человека, отдавшего всего себя служению России, стоят слезы.
> ОН [...] выходит в том самом тулупчике, прижимая к груди мешочек с горстью земли русской.
> [...] Он там наверху, залитый лучами восходящего солнца, поднимает тяжелую руку и размашисто медленно крестится, знаменуя Первый День Свободы.
> И все вокруг крестятся, целуются, размазывая слезы. (Sorokin 1995b, 86)

The oval doorway is reminiscent of the depiction of Christ in the mandorla; the poor clothing of a peasant is a reference to a monk's habit, imitating the poverty of Christ; the action of crossing oneself in a liturgically slow manner means professing one's adherence to Christ.

Scattered throughout the text of the novel are additional allusions to Christ, for example to the Christological number 30: at the time the story takes place, Marina is thirty years old (Sorokin 1995b, 24); her thirtieth love comes in her thirtieth spring (Sorokin 1995b, 78), that is, around Easter of the thirtieth year of her life. In Marina's dream, a troparion dedicated to a nameless imitator of Christ is sung:

> Having lo-o-oved Christ since my you-ou-ou-outh,
> I ta-a-a-ake His light yo-o-o-oke on myself,
> And I prai-ai-ai-aise thee, God, for ma-a-a-any wo-o-o-onders,
> Pra-a-a-ay for the redemption of our so-o-o-ouls …

> От юности Христа возлюбиииив,
> И легкое иго Его на ся восприяааал еси,
> И мнооогими чудесааами прослаааави тебе Бог,
> Моли спастися душам нааашиииим … [Sorokin 1995b, 127]

The dissidents also lay claim to imitation of Christ: Marina consoles and admires the dissident Mitia: "You are our martyr" ["Ты у нас мученик"], "Our sufferer" ["Страдалец ты наш"] (Sorokin 1995b, 93, 95). As with the Soviet hymn, the dissident message of a Christ-like suffering old Russia (Rus´) comes in capital letters:

> THE GREATNESS OF OUR GLORIOUS RUSSIA […] IN ORTHODOX MEMORY OF THE MILLIONS SHOT TORTURED MURDERED […] WITH GREAT ENDURANCE AND HOPE …

> ВЕЛИЧИЕ РУСИ НАШЕЙ СЛАВНОЙ […] С ПАМЯТЬЮ ПРАВОСЛАВНОЙ С МИЛЛИОНАМИ РАССТРЕЛЯННЫХ ЗАМУЧЕННЫХ УБИЕННЫХ […] С ВЕЛИКИМ ТЕРПЕНИЕМ И ВЕЛИКОЙ НАДЕЖДОЮ … (Sorokin 1995b, 127)

Mitia's eagerness to suffer and endure, however, has already waned; he has given up and is willing to emigrate (Sorokin 1995b, 94–5). In the late stagnation period, Christian self-sacrifice is yet another model of self-humiliation that has reached its limits.

This does not diminish the fact that in Sorokin's novel references to various holy women from the history of Christianity can be associated with the first name *Marina*—St. Margaret (in the Greek, and then in the entire Orthodox tradition: St. Marina), Gregory of Nyssa's sainted sister Macrina, as well as various Marian figures. Marina's prostitution creates a reference to two female sinners—to Mary Magdalene, the prostitute who followed Jesus, and to Mary of Egypt. Mary Magdalene's figure combines adherence to Christ and prostitution. This is quite comparable to Marina, who gives away her Eros to the dissident Mitia out of compassion. Mary of Egypt, the repentant sinner, who in the end finds the right path and leads a strictly ascetic life in the desert for forty-seven years, has inspired much of Russian apocryphal tradition and later works such as Aleksei Remizov's short story "Mary of Egypt" ["Mariia Egipetskaia"] (1915). Mary of Egypt experienced an upheaval very similar to Marina's: from Eros to asexuality. In the case of Sorokin's Marina, the only difference is that her celibacy is the asceticism of work and not of loneliness; her desert is the factory. Thus, two quite different conceptions of femininity are juxtaposed in Marina's relationship with Mary: on the one hand, the worldly sinners Mary Magdalene and Mary of Egypt before their repentance, and on the other, the pure Mother of God and the chaste Mary of Egypt (for more on Christian and Marian traces in *Marina's Thirtieth Love*, see Uffelmann 2010, 853–918).

As can be seen from these multiple connections to Christianity, *Marina's Thirtieth Love* offers a wide range of intertextual interpretations. Together with the illustrated play with psychoanalysis, gender, and sexuality, and with the investigation into non-conformist culture of the stagnation period, the Christian dimension makes the first 189 pages of *Marina's Thirtieth Love* an exercise in ambiguous novelistic writing inviting various interpretations. It adds a very different kind of writing, in this case a highly complex masterpiece of genre emulation, to Sorokin's portfolio.

Is this mimicry but an austere conceptualist game? Or does it have social or even political implications? While those researching the early Sorokin insist on his apoliticism, Petr Vail''s thesis about Sorokin as a "collector and conserver" of styles has clear political implications:

[Sorokin is] a collector and conserver [*sobiratel' i khranitel'*]. Of what? Well, of the same stylistic—non-ideological!—stereotypes and clichés that convey certainty and ease. These clichés are updated, being reborn through Sorokin's pen in diverse ways, not in the clownish costume of sots-art, but as symbols of stability, almost of timeless and limitless folkloristic constancy [...] (Vail' 1995)

Sorokin's feat of "conservation" is thus not only obvious in terms of genre, but also as a concept or even understanding of political and cultural history. In this context, the iteration of the device of self-submission describes a social practice that is sanctioned as it is the only viable alternative. If nothing remains but to reproduce submission under both individual and political paternal authorities again and again, then no rebellion against these authorities, as initially attempted by Marina, will ever change anything about this social structure (cf. Chernetsky 2007, 149). In this case, each revolt will only replace one authority with another, without ever breaking the pattern. This is not to say that Sorokin welcomes submission, but rather to state that his novel suggests the inescapability of iterated subjugation as reproduced in the individual both from within and without.

This victimization makes *Marina's Thirtieth Love* stand out among Sorokin's long prose texts. Against the backdrop of "The Cattle Plague" from *The Norm*, or *A Novel*, the "perpetrator text" ["Tätertext"] (Uffelmann 2003, 293) par excellence (chapter Five), and countless other scenes of violence, all related from the perpetrator's narrative perspective, *Marina's Thirtieth Love* forms an exception, a "victim text" ["Opfertext"] (Uffelmann 2003, 292) in which the victim's perspective dominates.

This difference also has an impact on the twofold structure of the novel. In *Marina's Thirtieth Love* Sorokin does not uncover the suppression of violence under a "seemingly smooth surface" (Engel 1999, 140) but constructs the smooth surface of the second half as both the concealment and the implementation of violence and victimization (cf. Kustanovich 2004, 307).

After her communist turn Marina habituates herself to voluntarily getting up in the morning at 6 a.m. (Sorokin 1995b, 191)—adopting Rumiantsev's self-congratulation at increasing the work quota. At this point all of the clichés of the Socialist-Realist production novel are activated (see Brougher 1998, 105). Rumiantsev for Marina is a model work hero much like the Socialist-Realist romanticizing of the jackhammer in the case of Aleksei Stakhanov, who in a staged propaganda stunt overfulfilled his work quota by a factor of fourteen on August 31, 1935: "Salutation to Stakhanov" ["Салют стахановцу"] (Sorokin 1995b, 210). The converted Marina toils at the workbench, having forgotten her old self and oblivious to the passage of time (Sorokin 1995b, 210). The Socialist-Realist fetishism of factory work prevails in Marina's new infantile enthusiasm for mechanical technology: she glories in "the wonderful music of the machines" ["чудесная музыка машин"] (Sorokin 1995b, 196).

Marina's entry into the factory is heralded by the announcement of the predefined norm of 350 pieces that a lathe worker must produce in a shift (Sorokin 1995b, 203). It shapes the pages that follow, which describe the process of Marina approaching and then overfulfilling this exclusively quantitative norm: 118 on the first day (Sorokin 1995b, 210), then 210 (223), 324 (226), and 371 (238)—"that's twenty-one pieces more than the set quota" ["то есть на 21 деталь больше положенной нормы"] (Sorokin 1995b, 238), finally 440 (247). This "initiation into the norm" is accompanied by her additional volunteering for an allegedly grass-roots-organized wall newspaper ["стенгазета"] (Sorokin 1995b, 214–5) and a purportedly voluntary Saturday workday (Sorokin 1995b, 231).

After crossing the factory threshold, Marina has relinquished her critical stance on Soviet conditions. She now approves of literally everything: the bright factory hall, the factory's cantina, the women workers' residence hall, the frugal snacks for dinner, and so forth (Sorokin 1995b, 196, 205, 213–4). As in exemplary Socialist Realism (cf. Siniavskii 1967, 419), there are no antagonistic conflicts in the factory brigade. This goes also for Marina Alekseeva's indolent, but repentant colleague Zolotarev, whom she successfully disciplines to perform more thorough work. When Alekseeva denounces drunkards in the street on Sunday afternoon, the narrator mentions only the gratitude expressed by the police (Sorokin 1995b, 233).

The price for all this model submission to the normative expectations imposed on a Socialist-Realist heroine is Marina's renunciation of female gender identity. Her worker's pass as a lathe operator uses the Russian masculine *rastochnik* (Sorokin 1995b, 209) and her colleagues refer to her only with the masculine *drug* [friend], not *podruga* (Sorokin 1995b, 227; cf. Obermayr 1999, 92). Soon, Marina gives up makeup and no longer pays any attention to how she dresses (Sorokin 1995b, 231). Thus her single heterosexual orgasm provides Marina with a female gender role only for a second before it then transforms her into a "face- and genderless being" (Stewart 2006, 260). Her newly acquired heterosexuality turns into a "zero sexuality" (Döring-Smirnov 1992, 560), eventually corresponding to the prudish norms of Socialist Realism. Marina's decorporalization borders upon machinization (Nedel′ 1998, 254).

Her last individual emotion in the novel is the joyful yelp she utters in the moment when she is integrated as an ordinary "worker" ["рабочая"] (Sorokin 1995b, 209) into the brigade.

The inner perspective of Marina Alekseeva gives way to officially pre-scribed speech acts such as Zolotarev's solicited self-criticism "I fully and unconditionally admit my guilt [...]" ["Я полностью и безоговорочно признаю свою вину (...)"] (Sorokin 1995b, 240) or emotional paradoxes such as the declaration of love to Soviet institutions: "I also feel great love for the Soviet Army [...]" ["я тоже испытываю большую любовь к Советской Армии (...)"] (Sorokin 1995b, 237). From this point on it is not Alekseeva or other fictitious characters speaking anymore; the "true [official] language speaks through her" (Wiedling 1999, 155). The characters' voices "fall victim to a community language ["einer gemeinschaftlichen Sprache zu verfallen"] which regulates all interpretations of the world and of human existence in the world, delegating responsibility, freedom, and their own judgements to it" (Leitner 1999, 96).

While the text becomes less and less readable, the reader's attention is drawn more and more to its formal aspects. These include the steps toward the reduction of Marina's individuality in the narrative: the last time her first name is mentioned alone (as in all the dissident part; Sorokin 1995b, 230); the last time first and last name occur together (Sorokin 1995b, 232); when and for how long only her last name appears (until p. 248). This transforms into a focus on the steps toward reduction of the novel's "novelness": the last time a fictional character is mentioned (Sorokin 1995b, 249); when the last direct speech is introduced with an em-dash (even if the signaled individual utterance already sounds like Soviet news; Sorokin 1995b, 255); where there is the last paragraph shift (Sorokin 1995b, 259) before a 27-page-long para-graph of reports on party activities from the Soviet central newspaper *Pravda*. The latter starts—obviously a special joke—with the totally irrelevant Communist Party of Luxemburg: "The plenary has made the decision to con-vene the next scheduled 24th congress of CPL in January 1984" ["Пленум принял решение о созыве очередного, XXIV съезда КПЛ в январе 1984 года"] (Sorokin 1995b, 259). Here Sorokin over-implements the practice of Socialist-Realist novels to include discursive elements from party documents in the fictional text. Sven Gundlakh, who read the novel in its samizdat form years before its Russian publication, is right in claiming that the final part of *Marina's Thirtieth Love* "is not meant for reading but for weighing in one's hands [*razveshivanie na rukakh*] the stack of neatly typed pages" (Gundlakh 1985, 77).

This means that the novel essentially contains two turning points: first from dissident perspective to Socialist Realism (Sorokin 1995b, 189), second from boring Socialist-Realist novel to official news (249). Thus, in contrast to *The Norm*, Socialist Realism is not spread out through several parts of the novel, but comes in suddenly after 189 pages. The first and the second part of *Marina's Thirtieth Love* are much more contextualized, referring to dissident narratives and Socialist Realism. Only the third, unreadable part continues the "white" tendency in Moscow Conceptualism by drawing attention to issues of genre (official Soviet news) and the interrelation between paper and text. This diagnosis is supported by a change in medium: in the original manuscript, the third, "Pravda" part was typewritten while the first part and second part were handwritten (Skakov 2013, 59).

Whereas Sorokin's narrator disappears in the third part, nowhere in the novel does the author, who typed twenty-seven pages of *Pravda* news and forced his translators to accomplish an analogous strenuous act (Wiedling 1999, 159–60), seem to display any form of partiality: his interest is equally devoted to the dissident narrative, Socialist Realism, and *Pravda* news. Even if the first two parts name-drop multiple figures from Stalin to Sorokin's fellow underground artist Oskar Rabin, a key representative of the Lianozovo group, Sorokin does this without any axiological partisanship or identification; the names come in as mere signals of a late Soviet (anti-)official discourses. Sorokin's non-axiological writing "questions the ideological function of literature in Russia, particularly the belief that a collective idea should transcend an individual's struggle for existence" (Lawrence 2015, 167–8). As a result "a feeling of false identity, of functional equality of thesis and antithesis, emerges" (Berg 2000, 106; cf. also Smirnov 1995, 142). Since "dissident literature dies" along with the first part of *Marina's Thirtieth Love* (Koschmal 1996, 25), this novel performs the "end of the aesthetics of responsibility" or "ethopoetics" (Koschmal 1996, 21; cf. also Monastyrskii 1985, 75; Weststeijn 1995, 38–9).

The threefold structure of *Marina's Thirtieth Love* is mirrored in other texts by Sorokin. A similar mechanism of gradual derailment (cf. Groys 2000b, 116) was evident in the "Letters to Martin Alekseich" from the fifth part of *The Norm* and will reoccur in *A Novel* (chapter Five), but in these longer texts the derailments are gradual. In contrast, diverse short stories by Sorokin can be likened to each other on the basis of a bipartite or "bipolar" (Berg 2000, 105) structure. This mechanism consists of deceptive emulation broken by a single unexpected (Buida 1994) "frame-break" (Chitnis 2005, 119), after which an "explosion of the plot" [*siuzhetnyi vzryv*] (Monastyrskii 1985, 75) follows— either through "flows of incomprehensible speech" or inserting violence (Kuritsyn 2001, 96). Many scholars have identified this technique as Sorokin's only plot-building trademark (Kenzheev 1995, 202; Danilkin 2002; Glanc 2017, 33–4), a scholarly uniformity already observed by Mark Lipovetsky (2000, 171) and Irina Skoropanova (2002, 211). The twofold structure applies to Lipovetsky's examples such as "Free Lesson" ["Svobodnyi urok"] (Sorokin 1992a, 82–92), in which authoritarian socialist pedagogy turns into child abuse (see Lipovetsky 2000, 174). The truism of sudden change, producing a bipartite structure, however, turns out to be already wrong from the outset, that is, even when looking at some of the early stories. For example, "Coming Home" ["Vozvrashchenie"], a Socialist-Realist-style puritanical love story, is all along permeated with vulgar language invading the decent family conversations, not only toward the end (Sorokin 1992a, 105–6). The plots of the novels *Four Stout Hearts*, *A Month in Dachau*, and *Ice* are also violent throughout without exhibiting any turning point, even if the violence in these cases can also be read as the materialization of vulgar metaphors (cf. Kustanovich 2004, 310).

CHAPTER 5

A *Novel* and Classical Russian Literature

The fourth long prose book by Sorokin to be discussed here in detail, *A Novel* [*Roman*], signals its genre not only in the subtitle like later editions of *Marina's Thirtieth Love* or the alleged novel *The Queue*, but also in the main title. *A Novel* was written between 1985 and 1989 and published in Russia in December of 1994 with a print run of 2,000. Thus, its "incubation period" in unpublished or unofficially published form was a bit shorter than with the previously explored texts.

The increasing accessibility of Sorokin's texts for Russian readers goes back to perestroika, the political reform process begun by the newly elected Secretary General Mikhail Gorbachëv in March of 1985. Intended as an attempt to rescue the Soviet system, whose looming failure was predicted by Soviet economists in the early 1980s, it brought the most eminent breakthroughs in foreign politics: the spectacular nuclear disarmament treaties signed by Gorbachëv and American Presidents Reagan and Bush senior in 1987 and 1991. Transparency in internal cultural politics became palpable in 1987 (Skillen 2017, 121). After Gorbachëv's speech to journalists about filling the "white spots" in Soviet history, in the late 1980s many twentieth-century literature works that had been prohibited for decades—by classic (anti-)Soviet authors such as Anna Akhmatova, Mikhail Bulgakov, Vasilii Grossman, and Andrei Platonov as well as émigrés such as Vladimir Nabokov, Aleksandr Solzhenitsyn, and many others—finally reached Soviet readers officially (cf. Nove 1989, 217–55).

Compared to the classics of Russian uncensored twentieth-century literature, Sorokin's works of the late 1970s and 1980s did not have a long prehistory of readers' demand. His first official publication in the Soviet Union after his unpretentious text in *For the Workers in the Petroleum Industry* was made possible in the periphery: the Riga-based journal *Spring*

[*Rodnik*] published Sorokin's story "Start of the Season" ["Otkrytie sezona"] in November of 1989 (Sorokin 1989). A few publications in more central periodicals followed until the end of the Soviet Union on December 31, 1991: the play "Pelmeni" ["Pel′meni"] in *Iskusstvo kino* in 1990 (Sorokin 1990), an excerpt from the tamizdat publication of *The Queue* in the popular magazine *Ogonek* (Sorokin 1991c), a segment from what would later become his book *The Norm* [*Norma*] in the journal *Volga*, a story in *Strelets* in 1991 (Sorokin 1991f), and the play "Confidence" ["Doverie"] in *Al′manakh LIA R. Elinina* (Sorokin 1991i). The large print run of *Ogonek* and also of the Soviet "thick journals" brought Sorokin to the attention of a larger audience. Telling in this respect, making the underground more visible, are the titles of the almanac *Herald of New Literature* [*Vestnik novoi literatury*] (Sorokin 1991f) and of the collection *Our Visibility* [*Vidimost′ nas: sbornik*], containing two more stories by Sorokin (1991g, 1991h).

Only after the dissolution of the Soviet state did Russia see the first autonomous publication of a thin book (128 pages) by Sorokin, *Collected Stories* [*Sbornik rasskazov*] (Sorokin 1992a) with a respectable print run of 25,000 copies. Sorokin's new visibility to a broader public was further enhanced by the fact that *Collected Stories* was short-listed for the Russian Booker Prize [*Russkii Buker*]. This eventually opened the door for book publications of his longer texts in the Russian Federation in 1994 and 1995: *The Norm* (Sorokin 1994c, 256 pages), *A Novel* (Sorokin 1994b, 398 pages), and *Marina's Thirtieth Love* (Sorokin 1995b, 285 pages).

The belated emergence of Sorokin on the Russian book market led to a very specific reception in post-Soviet Russia. Especially *Collected Stories*, *A Novel*, *Four Stout Hearts*, and *The Norm* were met with uproar by some reviewers, such as Vladimir Bondarenko who called Sorokin's writing "fecal prose" [*fekal′naia proza*] (Bondarenko 1995; see the overviews in Kasper 1999, 103; Wołodźko-Butkiewicz 2003, 71–3; Stewart 2006, 232–3; Paulsen 2009, 123–34). Apart from Sorokin's violation of literary taboos and decorum, some reviewers saw this kind of literature as an attempt to pander to "Western Slavists." The alleged reimport "from Germany," promoted by émigrés from "an American distance" (Remizova 1995), thus led to a first wave of negative reviews of Sorokin as a "foreign writer" (cf. Uffelmann 2000, 279). Later more sympathetic reviews appeared in Russia as well, but some fierce critics, such as Andrei Nemzer (for example 2003, 397–399), have continued to slam virtually every book publication by Sorokin.

Even a superficial glance at *A Novel* in the Russian original, which has not been translated into English thus far, gives the reader the convincing impression that this excessive story of rural life, sentimental love, and mass murder comes closer to a traditional novel. As with *Marina's Thirtieth Love*, this at least applies to the bulk of the novel, here 4/5 of the text: the graphical appearance of the novel's text is relatively homogeneous until page 332. It consists of an alternation of narrator's paragraphs in blockquote and fragments of direct speech, introduced with m-dashes. A second look at the chapter structure produces a similar impression: the novel seems classically structured in two parts with twelve and eight chapters each, all relatively evenly sized, apart from the lengthy eighth chapter of the second part (Russ. Sorokin 1994c, 242–398), whose end (pp. 332–98) consists only of narratorial blockquote with very few paragraph shifts.

A closer reading of the text reveals other novelistic devices. A relatively easily discernible technique is the Dostoevskiian trademark of creating suspense by letting somebody enter a room at the end of a chapter as—then still nameless—Tat′iana does at the very end of part one (Sorokin 1994c, 124). What follows is a device more often employed by Lev Tolstoi and Ivan Turgenev: the novelistic technique of retardation. The reader learns about Tat′iana and her future romance with the protagonist, Roman, not immediately, but only after three longish chapters that describe a hay harvest, mushrooming, a visit to the Russian sauna, and an excursion to a neighboring village (Sorokin 1994c, 125–65). These chapters are characterized by "sluggishness" that exhibits the "procedure of agony" of Sorokin's novelist narrative (Berg 2000, 107). Some readers might feel tempted to scan pages for potentially relevant information, but a truly attentive reading of these chapters allows to detect the classical structuring elements of a novel such as leitmotifs, loaded with symbolic meaning—the repeated appearance of velvet silk, in which the fateful axe comes wrapped later; the symbolic return of the first victim of Roman's killing, the wolf, as a fur on the floor of the bridal room (Sorokin 1994c, 319); and the little bear at Tat′iana's feet, all transparent symbols of violent passions hidden behind sentimental love (Sorokin 1994c, 193, 195, 233), supported by a great variety of direful allusions to death (Van Baak 2009, 465–7).

These leitmotifs are deliberately arranged by an omniscient authorial narrator who delivers historical background information (Sorokin 1994c, 25) and applies novelistic techniques, such as a frame tale leading to a retrospective that forms the main plot. In the frame narrative, a nameless visitor comes to a cemetery where he discerns the gravestone of a certain "ROMAN" (Sorokin 1994c, 4)—the eponymous protagonist of the novel, whose name also means "novel" and "romance" in Russian—a poignant prolepsis of the novel's fatal end. On the first page of the internal plot (Sorokin 1994c, 7) this very Roman returns to his home village Krutoi Iar after three years spent in the capital (St. Petersburg before World War I). After a few months in the village, he dies on the last page of the novel (Sorokin 1994c, 398).

The frame narrative consists of a cemetery idyll in the tradition of the graveyard poets of British pre-romanticism of the mid-eighteenth century: "There isn't anything prettier in the world than an overgrown Russian cemetery at the outskirts of a small village" ["Нет на свете ничего прекрасней заросшего русского кладбища на краю небольшой деревни"] (Sorokin 1994c, 3). The emphasized Russianness of the graveyard points to Nikolai Karamzin's canonical story "Poor Lisa" ["Bednaia Liza"] (1792), the most important text of Russian pre-romantic sentimentalism. In "Poor Lisa," the narrator recalls the fate of the eponymous peasant girl, who, seduced by the nobleman Erast, drowned herself. The Romantic heritage is later occasionally evoked again, for example, in associations with Lord Byron's *Childe Harold* (Sorokin 1994c, 14). However, in the embedded story, the realist classical novels of the second half of the nineteenth century provide the main guideline for Sorokin's emulation of earlier genres.

The beginning of the embedded story confronts the pastoral idyll with late-nineteenth-century means of transportation: Roman arrives by railway but is met by a coachman with his droshky. This evokes Russian realist novels with their confrontation of the railway as a symbol of modernization (Vojvodić 2012, 72) and the villages of rural Russia, which for centuries have remained unchanged. The asymmetry in the communication of blond thirty-two-year-old Roman Alekseevich Vospevennikov, who wears a moustache and side whiskers, with his coachman Akim speaks for a post-1861 (that is, imperial-Russia after the abolition of serfdom) hierarchy of the estates.

Akim speaks an old-fashioned, phonetically simplified non-standard Russian: "Wish you health, Roman Lekseich [...] I look—is this him coming? Thought, what Khrensh ambassador came here?" ["—Здравия желаем, Роман Лексеич! (...) Поглядел было—кто он это идет? Думаю, что ж это за хранцузский посланник сюды заехал!"] (Sorokin 1994c, 8). As this demonstrates, *A Novel* can compete with *The Queue* and *Marina's Thirtieth Love* in terms of masterful voice imitation. This time, the text imitates not the contemporary oral discourse, but historical forms of orality that differentiate the nobility and intelligentsia on the one hand from the peasantry on the other, as known for example from Tolstoi's "Master and Man" ["Khoziain i rabotnik"] (see chapter Eleven). While French serves as a prerogative of the nobility (Sorokin 1994c, 36), diminutives (Roma, Romushka) are used by elderly peasant women (Sorokin 1994c, 13).

The affectionate regression to historical modes of speaking and transportation that characterizes the late-nineteenth-century setting of the novel is doubled in the plot: in the first part of *A Novel* Roman nostalgically and joyfully recognizes the details of village life from his childhood in a sensual and tactile way (for example Sorokin 1994c, 25). He enthusiastically delves into pre-modern activities such as horse-riding (Sorokin 1994c, 58–60), hunting (Sorokin 1994c, 104–11), and manual harvesting. Never in the novel is pre-industrial rural life marked by its hardships, poverty, exploitation of the lower estates, insufficient hygiene, etc.

This longing for a pre-industrial world comes with many intertextual references, mostly from nineteenth-century Russian literature, but also from idealizations of peasant life in twentieth-century neorealism (such as the dissident Aleksandr Solzhenitsyn's "Matryona's Home" ["Matrënin dvor"], 1963; Sorokin 1994c, 26). For Sorokin's contemporaries of the 1980s, when *A Novel* was written, the main association from this nostalgia for a pre-industrial rural Russia was the work of the village writers [*derevenshchiki*] such as Valentin Rasputin or Vladimir Soloukhin.

In one of his early interviews Sorokin, however, attributed the range of inspirations rather narrowly when he claimed that "the novel *The Novel* [...] is written in a quasi-Turgenevian language" ["роман «Роман» (...) написан квазитургеневским языком"] (Sorokin, Rasskazova 1992, 120). At first glance this is convincing not only in stylistic terms, but also with regard to the character constellation. The gender distribution seems to look like that in many of Ivan Turgenev's novels: a young nobleman arrives in a village where he engages in a love affair with a young noblewoman. But the Turgenev suggestion is too narrow and has misled many researchers (Kasper 2007a, 473, 485). As a counterweight to this limited Turgenev reading, others have compiled an abundant list of additional allusions to classical Russian literature (Bibergan, Bogdanova 2014) and demonstrated direct textual analogies to various other classical Russian authors (Vojvodić 2012, 71–9). For Mikhail Epstein, in *A Novel* "'[t]he nineteenth-century Russian novel' exists as a generalized reality" on the reconstruction of which "Turgenev, Goncharov, Leo Tolstoy and Chekhov together could have collaborated" (Epstein 1995, 77). When it comes to the novel itself, not only is Turgenev explicitly mentioned as a measure of literary quality, but so are also Pushkin and Tolstoi (Sorokin

1994c, 141). Like Tolstoi's Levin in *Anna Karenina*, Sorokin lets his Roman philosophize about the meaning of life in his diary (Sorokin 1994c, 139) and reflect on Christ in his inner monologue (Sorokin 1994c, 68), during the Easter night mass (71–2), and in his conversation with the nihilist Kliugin (Sorokin 1994c, 89–90). During this conversation, Kliugin indulges in Dostoevskii-style political discourses about repression and anarchy (Sorokin 1994c, 177–8). The estrangement during the wedding ceremony as seen from Roman's perspective (Sorokin 1994c, 245–7) is again characteristic of Tolstoi (cf. Vojvodić 2012, 74–5). So is Roman's philosophical perception of the joy on the others' faces: "'They simply believe that everything will be fine'—he thought and was startled by the simplicity and might of this idea [...]" ["«Они же просто верят, что все будет хорошо!»—подумал он и, порази(лся) простоте и силе этой мысли (...)"] (Sorokin 1994c, 247). This is crowned by a typical Tolstoian self-persuasion with the help of the alleged simple clarity of a newly achieved insight (Sorokin 1994c, 249).

Also, the novel's gender interactions speak against the initial Turgenev direction: Roman is not a Turgenevian "superfluous man." A better embodiment of this type is his previous love Zoia Krasnovskaia who is alienated from Russia and its people and drowning in boredom ("скука"; Sorokin 1994c, 79–80) and hate for Russia. On the contrary, Roman pathetically rejects her with the unsophisticated Slavophile exclamation "I love Russia" ["Я люблю Россию"] (Sorokin 1994c, 80, see also 252). Later, Roman's reciprocated love for Tat´iana goes against the grain of Turgenev's pessimistic views of love affairs again: Turgenev neither would have depicted happy love shared by an urban intelligent man and a girl from the provinces. Never on earth would he have made them the joint perpetrators of mass murder, letting them "kill" also his beloved poetics of romance.

Roman's Slavophile rhetoric is no less contrary to the Westernizer Turgenev's views, but comes much closer to the idealization of rural life in a way that is reminiscent of Tolstoi's Levin from *Anna Karenina*:

> I was decaying in the city, in the capital. While here, it seems to me, I will live. Truly. [...] I will preoccupy myself with painting and farming. With agriculture and beekeeping.

> Гнил я в городе, в столице. А здесь, мне кажется, буду жить. По-настоящему. [...] буду заниматься живописью и хозяйством. Земледелием, пчеловодством. (Sorokin 1994c, 88)

Irrespective of the provenance of a certain motif, an ideological tendency, gender pattern, or style from Turgenev, Dostoevskii or Tolstoi, everything in *A Novel* feels uncannily familiar to the experienced reader of Russian classics of the nineteenth century. The reduction of rural activities, generational roles, and communicative routines between the estates to stereotypes extends as far as the characters' names—Tat´iana alludes to the ideal woman in Pushkin's *Eugene Onegine* [*Evgenii Onegin*] (1833), while Roman to Dostoevskii's axe murderer from *Crime and Punishment* [*Prestuplenie i nakazanie*] (1866).

The entire first part and the first two chapters of part two, fourteen chapters altogether, squander the reader's attention with a huge amount of superficial small talk—the political and philosophical passages are always short and their topics are not picked up again later—and descriptions of habitual activities like riding or hunting, a veritable "catalogue full of well-known realia from Russians' literature" (Kasper 1999, 107). Everything seems interchangeable (Danilkin 1996, 157), and nothing crystallizes into intrigue, conflict, or any passionate emotional constellation. Chapter eight of part two depicts at great length a stereotypical Russian rural wedding ceremony with drawn-out toasts, a suckling pig, female peasants singing, mass dancing, a peasant brawl, jumping over a fire, games for the newlyweds, passing the garland, and finally the retreat of the newlyweds to their bridal chamber, where they open their wedding presents (Sorokin 1994c, 256–318)—all of which seems anything but remarkable. The reader becomes exasperated, hardly learning anything new or being conveyed anything of special importance. The characters themselves hint at this predictability, epitomizing the entire ritual as typically Russian (Sorokin 1994c, 295). The huge percentage of useless information (Danilkin 1996, 158) causes boredom in the reader, making ongoing reading a considerable "task of endurance" (Skakov 2013, 52).

It is, however, worth imagining an unbiased reader who is not familiar with any other text by Sorokin and not rushing ahead by leafing through the book, thus also not recognizing yet that something will deviate from the usual graphical appearance of a novel after page 354. For such a theoretically imaginable reader *A Novel* does contain passages which allow not only a kind of ethnographic, folkloristic, "referential" reading (Groys 2000a, 237–8), but even some degree of fleeting emotional investment. The reader's involvement becomes possible beginning with chapter three of part two. While reflecting on his young love Zoia, Roman witnesses a wolf tearing apart a young elk (Sorokin 1994c, 165–6). Suddenly, not only do strong emotions emerge, but something unexpected happens: Roman is not attacked by the wolf, but the other way around. He chases the wolf and forces it into a deadly fight which Roman eventually wins with his knife, exulting many times: "Killed ... I killed you, killed ..." ["—Убил ... я убил тебя, убил ..."] (Sorokin 1994c, 167). Kliugin, who tends to the wolf bites on Roman's arms, becomes a mouthpiece for the reader's astonishment about the fact that the rural routine has been broken by something intense: "Huh! ... interesting. For our sluggish life this is really a heroic deed" ["Мда ... любопытно. Для нашей вялотекущей жизни это прямо подвиг..."] (Sorokin 1994c, 177).

But soon irony wins out again: Kliugin ridicules Roman's pathetic claim of everybody's "moral autonomy" ["автономная мораль"] and "compassion" ["сострадание есть в каждом"] (Sorokin 1994c, 177) as the pretext for his attack on the wolf. The doctor's counter-declaration of culture as a mere cover over violent passions falls into Turgenev's typical Schopenhauerian distinction between will and representation: "Bach, Beethoven, Raphael—that's all cover-ups, lids under which libido, thanatos, the thirst for murder is seething" ["Бах, Бетховен, Рафаэль,—все это ширмы, крышки, под которыми клокочет libido, tanatos (sic), жажда убийства."] (Sorokin 1994c, 178).

The story with the wolf has apparently left no traces on Roman—nor on the plot of the novel. The suggestion of Roman's moral infection by a kind of werewolf bite that would lead to his later murders (Smirnov 1994a, 337; Döring-Smirnov 1995; Gillespie 1997, 167) cannot be substantiated; it neglects the fact that by then, pathologically aggressive Roman has already attacked the wolf, not vice versa (cf. Bibergan, Bogdanova 2014, 309). But soon the next promising interaction evolves: the wounded Roman is nursed by Tat´iana (an allusion to Boris Pasternak's *Doktor Zhivago*, 1956), whom he spotted during the Easter mass before. He immediately falls in love (Sorokin 1994c, 187), quickly reveals it to her (Sorokin 1994c, 193), and asks her to become his wife (Sorokin 1994c, 216).

This love story gives rise to the third passionate development in the plot by bringing Roman into conflict with Tat´iana's ersatz father Kunitsyn, who initially does not want to lose his adoptive child and challenges Roman to a kind of Russian roulette duel (Sorokin 1994c, 199–200). Both turn the revolver drum once, put the revolver to their temple, and pull the trigger, but no shot goes off, so this intrigue falls short of sensational expectations again. Without psychological motivation, Kunitsyn then changes his mind and blesses the lovers (Sorokin 1994c, 217), which evolves into a tearful and long-winded scene depicting the unification of the families (Sorokin 1994c, 217–41).

The fourth moment of possible emotional involvement arises during the wedding: even if Roman is at first estranged by the church ritual, he becomes emotionally drawn in by Tat´iana's seriousness and tears of emotion. The culmination of affection comes with Tat´iana opening a letter from Roman's deceased mother to his future bride: "They cried, shivering and pulling each other in a tight embrace. 'This means, [...] you too are an orphan like me ...'" ["Они плакали, вздрагивая и прижимаясь друг к другу. / — Значит, (...) и ты тоже сирота, как и я..."] (Sorokin 1994c, 254).

The newlyweds' protestations of love are repeated eighteen more times, but already with "mantra"-like (Wawrzyńczak 2007, 192) mutual declarations ("'I love you!'—Roman whispered. [...] 'I live by you!'—she whispered" ["— Я люблю тебя! — прошептал Роман. (...) / — Я жива тобой!— прошептала она."] (Sorokin 1994c, 261; cf. Skakov 2013, 53). Given the sheer number of repetitions, the emotional tension of this exchange slides away and the reader's expectation for remarkable deeds or strong passions is again disappointed by an exhausting description of ritualistic wedding performances. Becoming tired from the repetitive plot, the reader's attention is conceptually drawn to his own expectations and to the novelistic device of suspense.

When the wedding is practically over, and the reader is just as tired of the whole ordeal as are its fictitious participants, the young couple retires to the bridal chamber in the house of Roman's uncle. There a textual "event" finally takes place that changes everything—without any psychological motivation whatsoever (Groys 2000a, 242; Lachmann 2004, 47). The sudden twist externally relies on Kliugin's wedding present that Roman unwraps on p. 321, an axe:

Roman unwrapped the velvet, and he held in his hands a beautiful axe with a thick blade like that of a chopper and a long oak handle.

On the blade was engraved:

Once swung—chop!

Roman contemplated the axe with a smile [...]

Роман развернул бархат, и в руках его оказался красивый топор с толстым, как у колуна, лезвием и длинным дубовым топорищем.

На лезвие было выгравировано:

Замахнулся — руби!

Роман с улыбкой разглядывал топор [...] (Sorokin 1994b, 321)

What follows is presented as both an outpouring of Roman's and Tat′iana's sincere love (in stereotypical confession formulas; Sorokin 1994c, 323) and as Roman's final abrupt epiphany (cf. Pavlenko 2009, 268):

> "That's true, that's true, my love!"—he joyfully replied. "You know, it seems, I understand everything. I understand everything! [...] I know what to do. Let's go."

> — Правда, правда, любовь моя! — радостно ответил он,— Знаешь, мне кажется, я все понял. Я понял все! [...] Я знаю, что делать. Пойдем. (Sorokin 1994c, 321)

What is the content of this insight? The subsequent actions tell us that in view of the "wedding axe" the newlyweds reinterpret the expectation of being together all the time (Sorokin 1994c, 328) as collaboratively committing a series of murders. In *A Novel* "the marriage is consummated through the bloody act of murder" (Skakov 2013, 54). Tat′iana keeps ringing a little wooden bell, which she received as a wedding present earlier, while Roman relentlessly brandishes the axe (Sorokin 1994c, 322–84). Their romance (and the genre of novel) ends in serial murder.

Roman's long line of murders, almost invariably introduced with Tat′iana's ringing the bell, exaggerates the novelistic device of leitmotif by "merely additive repetitions" (Kasper 1999, 109). While the fact that the orphans first murder their ersatz fathers could still be attributed some kind of psychoanalytical significance (Sorokin 1994c, 322–3), it is hard to think of any plausible motivation for hundreds of subsequent killings. The more it becomes clear that the murderous rampage will go on endlessly, the more the level of narratorial detail decreases. First, the ten inhabitants of Roman's uncle's house are slaughtered over eight pages (Sorokin 1994c, 322–30). Roman's attempt at tricking Kliugin, who initially provides the axe, out of the room where he is playing cards is even met with real resistance and culminates in a deadly fight (Sorokin 1994c, 326–8). But when Roman and Tat′iana have butchered all the members of the nobility in the uncle's house, the narration picks up speed: six domestic servants are quickly murdered on p. 331, before the couple heads off for the neighboring peasant huts, where Roman hacks to death the rest of the 247 inhabitants of the village (see Skakov's reference to Sorokin's private index "The list of victims slaughtered by Roman Alekseevich Vospennikov"; Skakov 2013, 64). This begins on

p. 332 and ends with the arrival of the murderous couple at the church on p. 364. For the following twenty-two pages Roman brings intestines from the peasants' huts nearby (Sorokin 1994c, 364–82)—an action that would have taken hours if interpreted as a realistic account—and desecrates the church's icons with these viscera (1994c, 384). Having committed most of the murders in Tat´iana's presence, he eventually also kills his spouse, chops her into small pieces (Sorokin 1994c, 384–5), and uses them to further desecrate the church (Sorokin 1994c, 385–8). With nobody left, Roman turns on himself, mixes his own vomit, feces, urine, and semen with pieces of Tat´iana's body, swallows the mix and vomits it up again (Sorokin 1994c, 392). After that he totally deteriorates to bestial behavior (creeping, sniffing, crying), before he finally expires in the last sentence.

Given the serial acceleration, the physical violence destroys not only all characters in the text, but also the text itself, the very readability of the "novel" (cf. Stewart 2006, 254). To be sure, this destruction of the text is not immediate, but develops in steps of deterioration, corresponding to the accelerating narration of the series of murders. The text becomes unreadable as soon as Roman leaves his uncle's house on p. 332. What follows thereafter compels the reader to a detective type of reading, with changes in the action of the story identifiable predominantly through changes in the graphic appearance (see Vojvodić 2012, 80–1). The last paragraph shift can be found on p. 354; the last direct speech is introduced with an em-dash on p. 362 (but already included in a sixty-five-pages-long paragraph of narratorial discourse); the last hypotaxis, signaled by a comma, comes on p. 381; the last parataxis ("and" between two finite verbs) follows on p. 385; the last tripartite sentence out of subject, verb, and object stands on p. 394. After that the last four pages of *A Novel* consist of bipartite sentences built only out of the subject "Roman" and a verb, repeated with increasing frequency. The final four lines are:

> Roman jerked. Roman moved. Roman jerked. Roman shook. Roman jerked. Roman shook. Roman moved. Roman shivered. Roman jerked. Roman moved. Roman jerked. Roman died.

> Роман дернулся. Роман пошевелил. Роман дернулся. Роман качнул. Роман дернулся. Роман качнул. Роман пошевелил. Роман дернулся. Роман застонал. Роман пошевелил. Роман вздрогнул. Роман дернулся. Роман пошевелил. Роман дернулся. Роман умер. (Sorokin 1994b, 398)

The unprecedented orgy of violence in the end of A *Novel* destroys both the textual world of Sorokin's stylization of a classical Russian novel and the nostalgic longing for pre-modern rural idyll. The explosion of the idyllic surface could be interpreted as a critique of the aesthetically conservative neorealism of the twentieth century and the retrograde program of the village writers. But the destruction of the narrative points to more than the mere deconstruction of an ideology: by throwing even the most avid reader off course, precluding any full reading of the entire text, Sorokin assaults the genre of a novel itself. The final sentence "Roman died" obviously invites a triple reading, given the pun based on the homonymy of the name "Roman" with the Russian words for "novel" and "romance." The laconic metaliterary statement "the [romance] novel is dead" (see Isakova 2003, 161) is ostentatiously stressed by its position in the last sentence, pointing to nothing less than the "decay of the novelistic form as such" (Remizova 1995). Ulrich Schmid interprets this as the postmodernist credo that "the only novel still possible had to deal with the depiction of its own literary impossibility" (Schmid 2015, 71). Most trenchantly, Nariman Skakov likens the end of A *Novel* to a "ritualistic practice of (self-)*exorcism*" (2013, 49, emphasis in the original). This gives rise to the interpretation that the violent plot should not be taken at face value but regarded as a detached exploration of the "memory of the genre" ["Gedächtnis der Gattung"] (Lachmann 2004, 48) of the novel.

With this fundamental thrust—how a novel is built and how it can be destroyed—A *Novel* revives the spirit of "white" conceptualism. For Skakov, A *Novel* "belong[s] to the realm of visual-textual conceptual art" (2013, 59), for Johanna Renate Döring-Smirnov, it is the equivalent of Kazimir Malevich's suprematist "Black Square" in the field of literature (1995).

With its two clearly distinguishable parts A *Novel* also appears as the most comprehensive demonstration of the bipartite plot-building mechanism that Sorokin also applied in many of his early short stories (see chapter Four). What is more specific for this work is the combination of violence and "performative incantations" (Noordenbos 2016, 64). This can be found in several short stories as well: "Start of the Season" ["Otkrytie sezona"] follows Sergei and Eger' (the archaic job title is derived from the German word for "hunter," "Jäger"), into an idyllic forest, where they listen to war songs by famous singer and songwriter Vladimir Vysotskii on a tape recorder. The Russian story phonetically reproduces Vysotskii's trademark rolled r, which is omitted in Sally Laird's English translation: "'The German sni-i-per finished me o-off, killing the o-one who fa-ailed to shoo-oot!'" ["— Немецкий снайперррр дострррелил меняяя, убив тогоооо, которрый не стрррелял!"] (Eng. Sorokin 1986a, 45; Russ. 1992a, 45). These lyrics provide the performative command for Eger´ to shoot at a figure standing in the thicket. His shot is successful, and only from the fact that the figure is dressed the reader understands with surprise that the unarmed victim of Eger´, this Germanized sniper in a hunter's disguise, is a young man. The two fictional hunters, however, are not surprised at all. Vysotskii singing ends: "'That's only the sta-art—now he-ear the rrrest!'" ["Это только пррисказкааа,—скааазка впередиии!"] Accordingly, the hunters outdo their murder—with cannibalism, beheading the corpse and eviscerating it in order to grill the man's liver (Eng. Sorokin 1986a, 46; Russ. 1992a, 47–8). Stories built around executed commands such as "Start of the Season" display performative twists comparable to *A Novel*: always already "violent speech action" [*nasil´stvennoe rechevoe deistvie*] becomes performative in Sorokin's plots (Ryklin 1992, 206); a slogan is not used for designating reality, but for prescribing an action (Stewart 2006, 240, 253–4).

This meta-performative dimension is not grasped by the explicitly or implicitly negative reception of Sorokin's violent plots also beyond the Soviet context, such as the assumption that they constitute a mere "shock" (Porter 1994, 39; Poyntner 2005, 35) or "idealess destruction" (Wawrzyńczak 2007, 196). Even observers well-disposed toward Sorokin cannot avoid characterizing him as a "cruel talent" (Groys 1992, 99) or "enfant terrible" (Genis 1997, 222). Plot-fixated studies, however, either underestimate or fully ignore the textual triggers for violence and the performative twists that motivate the outbursts of violence, desecration or indecency in the early Sorokin. In *A Novel* the respective commands are—in contrast to *The Norm* (chapter Three) or *Blue Lard* (chapter Eight)—present explicitly, as an emphasized or repeated slogan.

In *The Novel*, the central turning point is the saying "Once swung—chop!" ["Замахнулся—руби!"]. Later in the text the fouling of icons with the intestines of Roman's victims on pp. 382–4 is preceded by the meta-literary zeugma "Roman took the axe to the gospel / Roman assaulted the gospel" ["Роман положил топор на Евангелие."] (Sorokin 1994c, 382). In *A Novel* Sorokin even gives an explicit hint that proverbs—such as one taken from a context of Germanized hunting again—can be materialized literally in practical action: "The famous hunter's saying 'Shooting is easier when the hunting bag becomes heavier' he understood literally" ["Известную охотничью поговорку «Стрелять легче, когда в ягдаше тяжелее», он понимал буквально (…)"] (Sorokin 1994c, 111).

Irrespective of this meta-motivation of violence via performative speech, *A Novel* is clearly outstanding with its seriality of accelerated murders. In terms of quantity, but perhaps not quality, it supersedes even Sorokin's *Four Stout Hearts*, a novel with arguably the most disgusting singular scene of violence in world literature (it suffices to briefly imagine the detailed depiction of a "mind fuck," the penetration of a brain meticulously opened by surgery with obviously lethal consequences for the victim). The utterly violent plots of these novels justify Viktor Erofeev's attempt to inscribe Vladimir Sorokin as the "leading monster" into an a-Soviet "New Russian Literature" which shook "humanistic" norms by planting Baudelairian "flowers of evil" (*Tsvety zla*; Eng. Erofeyev 1995, xxviii; Russ. Erofeev 1997, 28–9). Still, Erofeev's allusion to ethical evil in no way exhausts the variety of violations of taboos—political, sexual, scatological—in Sorokin, and their meta-linguistic and meta-aesthetic thrust.

CHAPTER 6

A *Month in Dachau* and Entangled Totalitarianisms

S orokin's texts from the 1990s that follow in line after *A Novel* (1985–1989), which draws upon classical Russian literature of the nineteenth century, take yet another step away from the Soviet context, bringing the predominant focus on Socialist Realism to a definite "closure" (Kustanovich 2004, 310). The works of the 1990s even partially relinquish the Russian context, but like the "pre-Soviet" *A Novel*, they delve into history, in this case into the entangled history of totalitarianisms in Germany from 1933–1945 and the late-Stalinist Soviet Union in the period leading up to 1953.

Since World War Two, Germany had remained a loaded topic for Soviet writers. The scandalous closing of ranks between the two totalitarian regimes in the so-called Ribbentrop-Molotov or Hitler-Stalin pact of August 23, 1939, which paved the way for the joint effort to bring down the Polish state at the beginning of World War Two, remained a problematic fact for Soviet politics of memory after 1945. What is more, the counterfactual construct of a homogeneous Soviet people made it impossible to acknowledge the fact that between 1941 and 1945, the Jewish population in occupied Soviet territories had been the main target of the German genocide in the Shoah. Publications that documented the special German terror campaign against Soviet Jews, such as Il´ia Erenburg's and Vasilii Grossman's *Black Book* [*Chërnaia kniga*] (1946–1948), were repressed. On the other hand, censorship also prevented writing about totalitarian features of the Soviet regime until 1953, so that in later Soviet times there emerged a longstanding discursive tradition of exploring totalitarian Nazi rule in a way that could be read as an allegory of Soviet totalitarianism. This led to a subversive vernacular reception of reports and fictional works of art about German totalitarianism in the postwar Soviet Union, for example Iulian Semenov's books and Tat´iana Lioznova's TV series about the Soviet spy in the German SS, Shtirlits, which served as material for endless jokes. In his scenario for Tat´iana Didenko's and Aleksandr Shamaiskii's documentary collage *Mad Fritz* [*Bezumnyi Fritts*] (1994), Sorokin contributed to this tradition as well (see Hänsgen 1999, 217–21).

This mid-1990s film script falls into a period when Vladimir Sorokin traveled to Germany several times on German grants and wrote both "commissioned literature" and fantastic hyperboles about Russian-German relations, adding a novel topic to his portfolio (Ryklin 1998, 744), a new "mode of heterotopic writing" (Chernetsky 2007, 79). These trips included his participation in a conference at Munich University in March 1991 (Hansen-Löve 1992), a fellowship from the German Academic Exchange Service (DAAD) in 1992 (Sorokin, Shapoval 1998, 8; Kustanovich 2004, 311), and a Samuel Fischer Visiting Professorship at Freie Universität Berlin in the summer semester of 1998. After a short visit to Berlin in 1988, Sorokin's first longer trip to Germany took place during what was still the late perestroika period: in 1990 he spent several months in a writer's residency at Künstlerhaus Villa Waldberta in Feldafing, at the Lake of Starnberg south of Munich.

The main product of this trip was Sorokin's novelette (which in Russian is called a *povest´*) *A Month in Dachau* [*Mesiats v Dakhau*]. The first, poorly proofread publication of the text in Peter Urban's flawed German translation was released by the Zurich-based publisher Haffmans in 1992 (Sorokin 1992d). Almost simultaneously a gray Russian edition (without pagination, publisher, place, or ISBN) appeared in sophisticated, 16.5 × 30 cm tall, right-page-only book design by Igor Sacharow-Ross, featuring twelve narcissist photographs of the handsome author which, when leaved through, form a motion picture, framed by conceptualist photos of fresh meat and cloudy sky (Sorokin 1992c; cf. Smirnov 1994b, 286; Deutschmann 1998, 325 note 4). An English translation by Jamey Gambrell followed in the American magazine *Grand Street* in 1994 (Sorokin 1994a). Russia saw the first reprint of the tamizdat original in the two-volume edition of Sorokin's collected works in 1998 (Sorokin 1998a, I 745–65).

Unusual for the early Sorokin, *A Month in Dachau* can clearly be traced to his own experience, specifically his 1990 trip to Bavaria. The fictional date of the protagonist's departure from Moscow to Munich, May 2, 1990, is very close to the start of the real journey. Other dates provided for the writing of the fictional text and the journey undertaken by the author are also very similar. Moreover, Sorokin and his protagonist travel to almost the same place—to the Munich region, of which Dachau is a northern suburb. at almost the same time. This biographical exactitude is an exception in Sorokin's writing. What is more, in *A Month in Dachau* the protagonist, a Russian writer, shares his first name, patronym, and last name with the author, creating further biographical parallels (see Vassilieva 2014, 136). This fictional character must of course not be mistaken for the author of the same name, who—according to his essay in the German left-wing newspaper *die tageszeitung* (*taz*) from 1991—stayed in Dachau only for one night and visited the camp territory for just two hours (Sorokin 1991j, 26). He also preferred oysters with Chablis on Munich's picturesque Viktualienmarkt (Sorokin 2009a) while he sent his eponymic protagonist to experience physical and mental torture in a fictitious still-functioning concentration camp called Dachau, which had not been liberated by the US Army in April 1945. Thus, Sven Gundlakh's conceptualist notion of "author-character" (Gundlakh 1985, 76; cf. Eng. Sorokin, Roll 1998, 79; Russ. 1996, 123) is more applicable to *A Month in Dachau* than to the rest of Sorokin's oeuvre (Sasse 2003, 203). The German part of the plot is entirely non-autobiographical, making *A Month in Dachau* rather an experiment with diaristic style, a first-person narrator, and a poetics of internal experience, feelings, and fantasies as championed in James Joyce's technique of stream of consciousness.

The first-person narration of *A Month in Dachau* is obviously "untrue" (Deutschmann 1998, 328). The non-referential nature of the narrative becomes evident from distorted historical facts such as the "torture spa" concentration camp Dachau functioning in May of 1990. Only the fictitious alter ego travels into an "anachronistic and fantastic" (Vassilieva 2014, 140) alternative history in which Hitler's foreign minister Joachim von Ribbentrop (1893–1946) is alive in 1958 (Eng. Sorokin 1994a, 235; Russ. 2002, I 747) and the veneration for Hitler in his Upper-Austrian birthplace Braunau is hyperbolically exaggerated (in the fictitious plot a 10,000 square meter relief of Hitler's face marks the Austrian-German border crossing; Eng. Sorokin 1994a, 237; Russ. 2002, I 749). The most important deviation from history is a long-term alliance between totalitarian Germany and the Soviet Union, which was not broken by the historical German attack on the Soviet Union on June 22, 1941, a motif Sorokin will also pick up later, in *Goluboe salo* [*Blue Lard*] (1999).

The reader learns the protagonist's name from a Soviet departure visa (ordinary citizens could not travel outside the Soviet Union until the late perestroika years) on the first page of the short novel, which sounds more like a sentence of incarceration:

PERMISSION
Is hereby granted to Sorokin, Vladimir Georgievich, born 8/7/55, Russian, non-Party, to exit the USSR without hindrance for the German

Empire in order to spend his summer leave (28 days) in the concentration camp of the city of Dachau.

РАЗРЕШЕНИЕ
Сорокину Владимиру Георгиевичу, 7.8.1955 г. рождения, русскому, беспартийному, разрешается беспрепятственный выезд из СССР в Германскую империю для проведения летнего отпуска (28 суток) в концентрационном лагере города Дахау. (Eng. Sorokin 1994a, 233; Russ. 2002, I 745)

To obtain this permission the fictitious Vladimir Sorokin had to go through "most horrible torment, tensions. And humiliation. Megatons of humiliation" ["Все со страшными муками, напряжением. И унижением. Мегатонны унижения"] (Eng. Sorokin 1994a, 233; Russ. 2002, I 745). This and the memory of historical suffering of the population in the Soviet state are presented with pathos as institutional terrors like in dissident literature:

> For a half century we've been legless, they beat us and we stand up, they urinate in our faces, like [the Soviet consular officer] Nikolai Petrovich did in mine at the first interrogation, and we wipe ourselves off.
>
> Уже полвека мы без ног, нас бьют, а мы встаем, нам мочатся в лицо, как мочился мне Николай Петрович на первом допросе, а мы утираемся. (Eng. Sorokin 1994a, 234; Russ. 2002, I 746)

This aphorism-like saying vulgarizes common complaints about lopsided interrogations by the police, the secret service, or at a court trial: "they urinate in our faces" [*nam mochatsia v litso*]. Similar humiliation is repeated when the protagonist crosses two borders by train—the Soviet-Polish border and (pointlessly) the Austrian-German.

The victim's perception, however, changes as soon as the protagonist reaches the imagined still-functioning Dachau concentration camp of 1990. Here Sorokin inverts the foundational perception of Soviet people: "'abroad' was always a representation of paradise; hell was a [Soviet] concentration camp" (Vail′ 1994, 254). On the contrary, the protagonist of *A Month in Dachau* travels to hell abroad—and enjoys it: he adores "the *CAMP SMELL*, sacred, beloved, familiar" ["запах ЛАГЕРЯ, святой, родной, дорогой"] (Eng. Sorokin 1994a, 239; Russ. 2002, I 751, double emphasis in the original).

The stay at the Nazi model concentration camp shall provide the masochistic subject with "wine of pleasure" ["вино наслаждения"] (Eng. Sorokin 1994a, 239; Russ. 2002, I 751). The camp torturers appear personified as stereotypically German female heroine(s) from Goethe's *Faust* (1790/1832): "SHE, the two-headed woman in the black gestapo uniform, My Hellish Lovely: on the left, Margarethe; on the right, Gretchen" ["ОНА, двухголовая женщина в черной гестаповской форме. Моя Адская Прелесть, слева—Маргарита, справа—Гретхен"] (Eng. Sorokin 1994a, 240; Russ. 2002, I 752), who are additionally underpinned with facets of many other "super-women" of world literature (see Deutschmann 1998, 332), including Bulgakov's broom-riding witch Margarita. Both parts of the Janus-headed double woman, Margarita and Gretchen, are members of the SS and comprise masochist and sadist perversion: "the obstinacy of Sacher-Masoch's Wanda, the license of De Sade's Justine" ["непреклонность захермазоховской Ванды, расторможенность садовской Жюстины"] (Eng. Sorokin 1994a, 240; Russ. 2002, I 752). The Soviet citizen's submission to torture in the neo-Nazi camp is authorized by the founder of the Soviet Union, Vladimir Il´ich Lenin

НЕ

НАДО

НЕНАДО

НЕНАДОНЕ

НАДОНЕНАДО

НЕНАДОНЕНАДОНЕ

НАДОНЕНАДОНЕНАДО

НЕНАДОНЕНАДОНЕНАДОНЕ

НАДОНЕНАДОНЕНАДОНЕНАДО

НЕНАДОНЕНАДОНЕНАДОНЕНАДОНЕ

НАДОНЕНАДОНЕНАДОНЕНАДОНЕНАДО

НЕНАДОНЕНАДОНЕНАДОНЕНАДОНЕНАДО

НЕНАДОНЕНАДОНЕНАДОНЕНАДОНЕНАДОНЕ

НАДОНЕНАДОНЕНАДОНЕНАДОНЕНАДОНЕНАДО

ПРОТИВИТЬСЯГНОЙНОБЕЗУМНОМУРАЗЛАГА-

ЮЩЕМУСЯКРОВАВОЙСПЕРМОЙНАСИЛИЯХУЮ-

ТОТАЛИТАРИЗМА.АНАДОУМЕТЬОТДАВАТЬСЯЕМУСНА-

СЛАЖДЕНИЕМИСПОЛЬЗОЙДЛЯОБЩЕГОДЕЛА В.И.ЛЕНИН

(Eng. Sorokin 1994a, 240; Russ. 2002, I 752)

shouldnotnotresisttheputrefyinglyinsanedecayingprickofto
talitarianismoozingwiththebloodandspermofrapebutlearnhow
togiveoneselfoverwithpleasureandwithusefulnessforthesake
ofthecommoncause.   V. I. Lenin

The phantasmagoric "masochist vacation" which the fictitious protagonist spends in Dachau is split into twenty-five sections, each devoted to the protagonist's time in one of twenty-five torture cells; violence, sexuality, forced cannibalism, and defecation, but also multiple literary references are scattered throughout this fragment. In cell 1 "Vladimir Sorokin" is "only" beaten by his German "lover" ["любовь моя"] with a bat, has his nails torn off, and is forced to eat them (Eng. Sorokin 1994a, 241; Russ. 2002, I 753). Much more phantasmagoric is the torture in cells 6 and 20, where the author's alter ego is forced into cannibalizing a Russian girl (Eng. Sorokin 1994a, 242; Russ. 2002, I 754) and a Jewish boy (Eng. Sorokin 1994a, 247–8; Russ. 2002, I 759). Cell 7 adds an anal rape by a stereotypically German shepherd dog (in Russian: "немецкая овчарка"; Eng. Sorokin 1994a, 242; Russ. 2002, I 754), and in cells 9 and 10 "Vladimir Sorokin" is force-fed while his anus is obstructed, which leaves him with no choice but to eventually defecate on a photo of his deceased mother (Eng. Sorokin 1994a, 243–4; Russ. 2002, I 755–6), thereby combining two Russian idioms: the rather harmless "I shit at it" [*nasrat' mne na eto*] with the most frequent (and tabooed) aggression in Russian vulgar language, the desecration of the addressee's mother, "fuck your mother" [*ëb tvoiu mat'*]. Several forms of torture draw on the sacrifice of Christ (cell 15) and Christian martyrdom (cell 24): the fictitious Vladimir Sorokin is crucified "like [Apostle] Peter" ["как Петра"] upside down (Eng. Sorokin 1994a, 249, sic; Russ. 2002, I 761). Both the phantasmagoric series of tortures and the inscription into the traditional Christian sanctification of sufferers qualify *A Month in Dachau* as the second "victim text" in Sorokin's oeuvre, after *Marina's Thirtieth Love*.

However, toward the end, the protagonist's fantasies turn into a sadistic vision of "peaceful coexistence of two despotic superpowers" (Vassilieva 2014, 145), of joint Soviet-Nazi total rule over the world. The totalitarian allies have slaughtered victims from all over the world and now are occupied with cannibalizing them:

English, African, Russian, Jewish, German, Chinese ears, recently heeding the menacing chorale of our epoch, now baked with the brains of their former masters.

английские, африканские, русские, еврейские, немецкие, китайские уши, еще недавно внимавшие грозному хоралу нашей эпохи, теперь же запеченные с мозгами своих бывших хозяев. (Eng. Sorokin 1994a, 251; Russ. 2002, I 763)

Notwithstanding the carnivalesque impression from this cannibalistic feast (Sokolov 2005, 174), the hitherto masochistic plot transforms into a "perpetrator text" when the fictitious Vladimir Sorokin encourages Gretchen, whom he has just married, to "press the trigger of Red Desires, shoot, shoot, shoot, shoot from the Machinegun of Blond Elation at Friends and Colleagues" ["нажми на Спусковой Крючок Красных Желаний, стреляй, стреляй, стреляй, стреляй из Пулемета Белокурой Радости по Друзьям и Соратникам"] (Eng. Sorokin 1994a, 252; Russ. 2002, I 764). If transcending the level of the fictitious characters and including the extratextual author, *A Month in Dachau* appears far from exclusively masochist: it is the empirical author who—sadistically—inserts his fictitious alter ego into situations of phantasmagoric torture: "With sadistic consistency the writer Sorokin the First designs a torturous world, in which the writer Sorokin the Second finds his masochistic happiness" (Smirnov 1994b, 285).

Depicting both ends of the psychosexual spectrum, the masochistic as well as the sadistic orgies imagined in *A Month in Dachau* are hyperbolic implementations of phantasmas of Soviet war propaganda about German atrocities and the demanded Soviet retaliation (Il′ia Erenburg's "Kill [the German]" / "Ubei [nemtsa]," 1942), translated into the glossary of sexual perversion. German-Soviet entangled history appears as an exchange of exaggerated atrocities that are automatized in the historical discourses of both countries to a degree that—*A Month in Dachau* suggests—they have long become pathologically internalized in Russian and German minds, which interlock in "complementary contrast" (Brockhoff 1992, 142).

Against this fatal backdrop of entangled victimhood and perpetration, i.e. both committing and being subjected to torture, the only possible solution in *A Month in Dachau* is the unification of the masochist-sadist: the fictitious torture tourist "Vladimir Sorokin" must marry his fictitious torturer in an act of hierogamy. The transition between the masochist and the sadist parts is marked by the inter-totalitarian wedding between the Russian protagonist and the two-headed Gretchen-Margarethe to whom he proposes in cell 22 while overwhelmed by pain (in German: *Schmerz*): "schmerz schmerz i proposed to margarethe and schmerz schmerz but gretchen paleschmerz" ["шмерц шмерц сделал предложение Маргарите и шмерц шмерц а Гретхен побледнешмерц"] (Eng. Sorokin 1994a, 248; Russ. 2002, I 760). The couple travel to Munich's register office, decorated with swastikas (forbidden in post-war Germany since 1945), visit the Soviet consulate, and return to a neutralized German-Soviet concentration camp (Eng. Sorokin 1994a, 251; Russ. 2002, I 762–3)—the place of no return when it comes to German-Soviet entangled history.

Sorokin would not be Sorokin, however, were his text not to leave loop-holes for a non-literal reception on a conceptual meta-level. The most obvious device of estrangement is once again graphic. The Russian prose text acquires qualities of visual poetry when the masochist imperative attributed (of course wrongly) to Lenin is typed in the form of a pyramid without blank spaces (Sorokin 1994a, 240; cf. Kuritsyn 2001, 113). Following this pyramid, the phan-tasmagoric experiences of the fictitious subject in the twenty-five torture cells are recounted without punctuation and exclusively with lower-case letters (Eng. Sorokin 1994a, 241–50; Russ. 2002, I 753–62), simulating orality (Murašov 2016, 228). After the torture series comes another pyramid, now top-down. It is composed of two Catholic church hymns (see Vassilieva 2014, 180–1), the first also providing a liturgical formula from the Catholic Corpus Christi proces-sion, which is particularly popular in Bavaria (Eng. Sorokin 1994a, 250, typos corrected; in Russian exclusively in Cyrillic letters: Russ. Sorokin 2002, I 762):

CELL 25: durch das lamm das wir erhal-

ten wird hier der genuß des alten os-

ter[ ]lammes abgetan und der wahr-

heit muss das zeichen und die

nacht dem lichte weich-

en und das neue fängt

nun an dieses brot

sollst du erheben

welches lebt

und gibt

das

l

e

b

e

n

KAMEPA 25: дурх дас ламм дас вир эрхальтен вирд хир
дер генусс дес альтен остерламмес абгетан унд
дер вархайт мусс дас цайхен унд ди нахт
дэм лихьте вайхен унд дас нойе
фэнгт нун ан дизес брот зо-
льст ду эрхебен вельхес
лебт унд гибт дас

л

е

б

е

н

Another already well-known trademark of the early Sorokin is the destruction of the very textuality of the literary text by means of repetition: cell 14 consists of thirty-three repetitions (without punctuation and with only tiny variations) of "there you viscous swine" ["так свинья жидкая"], a piece of verbal abuse which, as the reader understands, is accompanied with thirty-three blows to the protagonist's body (Eng. Sorokin 1994a, 245; Russ. 2002, I 757). The perpetrator's exclamations are echoed in cell 12, where the protagonist declares himself ready to sign any conceivable invented indictment (Eng. Sorokin 1994a, 244; Russ. 2002, I 756), and in cell 19, where we only hear the subject crying "no" in German ["найн" in Cyrillic letters] twenty-nine times (Eng. Sorokin 1994a, 247; Russ. 2002, I 759), not knowing which kind of iterated torture he is undergoing just then.

A Month in Dachau is also rich in its play with different languages: many German parts are inserted into the "Russian-German macaronism of Sorokin's short novel" (Smirnov 1994b, 286). This peculiar "language contact" (Deutschmann 1998, 341) renders parts of the text incomprehensible to the average Russian reader (even more than to the American reader for whom the translator Jamey Gambrell preserved the relative incomprehensibility by reproducing the sections in German, which at least shares a language group with English). German words are estranged in Cyrillic phonetic transcription throughout the short novel (unlike the German translation [Sorokin 1992d, 41], on which Murašov bases his misleading observation of an "oscillation" between the alphabets; 2016, 231). This indicates that the text does not deal with "real German," but with that variety of German that was constructed by Soviet anti-German propaganda and Socialist Realism (see Ryklin 2001a).

After the twenty-five cells have been heard through the subject's ears in a stream of consciousness (cf. Poluboiarinova 2004, 7), lacking any punctuation (reminiscent of Hermann Broch's *The Death of Virgil* [*Tod des Vergil*]; 1945), standard language briefly returns with the inter-totalitarian wedding, but disappears again with the turn of the protagonist from masochism to sadism. The dramatic end lays bare the imagined nature of all the preceding tortures, the masochistic joy in self-destruction, and the Soviet-German perverse hierogamy by using the subjunctive and destroying language again:

> i would prefer the following sequence:
> 1. fill my stoma with worms gnawin gretchen's head
> [...]
> 7. shootin my body big bertha canno heavn great germany"

> я предпочёл бы следующую последовательность:
> 1. наполне моего желуде червие обглодавше голову гретхен.
> [...]
> 7. выстреле мой тело большая берта в неб велик германия.
> (Eng. Sorokin 1994a, 253; Russ. 2002, I 765)

Thus all the detailed invention of phantasmagoric tortures, masochistic and sadistic pleasures can be read meta-discursively, as a collage "compiled entirely from discursive fragments of other discourses" (Deutschmann 1998, 329). They refer both to Soviet war literature and to Russian dissident and émigré discourses of anti-totalitarian critique, especially to Aleksandr Solzhenitsyn's pathetic camp literature (see Vassilieva 2014, 180), amounting to an alleged national psychopathology that Russians have purportedly internalized. In *A Month in Dachau* the latter intertextual trace is laid bare explicitly with the affirmation of a quote from the émigré philosopher Nikolai Berdiaev: "Berdyaev is right: 'Russians are inclined to perceive everything in a totalitarian light" ["Прав Бердяев: «Русские все склонны воспринимать тоталитарно»"] (Eng. Sorokin 1994a, 238; Russ. 2002, I 750). With his characteristic hyperbolic technique, Sorokin materializes the pathology attributed to both German and Soviet totalitarian minds in fictitious sadistic tortures and masochistic pleasure from being tortured. This enacted double psychopathology is no more than a materialized metaphor from other discourses again, among others, the German *Historikerstreit* from 1986–1989 between Ernst Nolte and Jürgen Habermas about their disagreement over whether the German responsibility for Shoah was entirely singular or whether it could be legitimately compared to other totalitarian regimes of the twentieth century. Sorokin's shifts from masochism to sadism clearly perform comparability. The apex of meta-distance is reached in a meta-theoretical reference to the French poststructuralist philosopher Jacques Derrida, informing the reader that every text is totalitarian (cf. Roll 1998, 158–9; Isakova 2003, 159; Noordenbos 2016, 60, 82)—but also nothing more than text:

> derrida is right [...] every text is totalitarian we are in the text and therefore it follows in totalitarianism like flies in honey and the exit exit could it really be only death no prayer

> деррида прав [...] каждый текст тоталитарен мы в тексте а следовательно в тоталитаризме как мухи в меду а выход выход неужели только смерть нет молитва (Eng. Sorokin 1994a, 246; Russ. 2002, I 758)

Astonishingly, Sorokin relinquishes his meta-literary position when talking about Russian-German relations in interviews as he did several times in the 1990s. In his referential statements from the interviews he even assigns his literary texts clear-cut propositions about psycho-history, thus reducing the double-headed and contradictory heroine Gretchen from *A Month in Dachau* to "a drastic example of German sadism" ["krasses Beispiel für den deutschen Sadismus"] (Sorokin, Drubek-Meyer 1995, 70). In the quoted interview with Natascha Drubek-Meyer for the Erfurt-based magazine *Via Regia* in spring 1995, Sorokin proposed a rather mechanic dichotomy of national psychologies:

> [...] the relations between Germany and Russia resemble a love affair. It is an affair between two psychologically different types: Germany represents the anal-sadistic type, Russia the masochistic-genital one.

> [...] die Beziehungen zwischen Deutschland und Rußland gleichen einer Liebesbeziehung. Es ist eine Beziehung zwischen zwei psychisch verschieden veranlagten Typen, das heißt: Deutschland stellt den anal-sadistischen Typus dar und Rußland den masochistisch-genitalen. (Sorokin, Drubek-Meyer 1995, 67; similarly in Sorokin, Laird 1999, 156; Sorokin, Shapoval 1998, 15)

While this simple-minded binary might, if taken with a grain of salt, reflect the fictitious plot of *A Month in Dachau*, the dichotomy is inverted a few years later in a play that draws on Russian-German entangled totalitarianisms again. In the case of *Hochzeitsreise* [*The Postnuptial Journey*] the fact that the play was been commissioned by a German institution becomes so palpable that even the title is given in German and translated in a footnote in the Russian editions (see Sorokin 1998, II 599; Sorokin 2007b, 199). Written in 1994/1995, the play was staged by famous scandal-provoking director Frank Castorf at Volksbühne im Prater in Berlin on November 2, 1995, while awaiting its first edition in Russian in *Mesto pechati* in 1996 (Sorokin 1996). The German translation, which had been utilized for the premiere, appeared a year later (Sorokin 1997b). The original was reprinted in the first edition of Sorokin's *Collected Works* from 1998 (Sorokin 1998, II 599–629) to be later included in the collection of plays *The Capital* [*Kapital*] (Sorokin 2007b, 199–242).

In *The Postnuptial Journey* the incurable masochist equivalent of *A Month in Dachau*'s Russian writer "Vladimir Sorokin" is the German Günther von Nebeldorf, grandson of an SS torturer, and the sadist role in the inter-totalitarian sexual encounter is played by the Russian-Jewish Masha Rubinshtein, granddaughter to a KGB tormentor. What is more, in *The Postnuptial Journey* the female Russian character is split into two halves, Masha-1 and Masha-2 (staged in act one; Sorokin 2007b, 199–205; cf. Douzjian 2013, 160–3), resembling *A Month in Dachau*'s German Janus-headed Margarethe-Gretchen. Thus, contrary to the author's claims from his interviews with Sally Laird and Natascha Drubek-Meyer and their referential implications, for poetic purposes he treats both of the totalitarian experiences (Douzjian 2013, 155) and the psycho-cultural roles as interchangeable (cf. Poluboiarinova 2004, 9). As Igor' Smirnov states: Sorokin's fictional "psychotherapy is carnivalesque [...] it exchanges the patiens and agens of guilt" (Smirnov 1995, 143). This observation about the different fictional texts from Sorokin's "German" period in the 1990s refutes any attempts at a serious psychoanalytical reading such as Mikhail Ryklin's (2001b, 251–2; cf. Stryjakowska 2017, 99). For Sorokin, Freud's psychoanalysis cannot be interpreted referentially, only metaphorically (Sorokin, Laird 1992, 155–6; cf. Stelleman 2016, 519), even if this meta-theoretical insight does not undo the shocking effect of a primary referential reading of torture and perversion.

In *The Postnuptial Journey*, however, another layer of German-Russian relations is free from such primary shock effects that delay the meta-discursive analysis: mutual stereotypes about food. Act three of the play, an unusual anti-climax in a five-act drama, is in its entirety devoted to intercultural stereotypes about food (cf. Stelleman 2016, 530): Masha boasts about the correct way to drink vodka (from water glasses, before the meal, with a snack to be first sniffed and then eaten immediately after consuming 100 ml) and how to prepare "culturally correct" cucumbers (soft-salted, not marinated). She then supervises how her German pupils perform the orthopraxy of consumption (Sorokin 2007b, 217–22). The carnivalesque banality of this act overshadows the hyperbolic torture scenes from *A Month in Dachau*, which in the play reappear only in rather domesticized form, when Masha scourges Günther upon his request (Sorokin 2007b, 210–1).

The Postnuptial Journey thus separates the intercultural psychopathology of the entangled totalitarianism of the twentieth century from culinary issues. It is therefore not the case that in Sorokin eating and drinking is always connected to sexual transgression (Qualin 2015, 176, 182), violence (Beumers, Lipovetsky 2009, 93), or disgust (Wiedling 1999, 231). Especially in the second half of the 1990s and early 2000s, Sorokin repeatedly rolled out detailed panoramas of opulent feasts (cf. Ryklin 1998, 750). While the early play *Pelmeni*, published in samizdat in 1987 (Sorokin 1987b), destructively connects eating with cannibalism and the 2007 illustrated book *Horse Soup [Loshadinyi sup]* (Sorokin 2007c) with psycho-torture, in *Shchi [Cabbage Soup]*, premiered at Moscow's Iugo-Zapad theater in April 1999, bandit-chefs rather conservatively defend a wide range of Russian traditional meat dishes against totalitarian vegetarians (Sorokin 2007b, 243). The manifold scenes of oral consumption in Sorokin's oeuvre can therefore be subdivided into quite different registers (Uffelmann 2013a): Sorokin materializes political allegories of forced swallowing (like in *A Month in Dachau*, but also in the first part of *The Norm*); he deconstructs inter-culinary stereotypes (as in *The Postnuptial Journey*); he savors opulent feasts (as in *A Novel* and *Blue Lard*), not excluding certain altruistic implications (as with Liuda feeding Vadim in *The Queue*). In his later works he will also envisage fantastic forms of metaphysical absorption (in *Blue Lard*, the *Ice Trilogy*, and *Telluria*).

The volume *The Feast [Pir]* from 2001, with its programmatic culinary title (Sorokin 2001b), reads as a set of variations on Sorokin's different poetics of consumption, returning even to "white" conceptualist investigations of 391 possible combinations of the verb "gorge" [*zhrat'*] with different syntactical patterns (2001b, 411–443; cf. Vojvodić 2012, 62), which is not by chance dedicated to Lev Rubinshtein (2001b, 411).

Eventually Sorokin's columns in *Snob* from May 2009 to December 2010 (see Kubasov 2012) rather straightforwardly reveal the author's personal culinary preferences and experiences (Sorokin 2009b; see Uffelmann 2013a, 246–7); they contribute to the second, extra-fictional image that Sorokin created of himself as a publicist, interviewee, and even public figure in post-Soviet times. This extra-fictional self-image will be scrutinized in the second semi-biographical block of this Companion, in the following chapter.

CHAPTER 7

Sorokin's New Media Strategies and Civic Position in Post-Soviet Russia

The last Secretary General of the Communist Party of the Soviet Union, Mikhail Gorbachëv (b. 1931), failed to accomplish the top-down reforms through which he intended to preserve the socialist system. A veritable sorcerer's apprentice, he could no longer control the forces that he had conjured in the late 1980s. Facing internal traditionalist opposition within the Communist Party (such as Egor Likhachev), he increasingly had to rely on support from other societal forces outside the Party, even former dissidents such as Andrei Sakharov (1921–1989), the father of the Soviet nuclear bomb and later prominent human rights activist. These extra-communist new alliances compelled hardliners in the CPSU to attempt a coup d'état on August 21, 1991. The civil resistance against the putschists, spearheaded by Boris El'tsin (1931–2007), then President of the Russian Republic within the Soviet Union, ultimately led to the coup's failure. El'tsin took the opportunity to publicly humiliate Gorbachëv, who resigned as Secretary General three days later and as President of the Soviet Union on December 25, 1991, a few days before the official dissolution of the Soviet Union on December 31, 1991 (Breslauer 2002, 108–40).

The confrontation between El'tsin and the now post-communist opposition continued throughout the 1990s, leading to another attempted coup in September/October 1993. While the 1990s was by far the freest time ever in Russian history (Skillen 2017, 187), the challenges of the rapid political and economic transformation, going from one-party rule to democracy and from socialism to market economy, overburdened the various short-term governments under Russian President El'tsin, which were vacillating between pro- and anti-Western policies (Breslauer 2002, 214–30). The basic security of a socialist public economy also vaporized, once prices and currency exchange rates were liberalized. Suddenly, the informal economy of late Soviet times transformed into a mafia-controlled disaster, giving rise to a perception in broad parts of the population of the 1990s as a catastrophe, in turn discrediting democracy and producing a wide-spread demand for a new leader with a "strong hand" (Kagarlitsky 2002, 92, 249–50).

This change came with the transition from El'tsin to Prime Minister Vladimir Putin (b. 1952) in 1999, who was elected President of the Russian Federation in March 2000 and seized control of the pluralist media landscape in post-Soviet Russia with an iron grip (Skillen 2017, 262–340), either forcing oppositional oligarchs into exile (Boris Berezovskii, Vladimir Gusinskii) or having them arrested under dubious allegations (Mikhail Khodorkovskii; cf. Zygar 2016, 23–66). The first targets were TV stations that aired critical material, then oppositional print journalists (Anna Politkovskaia), and eventually, the hitherto-borderline anarchic Russian Internet. Putin's attempts at resurrecting the former glory of the Soviet Union as a superpower in the international arena culminated in military campaigns against the Caucasus republic of Georgia in August 2008 and against South-Eastern Ukraine starting in March of 2014. These attacks against the color revolutions in Georgia and Ukraine were meant to prevent an analogous scenario in the Russian Federation, but did not stop the white-ribbon protests in the winter of 2011/2012 which failed in part due to self-marginalization of their urban proponents (Kalinin 2017). Traumatized by the creative protests that were largely directed against Putin himself, the regime strengthened repressions at home (Gabowitsch 2017, 244–51). After the slightly more liberal period of Dmitrii Medvedev's presidency (2008–12), as some political commentators find (Gessen 2017, 296–9), Putin's third presidency (2012–2018) displayed not only neo-authoritarian, but even neo-totalitarian tendencies. What is more, the annexation of the Ukrainian peninsula of Crimea in March of 2014 led to the international isolation of Russia, mitigated only by the necessity to somehow keep talking about the war in Syria (2011–) and other urgent conflicts around the world.

Parallel to the economic crisis and societal turmoil, the 1990s also saw the dissolution of the insular Moscow Conceptualism milieu. Many members of the former circle took the opportunity either of permanent emigration or at least shuttle migration in the wake of their art's international canonization. While for Sorokin the latter was the prime option in the 1990s—his most stable arrangement was when he taught at a university in Tokyo from 1999 to 2001—in the early 2010s he purchased an apartment in Berlin's bourgeois district Charlottenburg, where he has been spending more and more time in recent years (see Sorokin, Thumann 2014; Sorokin, Sobchak 2017), occasionally returning to his Moscow-region house in Vnukovo. The new international demand and new media opportunities led not only to spatial dispersion of the former underground artists, but also to the group's social disintegration, which, according to Igor´ Smirnov (2018, 63), Sorokin reflected in the defeat of the heartseekers' sect in his *Ice Trilogy* (2002–2005). Philosophers associated with Moscow Conceptualism had in 1993 co-founded Ad Marginem, their own publisher, which released most of Sorokin's work between 1998 and 2002, even assembling two- and a three-volume editions of collected works (Sorokin 1998; Sorokin 2002a), but this connection broke in 2002 when philosopher Mikhail Ryklin, one of Sorokin's first interpreters, attacked both Sorokin and Ad Marginem publisher Aleksandr T. Ivanov for cynical profiteering (Ryklin 2003). With the provocative addition of nationalist author Aleksandr Prokhanov to Ad Marginem (cf. Noordenbos 2016, 178, 180), Sorokin was on the lookout for new publishers, opting for big publishing houses such as Zakharov (2004–2007; see Sorokin, Bavil´skii 2004) and AST (2007–).

The 1990s were also a period of self-declared crisis in Sorokin's creativity, which occurred after his finishing the novel *Four Stout Hearts* in 1991 (cf. Sorokin, Laird 1999, 161; Sorokin, Arkhangel´skii 2003). While biographers uncritically embraced this self-perception (Kustanovich 2004, 311), his artistic output would suggest otherwise. What does seem true is that rather than writing new novels Sorokin turned to shorter prose, plays, and film scripts. With this trans-media excursion he artistically groped his way through the decade before finally returning to writing novels in the late 1990s and releasing his first bestseller, *Blue Lard* [*Goluboe salo*], at the turn of the millennium.

Without a doubt, Sorokin used this novelistic incubation period between *Four Stout Hearts* and *Blue Lard* to seek out a slightly broader public through new genres. Before the 1990s, the Soviet political and aesthetic censorship prevented his plays from being performed (Sorokin, Genis, Vail´ 1992, 139), and his early plays had proved too "static and visual" for the theatrical stage (Beumers, Lipovetsky 2009, 91). Thus, the perestroika plays *The Ditch* and *Pelmeni* had to wait for their first performance until 1992–1993 (Beumers, Lipovetsky 2009, 95–6). His shift to more dramatic and (pseudo-)psychological forms of theater allowed Sorokin to eventually reach the ephemeral, but public theatrical audience as a playwright. Thus, for him, the 1990s heralded more of a transitory shift in genre than a general crisis of creativity. In the 2000s and 2010s it would turn out that breaks of several years between long-prose book publications were becoming his usual practice (cf. Sorokin, Dolin 2013). He tended to fill these gaps with working in shorter genres (Sorokin, Dolin 2018), sometimes compiling them into episodic para-novels such as *Sugar Kremlin* and *Telluria*.

In the 1990s, Sorokin was especially prolific in producing plays such as *Dysmorphomania* [*Dismorfomaniia*] (1990, premiered 1997), *The Jubilee* [*Anniversary*] (1993), *The Postnuptial Journey* [*Hochzeitsreise*] (1994, premiered 1995), *Cabbage Soup* (1995, premiered 1999), *Dostoevsky-trip* (1997, premiered 1999; English translation Sorokin in *Koja Magazine* in 2000), and *Happy New Year* [*S Novym godom*] (1998), all collected later in *The Capital* [*Kapital*] in 2007 (Sorokin 2007b, 126–364; for more on the performances, see Beumers, Lipovetsky 2009, 95–9). He also broadened his scope by authoring an opera libretto for *The Children of Rosenthal* [*Deti Rozentalia*] (2003, premiering at Bolshoi Theater in March 2005, music: Leonid Desiatnikov), included in Sorokin's collection *4* (Sorokin 2005b, 94–134) and combined with three later librettos in the collection *Triumph of Time and Insensitivity* [*Triumf vremeni i beschuvstviia*] (Sorokin 2018b).

While his activity in the theater scene was put on pause between 1998 and 2007, Sorokin instead invested more time in film scripts. Whereas *Bezumnyi Fritts* from 1994 consisted of a montage of Soviet films about Nazi Germany, he now co-authored a number of original scenarios. In two films based on his screenplays, *Moscow* [*Moskva*], written together with director Aleksandr Zel´dovich (2000), and *Kopeck* [*Kopeika*], coauthored with director Ivan Dykhovnichnyi (2002), Sorokin also appeared as an actor. In 2004 Il´ia Khrzhanovskii directed *Chetyre* [*Four*], coauthored by Sorokin, and in 2011 Aleksandr Zel´dovich shot *The Target* [*Mishen'*], based on a screenplay written together with Sorokin. The films bear less avant-garde character than the early plays, trying to reach a slightly broader public. Thanks to later public accessibility of not-always-legal copies on the Russian internet, this was continuously becoming all the more available. Two of Sorokin's film scripts were published in textual form in *4* (Sorokin 2005b, 50–93) and *Kopeck* (Sorokin 2005b, 135–205). The second half of 2010 saw another bout of film activity. This period included scripts based on Sorokin's literary texts—*Marina's Thirtieth Love*, prepared together with director Angelina Nikonova (2016), and *Nastia*, with director Konstantin Bogomolov (2017)—but also newly written screenplays for *Matryoshka* [*Matrëshka*] (coauthor and director Nikolai Sheptulin, 2016), and *DAU*, written together with director Il'ia Khrzhanovskii (2019).

With his plays, his librettos, and the film scripts, Sorokin chose increasingly widely consumed genres that moved further and further beyond informal-public Soviet samizdat and tamizdat. The former underground artist became a member of the Russian PEN Club in 1993 (which he remained until 2017), thus professionalizing his authorship. Making use of Sorokin's increasing canonicity in Russian contemporary literature, his publishers brought forward a number of rearranged and reassembled new editions of his older works, combining different genres under one book cover in the 2000s and 2010s (for example, one essay, one novel, and one film script in *Moscow*; Sorokin 2001c; or a play and seven short stories; Sorokin 2018a). The writer himself served as editor of an anthology (*The Russian Cruel Short Story* [*Russkii zhestokii rasskaz*]; Sorokin 2014d). The commercial rules of professional authorship might also be seen as the motivation behind Sorokin's new mass media strategy. In 1997 he told Marusia Klimova: "[…] underground does not sit well with me anymore. I am now interested in mass art" ["(…) андеграунд меня больше не устраивает. Мне сейчас интересно массовое искусство"] (Sorokin, Klimova 1997).

The most widely visible sign of Sorokin's changed media strategy came in fall of 2001 with his guest appearance on the Russian version of the American reality show *Big Brother, Behind Glass* [*Za steklom*]. This reality show was produced by Grigorii Liubomudrov for channel TV-6 and broadcasted on TNT and TVS from fall 2001 to summer 2002, featuring seven continuous participants and several special guests. The guests included the nationalist political provocateur Vladimir Zhirinovskii (November 11, 2001)—and Vladimir Sorokin (November 23, 2001). The show was an enormous success with ratings of up to 40%, thus the biggest single step toward mass popularity in the career of a former Moscow underground writer, securing him for the first time an ephemeral, but truly mass public. The TV guest-role also marked a short period of Sorokin's self-promotion in motion pictures around the years 2000–2002, comprising his performances as an actor in *Moscow* and *Kopeck*. In March of 2002 Sorokin praised the continuous participants of *Behind Glass*, but simultaneously critiqued the empty "soap bubbles" ["мыльные пузыри"] of TV (Sorokin, Neverov 2002), yet again finding literature to be a better alternative. With this he relativized his 1997 diagnosis of a general shift from textual to visual electronic media (Sorokin, Klimova 1997).

After his short TV intermezzo Sorokin became interested in the visual-textual bimodality of the Internet. On July 16, 2003 his website srkn. ru was registered by Zina Design (which up to the present day administers the website). The design first followed what Dagmar Burkhart in the tradition of Karl Rosenkranz had called the "aesthetics of ugliness" ["Ästhetik des Häßlichen"] (Burkhart 1997), later replaced by an "aesthetics of marketing" ["Ästhetik der Vermarktung"] (Howanitz 2014, 211). The website hardly uses the backchannel constitutive of the Web 2.0, rather sticking to one-to-many communication. According to the blog researcher Gernot Howanitz, it is a "typical example of an established, internationally renowned author who uses the opportunities of the web above all for the purpose of marketing" (Howanitz 2014, 209). With the web presentation Sorokin now addressed a possibly continuous broad public (if not mass public like with *Behind Glass*). The picture has changed slightly since Howanitz's analysis from October 10, 2012: the contributions in the blog section srkn.ru/blog are still rather scarce, but the LiveJournal blog ru-sorokin.livejournal.com/, registered on November 4, 2004, has been significantly more active. Still, given the only 3,123 comments received upon the 1,893 journal entries (as of October 11, 2018; according to ru-sorokin.livejournal.com/profile), this blog is also predominantly a monologue of regular editors, the bloggers <jewsejka> (Aleksei Evseev) and <neonorma>, and not a dialogue between the author himself and his readers.

Notwithstanding the paucity of interactivity, srkn.ru is a rich resource for full texts of Sorokin's early works and thus extremely helpful for automatized search. The availability of full texts allows to conclude that the logic of marketing is not exclusively monetary here. Sorokin seems to be interested in open access (apart from more recent texts that are protected by the publishers' copyright), accumulating symbolic capital for the canonization of his oeuvre. In sum, since the early 2000s, Sorokin has to a certain degree—via his occasional appearance on TV and radio as well as with his website administered by others—been embarking on an electronic and digital media tour, but simultaneously renewed his preference for the written word.

The expansion of Sorokin's literary portfolio to drama, film, and opera as well as his accommodation to and appropriation of electronic media took their time. This process was accompanied by a new openness to popular media. While the guest appearance on *Behind Glass* remained a singular escapade, the writer much more systematically responded to interview requests from mainstream media, especially from newspapers and magazines. Over the late 1980s and entire 1990s, his rare interviews had mostly been published abroad, even though he gave several interviews from 1994 listed on the srkn.ru/interview/1994 section of his website (as of October 15, 2018).

In terms of Sorokin's interview activity, a veritable explosion took place in 2002, not only in connection with *Behind Glass* and the scandal stirred around *Blue Lard* (see chapter Eight). Obviously, the growing number of interview requests also met with Sorokin's new readiness to give interviews not only to select artist peers or specialists in Moscow Conceptualism such as Aleksandr Genis and Petr Vail´ (see Sorokin, Genis, Vail´ 1992), but also to high-circulation periodicals such as the newspapers *Izvestiia* and *Komsomol´skaia Pravda*, the glamor magazines *Esquire* and *L'Officiel* in Russia, the leading German political magazine *Der Spiegel*, the Viennese newspaper *Der Standard*, *Gazeta Wyborcza* and *Polityka* in Poland, the Madrilène *El Pais*, radio station *Ekho Moskvy*, and *Radio Liberty*, all of which made him almost a "beau monde" figure (Kukulin 2002, 253).

A selection of ninety-two interviews reposted in the srkn.ru/interview section of Sorokin's personal homepage (as of October 15, 2018) is highly incomplete. On the one hand, it omits frequently quoted interviews such as the ones with Sally Laird from 1987 and 1992 (Eng. Sorokin, Laird 1999), with Aleksandr Genis and Petr Vail´ from 1992 (Russ. Sorokin, Genis, Vail´ 1992), and with Serafima Roll from 1995 (Eng. Sorokin, Roll 1998; Russ. 1996). On the other hand, the selection obviously downplays unsophisticated interviews with mainstream media of the early 2000s, which used to be online on his website in the 2000s but were later removed (for example Sorokin, Neverov 2002 and Sorokin, Semenova 2002). So far it is unclear why the recently more stringent selection did not affect the peak of twenty-seven interviews from 2010 on srkn.ru/interview/2010 and srkn.ru/interview/2010?page=1 (as of October 15, 2018).

When reading Sorokin's interviews in chronological order, a shift in the interest of some mainstream media is visible after *Behind Glass*. The focus moves from the writer's poetics to the person Sorokin, and later to his political views. And for the first time, Sorokin complies with the demand for disclosing personal matters; contrary to his earlier clear division of literature and life, he begins to share unpretentious predilections. In February 1995 in the interview with Serafima Roll, Sorokin had still weaseled out of direct answers with very defensive formulations: "[…] it goes without saying that I'm not immune to all human pleasures" ["И вообще, ничто человеческое мне не чуждо"] (Eng. Sorokin, Roll 1998, 82; Russ. 1996, 128). Soon after his appearance on *Behind Glass*, Sorokin, in an interview for the Internet portal km.ru, readily shared various personal details about his childhood, wife, daughters, dogs, and food recipes (Sorokin, Gribkova 2003; Sorokin, Suranova 2006) with the broader audience, also answering a questionnaire about his quotidian preferences (fish, vodka, white wine, and chess) and aversions (gin, perfume, films by Andrei Tarkovskii; Sorokin, km.ru 2001), highlighted in his profile page of the *Snob* project since December 2008 (https://snob.ru/profile/5295, accessed August 28, 2018). At the same time, he began allowing the published interviews, in which he resorts to "tropes of honesty and openness" (Rutten 2017, 136), to be accompanied by photographs showing him as a loving husband and father of twin daughters, in his home office, with his dogs, etc., amounting to a "celebrity-style self-presentation" (Rutten 2017, 137). More scattered pieces of private information can also be found in Sorokin's columns on snob.ru (2009–2010). Around the late 2000s the list of his interviews bears traces of his travels, for example, to Israel in 2005, to Norway in November and to Denmark in December 2009, to Ukraine in September 2008 and again in October/November 2010 (https://www.srkn.ru/interview).

Up to the present day, Sorokin's proper fictional works have remained quite non-autobiographical. However, for the faithful reader of Sorokin, scattered fictional elements contain hidden biographical references, for example, about his international trips (such as a trip to Passau in December 2012 in *Manaraga*; Sorokin 2017, 37), and allusions to friends and researchers: *Hochzeitsreise* lets Masha-1 and Masha-2 seemingly randomly mention a home address in Cologne's Schwalbacher Straße—where the conceptualist theoretician Boris Groys lived at that time (Sorokin 2007b, 616); *Blue Lard* features a minor character bearing the last name of Berlin-based specialist of Moscow underground Georg Witte (Sorokin 1999, 113); Berlin's district of Charlottenburg, where Sorokin found his second home abroad, is referred to with details for insiders in *Manaraga* (Sorokin 2017, 13, 20–1, 32, 240); *Day of the Oprichnik* [*Den' Oprichnika*] has quite transparent ciphers of his former fellow conceptualist Groys and of the philosopher Mikhail Ryklin as well as his wife Anna Al'chuk—as viewed with hate through the eyes of the neo-totalitarian hangman Komiaga (Sorokin 2006b, 142–4).

Whereas many of these crypto-autobiographical hints—none of which say anything about the author's innermost thoughts or feelings—will remain closed to the unprepared reader, with his mainstream-media interviews and with his TV appearance Sorokin actively reached out to the general public. The new publicity replaced the semi-private and informal-public contexts of the underground, which existed roughly until the end of the Soviet Union, the limited-public genres he fostered in the 1990s, and the broader literary audience, which he addressed with his "bestseller" *Blue Lard* from 1999. The latter, however, was also promoted significantly by the 2002 scandal and mainstream interviews in periodicals. Eventually, the remediations of theater screenings, the reposting of interviews, and the (mostly illegal) posting of copies of films based on his scenarios produced an effect of scattered, but wide and continuous access to genres such as theatrical performances or print newspaper interviews, which, when first produced, had a more confined range of addressees). However, this later development goes beyond his own strategies and is due to the general technological culture of the digital age.

Up until 2004, Sorokin's interviews put repeated emphasis on his previous attitude of "remaining in principle non-partisan" (in 1987; Sorokin, Laird 1999, 149) and "absolutely apolitical" ["абсолютно аполитичен"] (Sorokin, Rasskazova 1992, 123). In this vein, he maintained complete civic disinterest in his 1992 conversation with Tat´iana Rasskazova: "I do not have civic interests. It's all the same to me—stagnation or perestroika, totalitarianism or democracy" ["У меня нет общественных интересов. Мне все равно—застой или перестройка, тоталитаризм или демократия"] (Sorokin, Rasskazova 1992, 121). But the same year, in his conversation with émigré writers Aleksandr Genis and Petr Vail´, Sorokin declared to have grudgingly given way to a pressing feeling of civic obligation at least once in 1991: "during the coup I forced myself to go to the White House" ["Во время путча я сделал над собой усилие и поехал к Белому дому"] (Sorokin, Genis, Vail´ 1992, 143).

Correcting his previous apoliticial rhetoric, Sorokin's early outspoken political statements from the mid-2000s are rather broad, brashly condemning Russian political culture in its entirety (Sorokin, Sokolov 2005, reprinted in Sokolov 2005, 184–6). Over the 2010s Sorokin has proceeded to a more focused and concrete critique of Russia's neo-imperialist geopolitics (Sorokin, Ahrest-Korotkova 2010; Sorokin, Pavelka 2010), especially when it comes to President Putin's policy on Ukraine (Sorokin, Piotrowska, Sobolewska 2014).

The most frequently quoted interview with Sorokin, for the German political magazine *Der Spiegel* "'The Sinister Energy of Our Country'" ["'Die finstere Energie unseres Landes'"] (Sorokin, Schepp, Doerry 2007b), is to my knowledge the only professional translation of a text by Sorokin into English made from a third language and not directly from the Russian original (which is available at srkn.ru online; Sorokin, Schepp, Doerry 2007a). The English translation replaces the German/Russian title with another quote from the *Spiegel* interview, "'Russia Is Slipping Back into an Authoritarian Empire'" (Eng. Sorokin, Doerry, Schepp 2014). Thus the 2014 American editors made

Sorokin's politicization even more terminological than did the German journalists in 2007. In this interview Sorokin recalls his own development and dates the decisive change in his civic position around the year 2005:

> The citizen lives in each of us. In the days of Brezhnev, Andropov, Gorbachëv, and Yeltsin, I was constantly trying to suppress the responsible citizen in me. I told myself that I was, after all, an artist. As a storyteller I was influenced by the Moscow underground, where it was common to be apolitical. [...] I held fast to that principle until I was 50. Now the citizen in me has come to life.

> Der Staatsbürger lebt in jedem von uns. In der Zeit von Breschnew, Andropow, Gorbatschow und Jelzin versuchte ich ständig, den mündigen Bürger in mir zu verdrängen. Ich sagte mir, ich bin doch Künstler. Als Erzähler war ich durch den Moskauer Untergrund geprägt. Dort war es üblich, unpolitisch zu sein. [...] Das habe ich so gehalten, bis ich 50 wurde. Nun ist der Bürger in mir erwacht. (Eng. Sorokin, Doerry, Schepp 2014, 279–80; Ger. Sorokin, Schepp, Doerry 2007b, 107)

In 2007 his previous generalist attitude gave way to concrete reactions against Putin's military politics: "As a citizen, this makes me sit up and take notice" ["Als Bürger horche ich da auf"] (Eng. Sorokin, Doerry, Schepp 2014, 281; Ger. Sorokin, Schepp, Doerry 2007b, 107). And Sorokin's new politicization is not only critical, but also cautiously partisan, given his positive association with figures of the Russian opposition such as former Prime Minister Mikhail Kas´ianov, chess veteran Garri Kasparov, and former candidate for President of the Russian Federation Irina Khakamada (Eng. Sorokin, Doerry, Schepp 2014, 281–2; Ger. Sorokin, Schepp, Doerry 2007b, 108). He even goes as far as demanding action—from every Russian citizen: "Everyone must awaken the citizen within himself" ["Jeder muss den Staatsbürger in sich selbst wecken"] (Eng. Sorokin, Doerry, Schepp 2014, 282; Ger. Sorokin, Schepp, Doerry 2007b, 108). He asks no less from the West: "The West should be even more vocal in insisting that the Russians respect human rights" ["Der Westen soll noch stärker die Menschenrechte anmahnen"] (Eng. Sorokin, Doerry, Schepp 2014, 283; Ger. Sorokin, Schepp, Doerry 2007b, 108).

In the wake of similar politicized interviews journalists invited Sorokin to contribute his own political essays to Western periodicals (Sorokin 2014b; 2014c; 2015b). And he did, applying some of the literary devices of his fictional texts in the service of sarcastic political commentary. In July 2014, the long-time Moscow correspondent of the leading German quality newspaper *Frankfurter Allgemeine Zeitung* Kerstin Holm asked Sorokin to comment on Russia's military campaign in South-Eastern Ukraine. In response, the writer offered a counterintuitive sexual metaphor, illustrating not the military invasion, but the psychological trauma of the Euromaidan revolution for a horrified Russia: "Ukraine Has Penetrated Us" ["Die Ukraine ist in uns eingedrungen"] (Sorokin 2014d). The title of the English translation published in *The New York Review of Books* three days later loses this paradoxical invasiveness: "Russia Is Pregnant with Ukraine" (Sorokin 2014c). Quoting a whole bunch of discursive units from Russian colloquial reactions to the Ukrainian civil uprising, Sorokin further elaborates the eponymous sexual metaphor of the German essay title:

> Russia became pregnant with Ukraine. The yellow-blue sperm of Independence Square did its manly job [...]. A new life stirred in her [Russia's] enormous womb: Free Ukraine. The authorities were horrified, the liberals were jealous, and the nationalists were filled with hatred. (Sorokin 2014c)

Sorokin manages to capture the Russian counter-aggression in his customary corporeal terms (see Borenstein 2019, 214) as well: "It's well known that pregnant women often crave raw meat. And there it was, a quickly bitten-off chunk of fresh flesh: the Crimea" (Sorokin 2014c). Only with the final conclusion of the essay do the physiological metaphors turn to political explicitness: "Birth is inevitable. [...] The infant's name will be beautiful: Farewell to Empire" (Sorokin 2014c).

As transpires both from the maieutic questions of the *Spiegel* journalists and the simultaneous translation of Sorokin's 2014 essay by *FAZ*'s Moscow correspondent Kerstin Holm and by Jamey Gambrell for *The New York Review of Books*, Sorokin's new politicized civic image has partially been solicited or even co-shaped by Western journalists. Western commentators also reflect on a reading of Sorokin, the artist, as a political prophet (Sorokin, Tetzlaff 2009; Mortensen 2017), in spite of all of his reservations against literature as pedagogy still repeatedly expressed in the 2000s (for example, Sorokin, Bonet, Fernandez 2002). This reduced scheme of a non-artistic (and avant-garde-insensitive) reception has dominated the mainstream reception of Sorokin both within and outside Russia since 2006.

And indeed, there is one undisputable factor in his artistic practice which has served as a gateway for such reductionist readings: his gradual moving away from the preoccupation with the past—from Soviet rule and Socialist Realism (1980s) through German-Soviet entangled totalitarianisms (1990)—to new topics situated in the near future (2020s—2060s), yet again enriched with elements taken from the past. Sorokin's first post-Soviet major prose text, the novel *Blue Lard*, which will be the subject of the next chapter, is half bound in the entangled totalitarian heritage, but with the other half reaches out into a fantastic future of 2068.

CHAPTER 8

Blue Lard and Pulp Fiction

In Siberia in the year 2068, a "biophilologist" writes fourteen intimate letters to his gay lover about an enigmatic substance produced in clones of classical Russian writers (Sorokin 1999, 7–121). On Hitler's Obersalzberg in 1954, Stalin wins the upper hand over Hitler and injects himself with a semi-fluid substance through his eye into his brain, which grows to the size of the universe (Sorokin 1999, 336–8). With this Sorokin opens and ends his bestselling novel from 1999. How can two such totally divergent plots connect? The answer is: through the eponymous substance *Blue Lard* [*Goluboe salo*]: produced by cloned Russian writers in 2068 and transferred to a counterfactual history of 1954, in which Stalin and Hitler are still alive.

Sorokin's 1999 fantastic novel is torn between these two diverging time vectors (cf. Deutschmann 2003, 289)—one into the future year 2068, another into the past of 1954. With its tension between the "futurist" poetics of the link-and-frame story and the various "passéist" stories within the main plot, *Blue Lard* can ostensibly be described as the literary embodiment of a statement that Sorokin would repeat in various interviews: "I've said it many times: we are living between the past and the future" ["Я много раз говорил: мы живем между прошлым и будущим"] (Sorokin, Shirokova 2006).

This is not only true of the two different time spans narrated in the novel, but also of the overlapping poetological paradigms of Sorokin's entire oeuvre (cf. Uffelmann 2006, 112–3). *Blue Lard* appears to be an "anchoring" (Uffelmann 2006, 115) or "turning point" (Lipovetsky 2015, 155) in Sorokin's oeuvre: "Beginning with *Blue Lard*, Sorokin has been reforging himself" (Smirnov 2004a, 177). Temporally close to the fundamental turn in post-Soviet Russian politics from El'tsin's chaotic liberalism to Putin's neo-authoritarianism, *Blue Lard* splits Sorokin's oeuvre (and this Companion) into two halves, as Sorokin scholars agree (Ryklin 1998, 740; Uffelmann 2006).

Two discernable poetological tendencies overlap in *Blue Lard*. On the one hand, this novel continues Sorokin's longstanding interest in the Soviet past from the 1980s and on to his works on the German-Soviet entangled totalitarianisms produced in the 1990s (see chapter Six). On the other hand, its "quasi-adventure plot" (Lipovetsky 2015, 156) turns to sci-fi and popular fantasy literature, as was the case with *Four Stout Hearts*, which David Gillespie saw as a "parody of the detective thrillers that flooded the Russian market in the 1990s" (Gillespie 1998, 780).

For the reader familiar with Sorokin's earlier works, it is the various stories within the story of *Blue Lard* which most faithfully sustain his tendency to conceptualize the historically specific poetics of nineteenth-century novelistic writing and Socialist Realism. In reproducing a poetics of the past, instead of the conventional satirical mocking, the early Sorokin resorted to extensive emulation—sometimes hundreds of pages long—of certain styles, often implying a cold but not antagonistic distance. In contrast to this, only a minority of the stories in *Blue Lard* (such as the story of the swimmer or the Tolstoi emulation; Sorokin 1999, 93–109, 137–44) qualify as austere and coherent conceptualizations: many observers see most episodes as rather blatant parodies (Shatalov 1999, 206). This diagnosis, however, is too simple: rather than launching direct parodies himself, in *Blue Lard*, Sorokin is interested in the literary dynamics of pulp fiction. The reproduction of other literary styles (written by the original writers' clones) in the novel at first glance looks parodic, but this is no satire of reality. Sorokin here explores parodic forms of literary expression, as evidenced by his aggressive parodies of Lev Tolstoi and even harsher ones of the dissident Soviet icon Anna Akhmatova.

The novel deploys a new metaphor for conceptualist reproduction: cloning. The first third of *Blue Lard*'s plot is built around the literary creations of seven writing clones: Tolstoi-4, Chekhov-3, Nabokov-7, Pasternak-1, Dostoevskii-2, Akhmatova-2, and Platonov-3. Asked by Elena Kutlovskaia why he so consistently elaborated on the problem of cloning, Sorokin pointed both to "convenience" and "artificiality":

> It is good for literature. I do not believe that you can clone a human being, but I do believe that an artist can clone history, for example, or a certain time. In this case cloning is a shield with which one can conveniently cover up the artificiality of this sort of move, because time machines do not exist; meanwhile, a clone is a very convenient crutch—the mechanism of the reanimation of time, of history, of this or that person.

> Она хороша для литературы. Я не верю, что можно клонировать человека. Но я верю, что художник может клонировать историю,

например, или время. В данном случае клонирование—это щит, которым удобно прикрыть искусность такого хода. Потому что машины времени не существует, а клон—это очень удобная палочка-выручалочка. Механизм реанимации времени, истории, той или иной личности. (Sorokin, Kutlovskaia 2005)

In contrast to the plot-building reproductions of other styles seen in early Sorokin, the embedded stories in *Blue Lard* are presented as the results of "bio-philological" experiments. On the level of the plot, this experimental nature explains the imperfect reproduction of various poetics from the past. For instance, the literary creation of the Dostoevskii clone shows traces of obvious technical problems, such as excessive reiteration:

> [...] two commoners, a student and an elderly woman, stood stone-still to the ground like pillars, pillars pillars pillar-pillars, indeed verst-pillars, and their eyes followed the strange pair with obvious trepidation right up to the very entrance.

> [...] двое простолюдинов, студент и пожилая дама остановились, как вкопанные в землю столбы, столбы, столбы столбы-с столбы, да, верстовые столбы, и с нескрываемым волнением проводили глазами удивительную пару до самого подъезда. (Sorokin 1999, 33)

Nabokov-7 begins with Tolstoi—with an inversion of the famous opening sentence from the 1878 novel *Anna Karenina*: "All happy families are unhappy in the same manner, every unhappy family is happy in its own way" ["Все счастливые семьи несчастны одинаково, каждая несчастливая семья счастлива по-своему"] (Sorokin 1999, 81). The textual creations by Akhmatova-2 (Sorokin 1999, 49–57), Nabokov-7 (81–9), and Pasternak-1 (90–2) include vulgarisms quite untypical of these authors. The brutality inherent in Andrei Platonov's plots is reflected in the text by Platonov-3 (Sorokin 1999, 58–69), where body parts burn in a steam engine, and pent-up aggression erupts in Chekhov-3 (79). As benevolent (Lipovetskii 1999, 209; Stryjakowska 2016, 108) and adversarial commentators (Shatalov 1999, 206; Zolotonosov 1999, 18; Anninskii 2001, 116; Ermolin 2003, 406) agree, the infelicities in most of the attempts at rewriting, with the exception of Tolstoi, hint that the failure of this literary cloning must be understood as premeditated.

In the late 1990s and early 2000s, Sorokin several times used cloning and fantastic substances as his preferred metaphors of intertextuality and literariness. His 1997 meta-literary drama *Dostoevsky-trip* (premiered at Teatr na Iugo-Zapade in Moscow on November 24, 1999) introduces drugs named after famous authors that trigger trips into the fictitious worlds of these authors' texts. One pill sends its consumers to an embedded story more than reminiscent of Dostoevskii's *Idiot* (Eng. Sorokin 2000, 36–47; Russ. 1997a, 14–41), which proves lethal for them (Eng. Sorokin 2000, 53; Russ. 1997a, 58). Cloning as a poetological device can be found in Sorokin's work as early as in his 1993 play *Iubilei* (*Anniversary*). This device resurfaces in the opera libretto *Children of Rosenthal* in 2005 (see below), where it is applied to composers. A meta-literary reading of the eponymous substance in *Blue Lard*

> [...] can bring the reader to the insight that he consumes a drug which
> tears him out of his familiar everyday world and recombines its elements
> in a totally new manner in the imaginary fictional world. (Deutschmann
> 2009, 158; cf. also Glanc 2005, 136)

From this distant point of view, the entire novel can be interpreted as "a single big juggling performance [jongleernummer] with Russian literature," a "self-referential structure" revolving around literariness itself (Brouwer, Noordenbos 2006, 37). The underlined, "narcissistic" meta-literariness in the plays as well as in the novel *Blue Lard*, "a type of literature that reflects on the process of its own creation and reception" (Noordenbos 2016, 74), renders the label "postmodernism" better applicable to these texts than to many of Sorokin's other books.

However, the device of cloning writers, which dominates the first hundred pages of the novel, turns out to have no essential narrative function in the course of the novel's plot. For the biopunk framework plot, the clones' textual creations are only by-products of a biochemical process of lard secretion, "the production waste" [*otkhod proizvodstva*] (Genis 2011, 425).

The main product, the fantastic blue lard, remains for the most part shrouded in mystery. It appears to be a somehow all-powerful fuel for which all strive, including a retrograde sect of "earth-fuckers" ["землеебы"], who steal it from Gloger's Genlabi-18, but the reader fails to understand what its practical application might be until the fantastic climax toward the end (Genis 2011, 424–5). The enigmatic nature of the substance, captured in the English translation "trick lard" (Sorokin 2003a), invites hyper-complex narratological and semiotic interpretations (Deutschmann 2003, 304–58), intended to solve the unsolvable narrative aporias in the text (such as the contradiction in the fact that Gloger dies in the fourteenth letter he writes—which he therefore cannot have written; Deutschmann 2003, 299).

Moreover, the textual "production waste" is hardly the only "alien" piece of montage inserted into the main plot(s) of *Blue Lard*. Several other nested stories are also embedded in the various, rather heterogeneous parts of the framework plot. The most obvious, perfectly conceptualist example is one of Sorokin's earliest texts, the swimmer story "The Swim," written in the traditional manner of Socialist Realism (cf. chapter One). Embedded in setting of the year 2068 is the nested story "Blue Pill" ["Синяя Таблетка"] (Sorokin 1999, 160–7). This short story depicts Moscow's Bol´shoi Theater as a futurist purification plant (Sorokin 1999, 163) and culminates in the beaming of the blue lard from 2068 back to 1954. The story is projected into a theater, which is filled with excrement, during a stage performance attended by leading members of the Central Committee. At this point in the 1954 half of the plot, a piece of avant-garde writing about a blood-drinking couple, which is called "A Glass of Russian Blood: A Play in Four Acts" ["Стакан русской крови: пьеса в четырех действиях"] (Sorokin 1999, 277–87) and ascribed to Stalinist war writer Konstantin Simonov, is read aloud by Stalin's wife Nadezhda Allilueva as she flies to Germany in the company of Khrushchev and the entire Stalin family.

The two main time periods of the novel are randomly linked together with the help of a so-called "time cone" ["воронка времени"] (Sorokin 1999, 159), which sends a piece of the enigmatic blue lard into the Bol´shoi Theatre on March 1, 1954 (Sorokin 1999, 169). The 1954 setting seems historical only at first glance. Sorokin accumulates an array of blatant anachronisms: Stalin and Hitler are still alive; together they have won the war. In this counterfactual history, Hitler is a pedophile who rapes Stalin's daughter (Sorokin 1999, 323); Allilueva has sex with Pasternak and her stepson; Stalin also has two transvestite sons (Sorokin 1999, 187), is addicted to drugs, mixes German exclamations (Sorokin 1999, 205) and English vulgarisms (Sorokin 1999, 213), and, as a crowning achievement to top off these anachronisms, has become the lover of an utterly unhistorical count Nikita Aristarkhovich Khrushchev, who has already been removed from office in 1954 and appears as a decadent aristocrat (Sorokin 1999, 272) reminiscent of de Sade. Together, Stalin and Khrushchev eat a cannibalistic fondue consisting of a young man tortured by Khrushchev (Sorokin 1999, 245–7), have sex, and discuss a cynical travesty of Solzhenitsyn's canonical short novel about Soviet camp life *One Day in the Life of Ivan Denisovich* (1962) about the Soviet Union's luxury LOVELAGs (Sorokin 1999, 260). The color epithet "blue" [*goluboi*] from the novel's title appears to carry different meanings in the text, but is also the most-used colloquial Russian word for "gay" (cf. Giliarov 2008, 9–10). Gayness comes into play with the letter writer of 2068, Boris Gloger, as well as the homosexual love scene between Khrushchev and Stalin (this fragment was translated into English by Arch Tait; Sorokin 2003a).

When Stalin informs Khrushchev of the blue lard he has received from the *zemleëby*, the plot turns toward German-Soviet relations, one of Sorokin's favorite topics, which he again "enriches" with a banal intercultural psychopathology as in *The Postnuptial Journey*. The Soviet leaders head on to an idyllic meeting between the families of Stalin and Hitler, who have been good friends since the beginning of German-Soviet friendship and the creation of a new world order at an alternative conference of Potsdam (Sorokin 1999, 302), on the Obersalzberg. This counterfactual event is not even the climax of the novel's trivialization of the two dictatorships: after an intellectual discussion about the reasons for the weak representation of philosophy in Russia (Sorokin 1999, 314), Stalin utters a sentence which, if not embedded in a fictional text and countermanded two pages later (Sorokin 1999, 318–9), would in post-war Germany be regarded as a punishable denial of the German guilt for the Shoah: "The Americans killed 6 million Jews" ["Американцы уничтожили 6 миллионов евреев"] (Sorokin 1999, 316). After Reichsführer-SS Heinrich Himmler turns out to be an accomplice of the Soviets, Stalin eventually manages to inject the blue lard into his own brain (Sorokin 1999, 336), which subsequently expands to the size of the universe.

From this last twist of the spiral of historical fantasy, we suddenly return to the framework plot set in 2068. Here an elderly Stalin wakes up as the butler of a certain F, who receives letters from the readers' old acquaintance, biophilologist Boris Gloger. The novel ends with the literal realization of Hegel's bad infinity, repeating the January 2, 2068 letter from Gloger with which the novel started (Sorokin 1999, 342–3).

Apart from the figure of Stalin and the traditional genre of the epistolary novel (cf. Sokolov 2005, 110), there is not much in the framework plot which calls to mind the conceptualist passéism of Sorokin's earlier works. Rather, the framework story follows the generic rules of science fiction by introducing foreignisms (mostly Germanisms, Anglicisms, and Chinese calques) and invented technological vocabulary:

> There's not even a sensor-radio here. Verbotten: all this media plus-gemein. All the equipment uses third-generation superconductors. Which … ? Right, which do not leave S-trash in the magnetic fields.

> Здесь же нет даже сенсор-радио. Verbotten: весь медиальный плюс-гемайн. Вся аппаратура на сверхпроводниках третьего поколения. Которые? Да. Не оставляют S-трэшей в магнитных полях. (Sorokin 1999, 9, sic)

Most of the invented terms refer to the imaginary research field of "biophilology." This branch of science is responsible for the clones who produce their blue lard while writing. Of the clone Akhmatova-2, we learn the following: "Incubated at GENROSMOB. First trial—51% correspondence, second—88%. […] M-balance. Restless behavior, automatism, PSY-GRO, yangdianfeng" ["Инкубирована в ГЕНРОСМОБе. Первая попытка—51% соответствия, вторая—88%. (…) М-баланс 28. Поведение беспокойное, автоматизм, PSY-GRO, яндяньфын"] (Sorokin 1999, 19). The glossary of related terms in the novel (Sorokin 1999, 348–50) does not clarify these. In fact, it adds even more enigmatic explanations: "Ask the LOB—commit an act of dis-question which might disturb the M-balance" ["Спросить в LOB—совершить акт dis-вопроса, способный нарушить М-баланс"] (Sorokin 1999, 350; cf. also Kovalev 2013, 152–3). No better understanding can be derived from the technical (pseudo-)instruction for use of the blue lard at the end of the novel (Sorokin 1999, 339–40).

The "biophilological" terms contribute to the dominant impression of macaronization, which poses severe challenges for a translation that "conveys the disorienting and jarring nature of the original text" (Hoffman, Korchagina 2006, 141). The very beginning of *Blue Lard* reads:

> 2 January
> Hi, mon petit.
> My heavy boy and tender bastard, my divine and abhorrent top-direct. Remembering you is a hellish thing, rips laowai, it's *heavy* in the literal sense of the word. And it's dangerous—for my dreams, for L-harmony, for the protoplasm, for skandhas, for my V-2.

2 января.

Привет, mon petit.

Тяжелый мальчик мой, нежная сволочь, божественный и мерзкий топ-директ. Вспоминать тебя—адское дело, рипс лаовай, это *тяжело* в прямом смысле слова. И опасно: для снов, для L-гармонии, для протоплазмы, для скандхи, для моего V-2. (Sorokin 1999, 7, emphasis in the original)

The biggest challenge for the average reader of Russian (and English) is Sorokin's scattered use of Chinese lexemes. In the twenty-first century proclaimed in the novel (Sorokin 1999, 115), Chinese is so omnipresent that it renders some of the epistolary parts of *Blue Lard* almost unreadable. This is in stark contrast, for example, to Sorokin's later novels *Day of the Oprichnik* (2006) and *Sugar Kremlin* (2008, for both cf. chapter Nine), or to Aleksandr Zel′dovich's film *The Target* (2010), based on a script by Sorokin, where Chinese lexemes are used only occasionally. Also riddled with Chinese words are two short texts by Sorokin, "Iu" and "The Concrete Ones" ["Сонкретные"], included in the compilation *The Feast* (2000). In "Iu," Chinese serves as coloring and is functional for the reader's comprehension, but in "The Concrete Ones" it has an obscuring effect (Filimonova 2014, 224). In *Blue Lard* the Chinese lexemes add to the overall impression of chaos and hampered comprehensibility (Uffelmann 2013b).

As vulgar Russian language ("Rusmat"; Sorokin 1999, 23, 92) is a taboo in the 2068 society depicted in the novel, some "Russian" sentences consist exclusively of Chinese words used as cursing (plus the enigmatic "rips"): "Beibidi xiaotou, geichidi liangmianpai, choudixiaozhu, kebidi huaidan, rips ni ma de ta ben!" ["Бэйбиди сяотоу, кэйчиди лянмяньпай, чоуди сяочжу, кэбиди хуайдань, рипс нимада табень!"] (Sorokin 1999, 17). Chinese names even serve as an act of linguistic violence in a literal sense reminiscent of Franz Kafka's "In the Penal Colony" ["In der Strafkolonie"] (1919): "I will turn you inside out and write on each of your inner organs its Chinese name in Russian with Japanese black ink. / Don't forget this, rips hushuo badao" ["(…) я тебя выверну наизнанку и на каждом твоем внутреннем органе черной японской тушью напишу по-русски его китайское название. / Думай, рипс хушо бадао"] (Sorokin 1999, 109).

Both *Blue Lard* (Sorokin 1999, 345–7) and "The Concrete Ones" (Sorokin 2001b, 98) are appended with Chinese glossaries. For readers, using the glossary means leafing through the book, which complicates, or at least delays, comprehension. After a while, most readers will stop leafing because semantically, it hardly helps. This prompted Maksim Marusenkov to hastily associate the Chinese embedded particles with phonetic transrational language (*zaum'*; Marusenkov 2012, 127). Although Sylvia Sasse is wrong to assume that Chinese in "The Concrete Ones" is "fictitious Chinese," she correctly diagnoses the uselessness of the glossaries (Sasse 2003, 225). Thus the predominant function of Chinese in *Blue Lard* and "The Concrete Ones" is exactly its incomprehensibility, which enhances communicational dysfunctionality.

This (dys-)function of Chinese elements challenges Ol´ga Bogdanova's opinion that *Blue Lard* is only one in a series of Sorokin's various "polystylistically constructed texts" (Bogdanova 2005, 41). In an artistic work such as this novel communicational dysfunctionality rarely does anything other than contribute to the work's specific poetics. The incomprehensibility of large parts of these texts is what makes them innovative.

This (dys-)functionality is overlooked by Sorokin's sworn enemy Andrei Nemzer who in his book review of *Blue Lard* complains: "There are a lot of words in Vladimir Sorokin's new novel—Russian, Chinese, French, and German words. Pseudo-terminological, invented, slang, and vulgar words" (Nemzer 2003, 397). To this list we may add that with Chinese and Western European languages, there are also alphabets other than Cyrillic involved. In contrast to *A Month in Dachau*, where all German utterances are rendered in Cyrillic transcription, in *Blue Lard* Sorokin makes ample use of foreign alphabets for the sake of estrangement. For instance, he includes complete German sentences written in the Latin alphabet such as Hitler's question to Allilueva: "I am so happy, my charming friends! Don't you mind losing the ground under your feet for a moment here in the mountains?" ["Ich bin so glücklich, meine bezaurbende Freunde! Macht es Ihnen nichts aus, dass Sie hier in den Bergen für einen Augenblick den Boden unter den Füssen verlieren?"] (Sorokin 1999, 302, sic).

The typography of the novel is also disturbed by the excessive use of capital letters ("BLUT UND BODEN"; Sorokin 1999, 300) or mathematical symbols. *Blue Lard* operates through ostentatiously primitive sexual symbols in bold (partially Latin) letters with sexist commentaries such as "everybody's **olo** (apart from Akhmatova's-2) erect" ["**olo** у всех (кроме Ахматовой-2) встают"] (Sorokin 1999, 89). Slightly less eye-catching is the enigmatic use of italics, which is typical of many different works by Sorokin, giving the action or entity in question an esoteric quality (cf. Marusenkov 2012, 130), such as in the episode where Adolf Hitler *"touches"* his dog ["*трогал*"] (Sorokin 1999, 305). Where these various devices are combined, as in some of Gloger's letters, the fragments turn into "veritable transrational language" (Marusenkov 2012, 130), which goes beyond the futurist devices of transrational poetry, forming a "Sorokinian 'neo-*zaum*'" [*Sorokinskaia* "*novozaum*'"] (Marusenkov 2012, 140).

Evidently, Sorokin packed too much both into the language and into the plot of his novel, and purposefully did not care to connect the parts. According to Elena Petrovskaia, *Blue Lard* is "not a novel" but an "accumulation" of "static scenes" (Petrovskaia 2000, 416–7). Elevating similar impressions of the novel's disoriented readers to the level of poetics, one might argue that Sorokin lays bare the dynamic compilation of scenes that forms the basis of any novel. But in *Blue Lard* he goes a step further: the scenes often follow each other in line with what one could describe as the domino principle. This associative connection replaces the usual logical-temporal hierarchy between the frame narratives and the embedded stories. With further nested stories, even the loose domino principle fails to work; the transitions become highly arbitrary. Only toward the end of the novel, as in Quentin Tarantino's *Pulp Fiction* (1994), is there a feeble attempt to arrive at a circle structure; the last letter by Boris Gloger is the same as his first one—dating from January 2, 2068 (Sorokin 1999, 7, 342).

The poorly connected parts not only depict highly different contexts but also display a huge degree of poetological heterogeneity. Norbert Wehr finds that this structure resembles a collection of divergent film scenarios:

> Sorokin's bad fantasy begins to go head over heels; he kidnaps his characters into scenarios by Hitchcock or scripts for the James-Bond series, into films by Riefenstahl, Eizenshtein or Chaplin, in spaces and settings that could be designed by Dali, Komar & Melamid, Japanese Manga cartoonists or by Arno Breker. (Wehr 2000)

Even poetological labels such as cyber-punk or biopunk manage to capture only some aspects of the framework plot (such as a sinister future world, the blending of history and science on the one hand, and fiction and materialized metaphors on the other). They do not encompass the entire framework plot, let alone the inner stories.

In 1999 and 2001, Lipovetsky positively associated *Blue Lard* with Bakhtinian potentially creative "polyglossia" [*mnogoiazychie*] (Lipovetsky 1999, 215; Leiderman, Lipovetskii 2001, 61). In his 2008 monograph

Paralogues [*Paralogii*], he made a contrary evaluation, following Wehr's filmic associations:

> The process of producing the fantastic blue lard unfolds against a "totalitarian" backdrop, in an unintelligible, convulsive way, without any reflection: [...] Practically every plot turn which is connected with the blue lard looks inexplicable in this part of the novel, like the twists and turns in a bad action movie. (Lipovetsky 2008, 426)

Here, Lipovetsky speaks of *Blue Lard* as a monstrously heterogeneous "*non-roaring* mixture" [negremuchaia *smes´*] (Lipovetsky 2008, 441, emphasis in the original). With *Blue Lard*, "Iu," and "The Concrete Ones," Sorokin has for a short time relinquished his former ideal of "the purity of an internal order" ["чистота внутреннего строя"] (Sorokin, Genis, Vail´ 1992, 141), jumping back and forth as much as possible in the mood of chaotic modernism (Uffelmann 2013b, 191) and the style of fantasy literature.

True to his meta-discursive attitude, Sorokin in this novel confronts his readers with the conceptualization of fantastic discourses and the poetics of pulp fiction action thrillers. The object of conceptualization has changed—from "classicist" Socialist Realism to "modernist" popular genres. Therefore, for *Blue Lard* we cannot apply Genis's classical equation for sots-art conceptualism ("Russian postmodernism = avant-garde + sots-realism"; Genis 1999, 206) anymore. We must see this novel as a work of pop-art conceptualism (cf. Petrovskaia 2000, 415). The new genres that inspire Sorokin's "conceptualist interest in mass-culture genres" are "espionage films and comics" (Wehr 2000). In *Blue Lard*, Sorokin's conceptual focus is on modes of writing such as inconsistency, associative plot structures, and incomprehensibility. Thus, *Blue Lard* borrows from the inconsistency and heterogeneity of contemporary discourses such as esotericism, occultism, utopian projects, and pulp fiction, at once mimetically adequate and adequately unreadable.

Thus, the innovation of *Blue Lard* is not its meta-discursive trajectory, but its sudden popularity. The typical readers of the pulp fiction genre, which Sorokin meta-discursively emulates, did not feel offended by this novel, as the advocates of Socialist Realism felt insulted by *The Norm*, or proponents of classical Russian literature, by *A Novel*. Instead, these readers went ahead and bought it! It was others who felt insulted this time. The book "managed to offend almost every group in contemporary Russia: nationalists and Communists, liberals and former dissidents, conservatives, radicals, the Church hierarchy, and devotees of the most sacred hierarchy of all—Russian literature" (Gambrell 2015, 210; cf. Anninskii 2001, 115).

Tellingly, these groups took offense at the vulgar metaphors materialized in the plot of *Blue Lard*. The retrograde ideology ascribed to the sect of "earth-fuckers," who, in 2068, practice their veneration of Damp Mother Earth by masturbating into holes dug in the earth (Sorokin 1999, 126–7, 144–6, 153–4, 157–8), satirically materializes the late Slavophile cult of the Russian soil known as *pochvennichestvo* (Stryjakowska 2016, 112), represented by Fëdor Dostoevskii, among others, and revitalized in the post-Soviet 1990s in the context of neo-Eurasianist ideologies (Filimonova 2014, 228). Even more attention was paid to the anal-sex scene between Khrushchev and Stalin, which appears as the materialization of the historical political metaphor for destalinization, "Khrushchev scolded Stalin" ["Хрущев выеб Сталина"; literally: "Khrushchev fucked Stalin"] (Eng. Sorokin 2003a, 207–8; Russ. 1999, 258–9; cf. Uffelmann 2006, 114). However, attempts to read this scene as pornography in the proper sense are unsubstantiated because the text in no way seems to be aimed at arousing sexual excitement, but instead "neutralizes all possible emotions" (Genis 2011, 429).

The really provocative element of *Blue Lard*, apart from Sorokin's usual violation of using vulgar language in print, is the mechanism of conflation (cf. Borenstein 2005, 250) used with the aforementioned materializations of historical vulgar idioms. It culminates in contamination: of hegemonic political leadership and passive homosexuality (Stalin; cf. Sorokin, Bonet, Fernández 2002; Marsh 2007, 447; Gierzinger 2009, 56–8); of terroristic rule and cannibalism (Khrushchev, Stalin); of moralistic literature and obscenity (Akhmatova; cf. Hofmann, Korchagina 2006, 136–7; Kovalev 2013, 159). All together, these contaminations advance into an indissoluble "history-porno-graphy" (Obermayr 2005, 118). It is not pornography proper, but *Blue Lard*'s defiance of all traditionalist borders that made it the number-one target for the artificial production of a "scandal." Salla Räsänen has demonstrated that the critics actually paid less attention to the anal sex scene than to Khrushchev's and Stalin's cannibalistic fondue and their conversation about a fake Solzhenitsyn camp-literature work (Räsänen 2005, 10).

Also telling is the fact that the "scandal" around the novel was fabricated only in 2002, triggered by a campaign against Sorokin and other avant-garde or post-modern writers by the pro-Putin youth movement *Walking Together* [*Idushchie vmeste*]. The group started with rallies and "book return actions" in January 2002. The artificially orchestrated rage culminated on June 27, 2002, after Sorokin signed a contract with the Bol'shoi Theater for a libretto. Young and elderly so-called activists from *Walking Together*, who were in fact paid to take part, tore copies of *Blue Lard* and other postmodernist books into pieces and threw them in a foam toilet they had erected as a "monument for Sorokin" in front of the Bol'shoi Theater. Manuela Kovalev points out that by materializing a metaphoric toilet to throw book copies in it,

> [...] *Walking Together* not only applied the same technique as Sorokin did in his infamous novel, namely a materialization of obscene metaphors, but they, too, *performed* the obscene by reading out the very text they condemned in order to convey their (non-obscene) message. (Kovalev 2013, 167, emphasis in the original)

On the eve of this action, Artem Maguniants, lawyer for *Walking Together*, had already issued a criminal complaint for pornography based on the Khrushchev-Stalin pages (Sorokin 1999, 252–62; chronology according to Murav 2003 and Räsänen 2005, 12–4).

To be clear, all this unfolded three years after the publication. Nothing in Sorokin's work could have shocked his experienced readers. The summer 2002 protests were fueled by the political climate, as the authoritarian attitude of the Putin administration intensified. The new government ideology made *Blue Lard* appear "far more transgressive than it did when it was first published" (Borenstein 2005, 249). This made it possible for the attorney's office of Moscow's Zamoskvorech'e district to commission several expert opinions (see Räsänen 2005, 72–5). However, the experts eventually discarded the accusation of pornography in April 2003, and the attorney's office dropped the case without taking it to court.

Instead of seeing the case being dropped as a victory for artistic freedom in post-Soviet Russia, some researchers argue that the so-called scandal had a paradoxical commercial effect in favor of the writer. Marusenkov proves that the sixth Russian edition of *Blue Lard*, with which the book exceeded a print run of 100,000 copies, appeared before the June 2002 attack (2012, 195 note 465) and Sorokin himself asserts that the scandal contributed little to the sales numbers (Sokolov 2005, 130). But other observers claim that thanks to the scandal—combined with his newly acquired popular guest role on *Behind Glass*—Sorokin ceased to be a writer known only to a small group of like-minded people, and instead became a well-known figure. Most prominently and unexpectedly, Mikhail Ryklin launched the allegation that Sorokin and his publisher were tacitly in cahoots with *Walking Together*:

> Many observers (who are quite smart, too) assume that the political technologists make use of the publishing house Ad Marginem for their own purposes, allowing it to derive commercial gain from staging political persecution. (Ryklin 2003, 183)

Ryklin's interpretation of the scandal as a sophisticated PR stunt arranged for Sorokin by the "political technologists" of the Kremlin confuses cause and effect (cf. Rutten 2017, 144). It is a surprising claim that the anti-avant-gardist intentions of the *Walking Together* led to dialectical symbolic and even economic advantages for the author and his publisher (cf. Räsänen 2005, 152). But still, this "scandal of success" (Obermayr 2006, 520) over a relatively high-selling novel, in addition to the formal recognition crystallized in the National Booker Award and Belyi Prize in 2001, suddenly made Sorokin's former underground art "convertible" into a product for the masses—at least in respect of its pulp fiction techniques.

The growing doses of mass convertibility meant increased and continuous public attention. A second artificial "scandal" had already been maturing since the new artistic director of the Bol'shoi Theater, Anatolii Iksanov, had commissioned an opera, eventually known as *The Children of Rosenthal* [*Deti Rozentalia*], from Sorokin and composer Leonid Desiatnikov in 2002. When the premiere was announced for March 23, 2005, the recently renamed Putin youth organization *Ours* [*Nashi*] picketed in front of the theater. 293 members of the Russian State Duma joined the "scandalizers" [Skandalierer] (Engel 2009, 713) and accused the opera's choir of prostitutes of being pornography despite its obvious lack of erotic elements. Only twelve members voted in favor of staging the opera. Sorokin replied by associating this attack with the repressive cultural policy of late Stalinism, the Zhdanov era (Engel 2009, 717 note 34).

In August 2016 Sorokin's short story "Nastia," which had first been published in *The Feast* as early as 2001 (Sorokin 2001b, 7–76), suddenly became an object of hostility when film director Konstantin Bogomolov announced his plans for screening it on his Facebook page. Now it was not top-down "scandalizers" who took action, but an unknown Orthodox activist called Irina Basina. Discerning in the cannibalistic plot of "Nastia" the mocking of Orthodox values, Basina set out to "counteract extremism" ("Aktivisty" 2016), and campaigned to prohibit its screening. This case illustrates the increasingly repressive role of self-appointed Orthodox zealots and hooligans in the Russian Federation since the early 2000s.

All these attacks show that Sorokin's works became a target as soon as they addressed a broader public—be it via pulp fiction, a production for Russia's most prestigious theater, or film adaptation. Moreover, time and time again it is Sorokin's provocative materialized metaphors that serve as the pretext for an attack: in the "Nastia" case this is the "fresh-baked" [*novoispechennaia*] sixteen-year-old birthday girl who is literally cooked in the oven (much as in the fairy tale "Hansel and Gretel" ["Hänsel und Gretel"]) and eaten by the birthday guests (see Kalinin 2013, 137). Given the highly specific nature of Sorokin's trademark of the materialization of metaphors, similar attacks on the freedom of literature have to date not led to serious legal consequences for the writer or mass mobilization against avant-garde art in post-Soviet Russia (Engel 2009, 714–5).

CHAPTER 9

Ice and Esoteric Fanaticism—a New Sorokin?

After the end of the Soviet Union many things have obviously changed, both in Sorokin's new media strategies in the 1990s and early 2000s (see chapter Seven) and in his turn toward popular culture with *Blue Lard*. At first glance the trilogy comprising the novels *Ice* [*Lëd*] (2002), *Bro's Path* [*Put' Bro*] (2004), and *23,000* (2005) still applies certain devices found in *Blue Lard*—the inspiration from popular crime thrillers and fantasy literature and a fantastic substance as the main connector. The second part, *Bro's Path* (Sorokin 2004b), forms a logical prequel to *Ice* (Sorokin 2002b) and was therefore included first when it was compiled together with *Ice* and the never separately published third part, *23,000*, under one cover with the title *Trilogy* [*Trilogiia*] in 2005 (Sorokin 2006a). Counting 685 pages, the *Trilogy* is Sorokin's longest coherent book so far. For the 2008 reissue Sorokin slightly rewrote the ending of *23,000* (Ågren 2014, 115–6).

The *Ice Trilogy* is also the most eagerly translated part of Sorokin's oeuvre. The earliest example is Andrew Bromfield's English translation of three fragments of parts one and three of *Ice* in *Index on Censorship* (Eng. Sorokin 2005a; corresponds to Russ. 2002b, 71–7, 209–14, 287–9), followed by the book publication of Jamey Gambrell's full translation of *Ice* in 2007 (Sorokin 2007a). Gambrell's efforts culminated in the complete *Ice Trilogy* edition (Sorokin 2011b, 231–478, where the first part was entitled "Bro," not "Bro's Path").

The eponymous substance *Ice* [*lëd*] is a specific piece of frozen water that fell down to earth with the historical Tunguska meteorite in 1908. Described as an "ideal Cosmic substance" ["идеальное космическое вещество"] (Eng. Sorokin 2007a, 219; Russ. 2002b, 214) and venerated fanatically in the novel (Eng. Sorokin 2007a, 255; Russ. 2002b, 251–2), it is reminiscent of substances from Sorokin's earlier texts. Most prominently, *Blue Lard* featured a mysterious blue semi-liquid, produced by clones of Russian writers. While their textual products were considered imperfect "production waste," the enigmatic blue substance kindled the desires of all antagonists in the 1999 novel. In *Four Stout Hearts* from 1991 Sorokin had introduced an even more indefinable substance, analogous to the *lëd* in the *Ice Trilogy*, and also connected to the protagonists' hearts. In *Ice Trilogy*, the frozen substance from the Tunguska meteorite can be used only by the chosen 23,000, whose living hearts may be freed from their earthly prisons by beating a hammer made of the cosmic ice against the character's breastbone. When all 23,000 have been cracked open, the primordial "Light" ["Свет"], currently lost by the humans who degraded into metaphysically dead "meat machines," will be restored. This, in short, is the intrigue of the three novels with their rather transparent binary distribution of actors (Novokhatskii 2009, 96), the "simplistic cast of heart singers and 'meat machines'" (Kiem 2007).

In accordance with the chronological structure of this Companion, the following analysis goes against the order of the eventual trilogy publication from 2005 and sticks to the chronology of first publications and the order in which the first Russian readers became acquainted with the three novels. Thus, my reading starts with the release of *Ice* in March 2002. This first part of the future trilogy is set in post-Soviet Moscow where certain blue-eyed and blond people are searching for other blue-eyed blonds whose "hearts speak" when they strike their breastbones with hammers made from the *lëd* from the Tunguska meteorite that landed in the Krasnoiarsk region in Siberia in 1908.

From the opening pages of *Ice*, the narrative seems homogeneous, far from the random structure of *Blue Lard*. At second glance, however, *Ice* also sins against some narratological rules of the novelistic genre. The first and longest of the four parts of *Ice* (Eng. Sorokin 2007a, 1–165; Russ. 2002b, 7–160) differs from conventional narration due to serialization, the repetition of similar actions with small variations. An obvious example are the repeated imperatives "Respond!" ["Отзовися!"] and "Speak with the heart!" ["Говори сердцем!"] (Eng. Sorokin 2007a, 5, 47; Russ. 2002b, 12, 51). Moreover, the narrative leaves the impression that it was made in a hurry, written in staccato, and remains unfinished. The hasty narrator does not bother to give a methodical description of his characters, only providing asyndetic enumerations of a few of their features (Eng. Sorokin 2007a, 4; Russ. 2002b, 10). Seemingly, the novel also invites its reader to a hasty reception as well. Bold emphases in the text are not indications of important ideas. Instead, they introduce new characters (doctor, female assistant, driver, etc.; Eng. Sorokin 2007a, 12, 25; Russ.

2002b, 18, 20, 31), as if facilitating accelerated skimming. This causes some initial doubts about the novel's metaphysical claims:

> The discursive syntactical simplicity and spontaneity contradicts the complicated task to be completed by brothers and sisters through meticulously prepared and carefully planned actions. The refinement of the mission clashes not only with the brutal acts but also with the primitive language used by many converts, including the spiritual leader. (Nazarenko 2003, 134)

The first story revolves around "brother Ural" (part one, subchapters 1–3). In section one, Iurii Lapin has his breast violently "cracked" with the *lëd* hammer and his heart tells his "proper name," Ural. Sections two and three describe Lapin's / Ural's psychological difficulties, as he comes to terms with his new "heart" identity. This tripartite structure sets the rhythm for the following two individual stories, those of Diar (I 4–6) and Mokho (I 7–10). Each subplot consists of three to four subchapters: the first section contains the cracking; the second, the awakening after the violence; and the remaining sections show the crisis triggered by the new sensibility in conflict with the characters' old social roles. All three of the newly awakened go through a rather troublesome farewell to physical sex, which is narrated with much physiological detail, showing contemporary post-Soviet life as hell on earth (Eng. Sorokin 2007a, 110–3; Russ. 2002b, 111–3; cf. Ågren 2014, 108), and a series of crying fits (Eng. Sorokin 2007a, 109, 147, 155; Russ. 2002b, 110, 144, 152), some provoked by dreams in italics that comprise motifs of crying (Eng. Sorokin 2007a, 105, 115, 143; Russ. 2002b, 106, 116, 141). After these "cycle[s]" of "[t]ears, sleep. Sleep and tears" ["цикл. Слезы, сон. Сон и слезы"] (Eng. Sorokin 2007a, 162; Russ. 2002b, 157), Ural, Diar, and Mokho can count as newborn and be initiated into the brotherhood (Eng. Sorokin 2007a, 164–5; Russ. 2002b, 159–60). Thus ends the first part, modeled on "pulp mystery novels" (Caryl 2007, 61). The three who have been successfully "cracked open" are admitted to a totalitarian sect (Sorokin's own description; Sokolov 2005, 128), modeled on historical Russian sects such as the *skoptsy* (Etkind 2009, 653). In *Ice*, the sect members press their hearts together instead of having sexual intercourse, and experience a state of supreme bliss and rapture. Even Borenboim / Mokho, an inveterate cynic, suddenly feels pity for the heart of a dying rat (Eng. Sorokin 2007a, 105; Russ. 2002b, 106).

The second part (Eng. Sorokin 2007a, 167–287; Russ. 2002b, 161–284) tells the prehistory of the post-Soviet search for those "alive at heart" and ends with Ural's, Diar's, and Mokho's initiation into the brotherhood (Eng. Sorokin 2007a, 287; Russ. 2002b, 284). Narrated in the first person by Varia Samsikova / Khram, the story follows the gradual gathering of the chosen 23,000 from World War Two, when it is just 153 of them, to January 1, 2000, when their number reaches 18,610 (Eng. Sorokin 2007a, 211, 283; Russ. 2002b, 205, 280). This more coherent part follows the genre rules of conversion narratives. It begins with an emotional autobiography that includes markers of orality, indicating an authentic evidence.

Another conventional literary device is estrangement from a child's perspective. For example, life in Varia's mother's house under the "funny" German occupants is presented as "cheery" ["смешные," "весело"] (Eng. Sorokin 2007a, 171; Russ. 2002b, 165); and when Varia, together with other girls from the occupied territories, is deported to "Greater Germany" ["Великая Германия"] for forced labor, the parade ground in a transition camp overwhelms the village child as an "enormous public square" ["огромадный майдан такой"] (Eng. Sorokin 2007a, 182; Russ. 2002b, 176).

While the estranging perspective of a child could be appreciated as conventional literature, after the first part, the reader already anticipates that this is all irrelevant and everything that counts must follow only after the usual metaphysical awakening with a *lëd* hammer. This is confirmed when what Varia first perceives as an execution of prisoners of war transforms into the *lëd* ritual known from part one (Eng. Sorokin 2007a, 183, 192; Russ. 2002b, 177, 186). The mechanism of positive disillusion is repeated for the last time when Khram's expectation of rape turns into her first "heart intercourse" (Eng. Sorokin 2007a, 197–8; Russ. 2002b, 192).

Later, Khram's conversion narrative, well in accordance with the genre rules, turns to sermon (Eng. Sorokin 2007a, 215–8; Russ. 2002b, 210–4), mission, vision, and prophecy. The sermon part—Bro's instruction to Khram—culminates in an esoteric cosmology, transposing the Prologue to the Gospel of John (1:1–5) into an esoteric metaphysics of light and its chosen bearers:

> In the beginning there was only the Light. And the Light shone in the Absolute Emptiness. The Light shone for Itself Alone. The Light consisted of twenty-three thousand light-bearing rays. And we were those rays.

> сначала был только Свет Изначальный. И Свет сиял в Абсолютной Пустоте. И Свет сиял для Себя Самого. Свет состоял из двадцати трех тысяч светоносных лучей. И это были мы. (Eng. Sorokin 2007a, 215; Russ. 2002b, 210)

This genesis would be incomplete without a gnostic teleology of return to the origin (cf. Scholz 2010), when the chosen 23,000 will unite in one circle and simultaneously pronounce all twenty-three words of the heart language: "Once again we will become rays of the Primordial Light" ["И мы снова станем лучами Света Изначального. И вернемся в Вечность"] (Eng. Sorokin 2007a, 218; Russ. 2002b, 213).

The culminating elements of the conversion narrative are visions and acts of prophecy. Khram, with her exclusive knowledge of all twenty-three words, claims, "I saw the hearts of ALL OUR PEOPLE on this gloomy planet" ["(…) я увидела сердца ВСЕХ НАШИХ на этой угрюмой планете"] (Eng. Sorokin 2007a, 273; Russ. 2002b, 270). She also prophesies that the reunification of the 23,000 and their return to the Light will take place within twenty months from January 1, 2000 (Eng. Sorokin 2007a, 283; Russ. 2002b, 280). The graphical representation of the privileged status claimed by the chosen is rendered in capital letters. Capitalization structures Khram's sharp distinctions between "MACHINES MADE OF MEAT" ["МЯСНЫЕ МАШИНЫ"] (Eng. Sorokin 2007a, 248; Russ. 2002b, 245) and "OUR PEOPLE" ["НАШИ"] (Eng. Sorokin 2007a, 272; Russ. 2002b, 269).

The eschatological vision crowns the mission for which Khram is chosen by the prophet Bro, the discoverer of the *lëd*. This mission consists of recruiting those "alive at heart" in the USSR. The search is supported by Stalin's secret service MGB; the chosen brothers and sisters become a part of Lavrentii Beriia's terror commandos (Eng. Sorokin 2007a, 218–42; Russ. 2002b, 214–238). With the political liberalization after Stalin's death, the accomplices of Beriia's terror themselves become victims of the destalinization movement (Eng. Sorokin 2007a, 264–76; Russ. 2002b, 256–73). Their interrogations are similar to the *lëd* hammer ritual: they are ordered, "Tell! Tell! Tell us!" ["Гово-ри! Гово-ри! Гово-ри!"]; Eng. Sorokin 2007a, 264; Russ. 2002b, 261. Thus, in a historical-political reading, the fanatic chosen few are an allegory of the mass murderers of Stalinism.

The third and fourth parts are much shorter than the first two. The third part is a user's manual for a technical device called "*Ice* Health Improvement System" ["Оздоровительный комплекс 'LËD'"], to which the promoters have added a series of reports compiled by testers of the device. Differing in length, tone, and vulgarity or business-like laconicism, the series of sixteen "comments and recommendations from the first users of the *Ice* Health Improvement System" ["Отзыва и пожелания первых пользователей Оздоровительной системы «LËD»"] (Eng. Sorokin 2007a, 293–314; Russ. 2002b, 291–310) show that all testers felt their hearts. Moreover, all reports end with the word "light" ["свет"], thus betraying the effectiveness of the transformation even if the testers have not yet realized it. The high-tech poetics of the user's manual and the rhetorical standardization of the "Counter-Indications" ["Противопоказания"] and "Warnings" ["Предостережения"] (Eng. Sorokin 2007a, 292–3; Russ. 2002b, 287–9) point to Sorokin's renewed quasi-conceptualist meta-interest in genres, this time non-literary speech genres from the context of user's manuals. The features of these genres are also seen in the seriality in the comments and the identical endings of the recommendations, which make the third part of *Ice* comparable to the serial parts of *The Norm*. Finally, *Ice* lays bare the mechanism of montage: like the signifier *norma* in *The Norm*, here the miraculous *lëd* forms the only link between the parts of the pseudo-novel.

Returning to fiction in the fourth part, the text ends with a short scene in which a little boy gets up in the morning and instead of his parents finds parts of the "*Ice* Health Improvement System" as described in part three and a small piece of *lëd*. As the boy does not know how to handle the device, the novel ends with a still life with toys and melting ice, open for the reader's interpretation: "The ice lay next to the dinosaur, jutting out from under the blanket. The sunlight shone on its wet surface" ["Лед лежал рядом с динозавром, высовываясь из-под одеяла. Солнечный свет блестел на его мокрой поверхности"] (Eng. Sorokin 2007a, 321; Russ. 2002b, 317). The sentimental and toylike (Lipovetskii 2008, 619) still life stands in stark contrast to the drastic language of part one, the pathos of part two, and the passion of the users' comments in part three of *Ice*. It is the most felicitous part of the entire trilogy, where the text reaches symbolic imagery of traditional literature.

If the text had ended with the user's manual in part three, one might have concluded that the end of *Ice* recalls the de-literarization at the end of *A Novel* or *Marina's Thirtieth Love*. But the linear narration of the second and most of the first part, together with the open ending of the final part, point away from such de-literarization. This feature compelled readers such as Konstantin Kustanovich or Christian Caryl to contend that with *Ice*, Sorokin "completes his transition to representational fiction" (Kustanovich 2004, 314) and "a more conventional mode of storytelling" (Caryl 2007, 63). It also earned Sorokin unexpected sympathy from hitherto hostile readers (Ermolin 2003, 408).

While former skeptical critics like Evgenii Ermolin expressed their opinions much more mildly this time, remarkably angry reactions came from other factions. This time, Sorokin's readers had more problems with ideology than language. American reviewer Elisabeth Kiem felt offended by "[…] the sheer sophomoric tedium of his never-ending sado-fantasy that provokes the book-burner in me" (Kiem 2007). Many reviewers asked themselves how to deal with the fanaticism, racism, and terrorism implied in the plot (Gorokhov, Shevtsov 2004; Latynina 2006, 137), noticing that the unlucky others, who are attacked with the ice hammer without responding to this drastic procedure with heart speech, are skipped over by the speedy narrator without the bat of an eyelid (Eng. Sorokin 2007a, 236; Russ. 2002b, 231–2). The fanatic sectarians regard their unresponsive victims as a minor race whose deaths do not matter because they are metaphysically dead from the start: "The absolute majority of people on this earth are walking dead. They are born dead, they marry the dead, they give birth to the dead, and die […]" ["Абсолютное большинство людей на нашей земле—ходячие мертвецы. Они рождаются мертвыми, женятся на мертвых, рожают мертвых, умирают (…)"] (Eng. Sorokin 2007a, 211; Russ. 2002b, 205). For the Soviet recruitment in 1950, we learn that only two out of two hundred "cracked" survived (Eng. Sorokin 2007a, 238; Russ. 2002b, 234). Thousands of non-chosen people, those who are found "empty" ["пустой"] and die in the course of the selection process, are dehumanized to waste: "how many of you empty ding-dongs they gone and multiplied" ["сколько же вас, пустозвонов, понастругали …"] (Eng. Sorokin 2007a, 6; Russ. 2002b, 12). Only before her transformation from Varia to Khram the protagonist of part two perceives what is going on as an execution and morally condemns the perpetrators as "beasts" ["Вот гады проклятые"] (Eng. Sorokin 2007a, 192; Russ. 2002b, 186).

Also challenging is Sorokin's identification of the heart seekers' "tour de l'URSS" in 1950–1951 with the "meat grinder" ["мясорубка"] of Beriia's "repressive state structure" ["репрессивный аппарат"] (Eng. Sorokin 2007a, 239; Russ. 2002b, 234). In a negative metonymy, Sorokin's totalitarian sect is linked to Hitler's SS and Stalin's NKVD (Höllwerth 2015, 205), although he refrains from any explicit moral condemnation of the main action element of the trilogy, the "cracking" with its 99% casualty rate. On the backdrop of the second part, the post-Soviet reader also readily recalls the contempt for mankind ascribed to Stalin by Anatolii Rybakov in his novel *Children of the Arbat* [*Deti Arbata*] (published in 1987; Eng. Rybakov 1988a, 559; Russ. Rybakov 1988b, 438), which Sorokin quotes in passing in one of the capital-letters sayings from subchapter I 3: "GET RID OF A MAN, GET RID OF A PROBLEM" ["НЕТ ЧЕЛОВЕКА—НЕТ ПРОБЛЕМЫ"] (Eng. Sorokin 2007a, 34; Russ. 2002b, 39).

Especially problematic seems the racial side-aspect of the selection. The in-group of people among which the search takes place is defined by the pre-condition of race: "We are blue-eyed and fair-haired" ["Мы голубоглазые и светловолосые"] (Eng. Sorokin 2007a, 218; Russ. 2002b, 213). Again, the narrator fails to offer any explicit condemnation of such racist fictions of Aryan supremacy, but the conversations in subchapter I 3 show the interconnection between Russian esoteric and conspiracy discourses and their link to antisem-itism (Eng. Sorokin 2007a, 35–8; Russ. 2002b, 40–4; cf. Aptekman 2006, 677; Marsh 2007, 371). With similar ambiguity, Sorokin will further develop the esoteric-racist idolatry of Siberia in the film *The Target* (2010), which draws on the Arkaim excavations next to Cheliabinsk (Kukulin 2013, 336), and in *Telluria* (2013) with its Altai mythology.

In the trilogy, however, the selection is fatally reminiscent of the National Socialist "Auslese" of the privileged Aryan race (see Smirnov 2004a, 178; Ågren 2014, 114). This concern is supported by the various Nazi motifs in the plot of *Ice*. For instance, Khram's conversion narrative departs from German-occupied Western territories of the Soviet Union in 1941. German phrases in Cyrillic transcription, with some grammatical mistakes, also in the American edition ("Das ist schöne Wien" ["Дас ист шене Вин"]; Eng. Sorokin 2007a, 201; Russ. 2002b, 195), serve as coloring of the occupation scenery. Next, SS men awake Khram and are thus the first "chosen" to appear in the entire future trilogy in the 2002 text, although in the 2004 edition Bro's Siberian conversion story was added as a prequel. Finally, the chosen Germans are explicitly identified as "blond" ["белобрысые"] with "blue" ["голубые"] eyes (Eng. Sorokin 2007a, 205; Russ. 2002b, 199).

Thus the normative good for which the fanatic chosen few strive in *Ice* is—viewed from a humanistic point of view—a fantastic evil. As the second part of the planned trilogy, *Bro's Path*, states explicitly, the chosen few are at "war against humankind" ["война против рода человеческого"] (Eng. Sorokin 2011b, 136; Russ. 2004a, 176). This part of the trilogy amounts to "a single monstrous vision" (Kalfus 2007) from an inner perspective of the perpe-trators (cf. Latynina 2006, 137), which the readers have to painfully re-produce (Bondarenko 2002, 243). Sorokin will perfect this literary technique in the hangman's discourse of *Day of the Oprichnik* in 2006. The critical question for the readers of the trilogy is whether Sorokin's meta-fascist narrative can remain uninfected by the very discourse it emulates. Does fascist ideology undergo a "subversive affirmation" in *Ice*, as was the case with Sorokin's reenactments of violence inherent in Socialist Realism? With *Ice*, this problem is aggravated by two factors: Sorokin's own statements about his intentions behind these texts, and the fact that he dwells on the motif in a 700-page-long trilogy.

Sorokin is of course well aware that the distinction between a chosen few and the ordinary people is totalitarian (Sorokin, Neverov 2002), but in his interviews from 2004 he repeatedly denies any association with the Aryan racism of the German Nazis. As Sorokin explains, the "brothers of the LIGHT" are blond and blue-eyed because this combination is allegedly inconspicuous (Sorokin, Kochetkova 2004; Sorokin, Reshetnikov 2004). For an author who has worked with German history discourses such as *Historikerstreit*, this claimed naivety appears highly unconvincing.

The prequel *Bro's Path* and the sequel *23,000* repeat the racist and fascist motifs of *Ice* rather than change the internal perspective from within a fanatic sect. *Bro's Path*, published in September 2004, logically constitutes the first part of the *Ice Trilogy*. It tells the story of the prophet Bro, who also appears in *Ice*, where he hands over the responsibility for gathering the chosen 23,000 to Khram (Eng. Sorokin 2007a, 218–9; Russ. 2002b, 213). Born on the day when the Tunguska meteorite came down, Bro is also the first man to touch its ice. His story is narrated in the same linear fashion and first-person perspective as the second part of *Ice*. The binary axiology and disdain for the "machines made of meat" remain unchanged.

For the reader acquainted with *Ice*, nothing in *Bro's Path* comes as much of a surprise (cf. Bogdanova 2005, 45). To the hitherto highly sympathetic reader Igor´ Smirnov, the two texts seem to be almost identical, built on the principle of "parallelism" (Smirnov 2004b). Violence, which was still present as something inevitable in *Ice*, fades into the background. Only the repeated strikes to the breastbones with the ice-hammer remotely remind the reader of Roman's axe in *A Novel*. Although the esoteric ice-hammer does not murder those capable of heart life, the serialization of the ritual seems familiar to anyone acquainted with Sorokin's early oeuvre.

The text pays for this repetition of patterns from part two of *Ice* with the reader's inattentiveness or even boredom, as an exasperated translator also admitted (cf. Gambrell 2011). The long biographical narration about the childhood and youth of Aleksandr Dmitrievich Snegirëv (Eng. Sorokin 2011b, 3–41; Russ. 2004b, 8–55), again underpinned with manifold mechanical estrangement effects (cf. Lipovetskii 2008, 625; Marusenkov 2012, 137–8) through the perspective of a child (for example Eng. Sorokin 2011b, 14; Russ. 2004b, 19), contains few hints about the subsequent esoteric metaphysics of the light, ice, and heart. The traditionalist linear writing strains the reader's expectations to the extent that the detailed description of the expedition to Tunguska (Eng. Sorokin 2011b, 41–72; Russ. 2004b, 56–95) serves as one long retardation. The reader familiar with *Ice* knows in advance that in the end, only the gradual intensification of Snegirëv's metaphysical premonitions of heart love, ice magic, and cosmic energy (Eng. Sorokin 2011b, 8, 21, 29, 34, 58; Russ. 2004b, 12, 28, 38, 46, 77) will remain relevant. Snegirëv's awakening will erase everything accumulated in the previous *Entwicklungsroman* and make the preceding ninety pages superfluous. Almost everything that follows—the contact with the ice, the awakening of Bro, the first hammer and cracking open, the first intercourse by heart, the cathartic crying fit, the search and serial finding of the first twenty-one—is again well known from *Ice*. Having read *Ice,* the readers of *Bro's Path* can—a peculiar inversion of the aims of Bertold Brecht's estrangement didactics—no longer be interested in the course of the action or even the literary devices of the prequel, as they routinely recognize the ice-cosmology. Thus de-automatization falls back into automatization.

No less long-winded is the description of the fascination with the newly discovered substance, including another half-hearted attempt at a cosmogony. Here Sorokin, in italics, partially self-plagiarizes the genesis narrative from *Ice* (Eng. Sorokin 2011b, 77–80; Russ. 2004b, 101–5). The metaphysics of *Bro's Path* differs from *Ice* only in tiny nuances: Bro claims to be the mouth through which the world soul Sophia speaks, introducing "Wisdom of the Light" ["Мудрость Света"] (Eng. Sorokin 2011b, 161; Russ. 2004b, 208). The rest—the cracking open, the cathartic crying fit, the pressing together of the chests and conversation of the hearts, the Aryan racial privilege, the discrimination against darker phenotypes, the vegan ideology of the sect, arrests by the Soviet intelligence service, and its complicity in terrorism and provision of the *lëd*—all these elements look to be copy-pasted from *Ice* (Eng. Sorokin 2011b, 86–8, 92, 102, 106, 122, 128, 146; Russ. 2004b, 113, 115, 120, 132, 137, 157, 165, 188). Even a pre-modern instruction for assembling the ideal *lëd* hammer mirrors the industrial user's manual from part three of *Ice* (Eng. Sorokin 2011b, 169–70; Russ. 2004b, 218–9). In the insignificant thematic differences from *Ice* one can observe the absence of variation, the chief virtue of classical rhetoric and literature, while the frequent use of italics for the metaphysical strivings, excessive emotions, and overstated pathos such as *"my heart's ecstatic state"* ["восторг сердца"] (Eng. Sorokin 2011b, 69, emphasis added; Russ. 2004b, 91; cf. Marusenkov 2012, 139) and capital letters for epiphanies like the insight "AN ICE HAMMER" ["ЛЕДЯНОЙ МОЛОТ"] (Eng. Sorokin 2011b, 102; Russ. 2004b, 132) may expose the primitivity of such literary devices.

One difference is that the awakened hearts in *Bro's Path* are more power-ful. Bro recognizes those who can be awakened from afar (Eng. Sorokin 2011b, 95; Russ. 2004b, 123), and Bro and Fer together are able to "scan" a whole town to see if there is another latent live heart in it (Eng. Sorokin 2011b, 118; Russ. 2004b, 153, 271). This produces significantly fewer casualties than the random search for Aryans in *Ice*. The awakened can communicate with each other through walls. Their hearts work together as a magnet which can hypnotically force a not yet awakened heart into a fainting spell (Eng. Sorokin 2011b, 124; Russ. 2004b, 160). The fantastic substance *lëd* seems to dominate everything, even more so than in *Ice*. It even takes on interactive qualities, stressed by italics: "And the Ice *answered* them" ["И Лед *ответил* им"] (Eng. Sorokin 2011b, 111; Russ. 2004b, 144). With the second novel of the future trilogy, the adherence to transforma-tive substances that "render metaphysics physical" (Smirnov 2004b) intensifies in Sorokin's writing. This impression was so strong that some readers expected a further intensification of the metaphysical element, possibly even something outright religious (Shevtsov 2004), from the third part of the trilogy.

The third novel, *23,000*, which was included in the trilogy volume pub-lished in December of 2005, picks up where *Ice* left off—in January 2000, with the abduction of the little boy Misha and the "orphaned" piece of melting *lëd*, depriving the end of *Ice* of its openness (cf. Romanova, Ivantsov 2004; Caryl 2007, 63). *23,000* begins as a tumultuous action thriller with the already well-known binary of the chosen brotherhood and the metaphysically dead "meat machines." Full of disdain for their stupidity and vulgarity, Merog, the soldier of the "Light," kills them in droves as if in a first-person shooter video game (Eng. Sorokin 2011b, 501; Russ. 2006a, 491).

In the meantime, the decrepit Khram awaits the arrival of the new juvenile Messiah Gorn, the boy Misha from the end of *Ice*, who is supposed to become the center of the mystical union of 2,300 brothers and sisters in the near future (Eng. Sorokin 2011b, 534; Russ. 2006a, 525). Khram, the old woman, and Gorn, the little boy, communicate with their hearts in close embrace like the Virgin Mary and Jesus in various Orthodox icons and Catholic depictions of the Madonna with the child: Adoration of the Child (Eng. Sorokin 2011b, 541; Russ. 2006a, 532), Hodegetria (Eng. Sorokin 2011b, 566; Russ. 2006a, 566), and Glykophilousa (Eng. Sorokin 2011b, 592; Russ. 2006a, 584). Together Khram and Gorn are yet far more powerful than Bro and Fer with their scan-ning of a single city in *Bro's Path*. The new duo can scan the entire globe for the remaining brothers and sisters: "[...] with my heart it's possible *to see THEM ALL AT THE SAME TIME!*" ["(...) вместе с моим сердцем можно увидеть

ВСЕХ СРАЗУ!"] (Eng. Sorokin 2011b, 577; Russ. 2006a, 568, emphases in the originals). Not all the other brothers and sisters possess the same strength of heart, and some need to be encouraged or calmed down by the others. The esoteric veneration of the fantastic substance culminates with the cheering advice: "Rely on the Ice" ["Надо положить себя на Лед"] (Eng. Sorokin 2011b, 523; Russ. 2006a, 514).

This and many other ritualized utterances such as reports about the "meat's" resistance against the already awakened 21,369 and Khram's italicized confirmation that she knows everything (by heart) are ostentatiously repeated throughout the text of the third novel: "'[…] The meat is resisting the Brotherhood.' / 'I *know*'" ["— (…) Мясо противится Братству. / — *Я ведаю*"] (Eng. Sorokin 2011b, 507; Russ. 2006a, 498, emphases in the originals). The repeated conjurations intensify during the final eschatological circle formed by all 23,000 chosen in eight sentences beginning with "And …" ["И …"] (Eng. Sorokin 2011b, 689; Russ. 2006a, 679). The repetitions continue even after the 22,998 brothers and sisters have all died in their circle and only the apostates B´orn and Ol´ga are still alive. Now it is time for them to use their own incantations: "By God" ["Богом"] (Eng. Sorokin 2011b, 693; Russ. 2006a, 684; also in the rewritten second edition, Sorokin 2009a, 701). The antagonists with their creationism appear infected by the metaphysical thrust of the brotherhood—and their monotony, and their theology reads in no way more convincingly than the esoteric teachings of the brotherhood (Lipovetskii 2008, 639–40). With the poorly written theological fragment, literariness approaches its end (Kalinin 2013, 146), at least if understood as the virtue of persuasion. With this final piece of deliberately bad writing, Sorokin displays a renewed interest in meta-exploration of certain discursive mechanisms. He lays bare the redundancy of conjuring speech acts and the conceptual insight that repetition does not intensify, but rather reduces and simplifies its object (cf. Bogdanova 2005, 47).

The most important—and in a sense unexpected—element of the plot of 23,000 is the opening of the "holistic" [*tsel´nyi*] (Sokolov 2005, 132) or even hermetic perspective from inside the sect. The third novel adds the external perspective (cf. Novokhatskii 2009, 178) of unwilling victims of the hammer violence who seek revenge: "Fuck off, Ice!" (Eng. Sorokin 2011b, 608; Russ. 2006a, 600, English in the Russian original). During their meeting at Tel Aviv, B´orn and Ol´ga try to guess the commercial interests of the enterprise *Lëd* (Eng. Sorokin 2011b, 572; Russ. 2006a, 563) and delve into the question of fascism in the fanatic sect:

"Maybe the Celts, for example, or maybe the Yakuts had a rite like that. [...]"

"Doesn't look like them. More likely—Fascists."

"And how is this connected to Fascism?"

"It's connected somehow. I'm certain. The German Fascists used ancient mythology."

— [...] Может, у кельтов, например, или у якутов был такой обряд. [...]

— Не похоже. Скорее—фашисты.

— И как это связано с фашизмом?

— Как-то связано. Уверен. Немецкие фашисты использовали древнюю мифологию. (Eng. Sorokin 2011b, 572; Russ. 2006a, 564)

The sect chapters in *23,000* are again repetitive, similar to each other and to the two previous novels. Yet, the third novel of the trilogy is different because it includes the counter-perspective of "normal humans"—victims and apostates. B´orn and Ol´ga's violent suppression by the fanatics forms the most intriguing story in the entire trilogy because they hesitate, conjecture, try out various solutions, and therefore exhibit a level of psychological depth inaccessible to the chosen, who are always much too confident and look "like dolls" (Bogdanova 2005, 48). The fanatics—much like the heroes of Socialist Realism—are devastatingly uninteresting in themselves, if not viewed from a conceptualist meta-perspective.

The conflict between the two camps in *23,000* even creates suspense: we do not know whether the eschatological termination of the "meat" world will succeed. As the chosen 22,988 die and only the two humans, Ol´ga and B´orn, survive, the reader may remember the legendary mass suicides of sects such as the Peoples Temple in Jonestown in 1978. Suddenly, the "meat machines," disdained throughout 95% of the three novels, have the last word. This makes *23,000* the least hermetic, although not yet "polyphonic" (Sorokin, Kochetkova 2004), part of the trilogy. This novel brings together a sectarian and an anti-sectarian discourse, implying an internal negation of the brotherhood's metaphysical claims. In this vein, Mark Lipovetsky reads the trilogy as a "meta-parody on philosophies of social, national, and religious chosen-ness [*izbrannichestvo*]" (Lipovetskii 2008, 623), while Alexei Pavlenko diagnoses Sorokin's use of supplementation as a device of deconstruction:

> [...] adopting a classic deconstructive gesture, Sorokin switches the sup-
> plemental element of his narrative structure with what was supposed to be
> its central part: Olga and Bjorn are saved because they have accepted their
> fallibility. (Pavlenko 2009, 275)

The dialogical and loving relationship between B´orn and Ol´ga refutes the brotherhood's preceding claims about the inhumanity of humankind (Ågren 2014, 110, 114) and inserts the counter-perspective into the esoteric ideology. Birgit Menzel argues in a similar way for Sorokin's *Ice Trilogy*:

> As to the uses of occult topics and their function in these novels, I see
> Sorokin's novels as a parody of post-Soviet political occult ideologies and
> at the same time as a Gnostic tale in popular disguise. (Menzel 2007, 13)

Scholars have provided a wide range of implicit references of the trilogy to hermetic, mystical, and esoteric literature such as the Kabbalah (Kukulin 2002, 266; Aptekman 2006, 676), Hindu philosophy (Menzel 2007, 14), Gregory Palamas's Hesychasm (Grigoryeva 2013, 118), Nietzsche's crypto-racist vision of the superman (Novokhatskii 2009, 82), Vladimir Solov´ëv´s late apocalyptic visions (Romanova, Ivantsov 2005), Gleb Bokii's occultist NKVD faction (Giliarov 2008, 29–30), Ivan Il´in's philosophy of the heart (Grigoryeva 2013, 125–6), Daniil Andreev's *Rose of the World* [*Roza mira*] (Ågren 2014, 102–4), Lev Gumilëv's ethnogenetic speculations (Marsh 2007, 369), and the coincidence with Hanns Hörbiger's World Ice Theory [Welteislehre], which influenced the German National Socialists (Ågren 2014, 101). For Dmitrii Novokhatskii, all these inspirations amalgamate in Sorokin's "idiosyncratic [...] synthesis of mythic traditions" (2009, 95). This secondariness and syncretism shows that Sorokin, even in his later works

> [...] continues to utilize his strategy of subversion by affirmation, a rit-
> ualizing depiction of a dominating ideology, which is adopted through
> mimicry, e.g., Socialist Realism in his Sots-Art prose and now the popular
> metaphysical discourse of the occult. (Menzel 2007, 14)

The first Russian reviewers of *Ice* and *Bro's Path* were divided over the question as to what they should prioritize in the trilogy. Is it the thematic innovation and the metaphysical aspirations (Shevtsov 2004; Shevtsov 2005a)—the pro-sectarian interpretation? Or the deconstruction of the hubris and inhumaneness of the fanatic brotherhood (Nazarenko 2003; Romanova, Ivantsov 2005)—the anti-sectarian reading (cf. Bondarenko 2002, 248)?

These diametrically contradicting interpretations resemble old dichotomies of literal reading ("disgusting") and meta-literary interpretation of Sorokin's works. Interesting here is the author's participation in the debate. As early as March 2002, in an interview given right before the publication of *Ice* under the title "Goodbye, Conceptualism" ["Proshchai, kontseptualizm"], Sorokin himself seemed to unambiguously support the metaphysical and ethical interpretation: "I was in the process of saying goodbye to conceptualism. I wanted to move in the direction of a new content and not the form of the text" ["Я попрощался с концептуализмом. Мне хотелось двигаться в сторону нового содержания, а не формы текста"] (Sorokin, Neverov 2002; cf. also Sorokin, Reshetnikov 2004). Not buying this, Ol′ga Bogdanova argues that Sorokin's reply was a sly reaction to similar theses by other critics. Among those are Mikhail Epshtein and Dmitrii Kuz′min, who diagnosed a lovingly nostalgic, re-individualizing "post-conceptualism" [*postkontseptualizm*] in contemporary Russian poetry (Epshtein 1990, 360; Russ. Kuz′min 2001, 463; Eng. Kuz′min 2019, 13; Kuz′min 2002; cf. Bondarenko 2002, 248 note 9; Kukulin 2002, 262). Among other reasons, this means that Sorokin's interviews are not to be "blindly trusted" (Bogdanova 2005, 49). Other scholars agree that Sorokin is playing with "new sincerity" in a manner of "conceptual confessionality," a false and mannerist gesture (Bogdanova 2005, 46). If this is the case, Sorokin is updating the well-known "conceptualist mythopoetics" (Smirnov 2004a, 181) of Moscow Conceptualism and Medical Hermeneutics as part of a postmodern performance (Brouwer 2006, 63).

Directly after the publication of *Ice* Sorokin was still open to various interpretations and did not offer his own version. He even commented: "Out came a strange book, not entirely comprehensible to me" ["Получилась странная книга, мне не до конца понятная"] (Sorokin, Alekseev 2002). In interviews from 2003 and 2004, however, he began to state that the metaphysical strivings are central to *Ice*: "[…] *Ice* is a book about the eternal" ["(…) Лед—книга о вечном"] (Sorokin, Kochetkova 2004); "*Ice* is a metaphysical novel" ["Лед— метафизический роман"] (Sorokin, Bavil′skii 2004). He seemed to be empathetic toward the totalitarian sect:

I am not a member of the brotherhood described in the novel; much in the protagonists is alien to me. I certainly feel with them as people who try to correct their nature. Their path from suffering to luck makes me cry. I simply pity them.

Я — не член описанного в романе братства, многое в героях мне чуждо. Я им, безусловно, сочувствую как людям, пытающимся исправить свою природу. Их мучительный путь к счастью вызывает у меня слезы. Мне их просто жалко. (Sorokin, Reshetnikov 2004)

But in the same interview he declared a contrary partisanship: "[…] I am not a brother of the Light, I am rather a meat machine" ["(…) я не брат Света, я скорее мясная машина"] (Sorokin, Reshetnikov 2004).

Sorokin's interviews also mention a desire for emotional authenticity, which resembles the sectarians' pathos for love at heart: "I want to be truly, metaphysically honest" ["Я хочу (…) (б)ыть по настоящему, метафизически честным"]; Sorokin, Samoilenko 2003). The author even imitated his fictional characters in opting for a vegetarian lifestyle roughly during the years of working on his trilogy (cf. Shevtsov 2004). For Ellen Rutten, Sorokin in the mid-2000s increasingly gave the impression of subscribing to a broader anti-postmodernist trend of new sentimentalism (Rutten 2006, 57). Eleven years later Rutten remarked that in Sorokin's interviews from that time "he articulates views eerily resembling those of the members of his [fictional] sect" (Rutten 2017, 130) and that he "unmistakably reverted to the classical vocabulary of artistic sincerity" (Rutten 2017, 131). Even if such statements can be picked from his interviews, they are usually accompanied by an ambiguous self-correction:

I love sincere people who are intrinsically non-mechanic and don't live like machines. […] as a result I remained on the side of the human beings, on the side of the "machines made of meat."

Я люблю искренних людей, которые внутренне не механистичны и живут не как машины. […] в итоге [я] остался на стороне людей, на стороне «мясных машин». (Sorokin, Kucherskaia 2005)

Similar phrases leave Sorokin's interpreters puzzled: are the ethical claims of cordial authenticity in the novels and in the interviews "[f]ake or real? That question runs throughout the history of the novels' reception as a basso continuo" (Rutten 2017, 141).

The aporia of sincere identification or conceptualist distance culminated when Sorokin directly engaged in a dialogue with scholars about the adequate interpretation of his intentions. Previously, he always denied that literary production can be interpreted according to an assumed authorial intention. Now, Sorokin reacted to the opinions of Vasilii Shevtsov (Shevtsov 2004; Gorokhov, Shevtsov 2004; Shevtsov 2005a; 2005b) and Igor' P. Smirnov (Smirnov 2004a; 2004b), insisting on the validity of his own interpretation of his works.

In the Festschrift for Dagmar Burkhart, Igor' Smirnov proposed a deconstructive reading of the new apparently unsophisticated writing for a mass reader: "behind the banal ideological equipage of the novel's subject about the chosen [...] Sorokin deconstructs the idea of saving humankind through the selection of its best representatives" (Smirnov 2004a, 181). After the publication of *Bro's Path* in October 2004, Smirnov even more rigorously denied the author's purported new interest in content and not form, declaring the metaphysical content as boring [*skuchnovato*] (Smirnov 2004b) and non-informative: "It seems that for one who is familiar with *Ice* (2002), *Bro's Path* does not provide any significant information at all" (Smirnov 2004b). Smirnov goes as far as maintaining that this "transinformative" novel is intended as a parody of literariness per se: "*Put' Bro* destructively parodies literariness itself [...]" (Smirnov 2004b). According to this interpretation, the second novel of the trilogy is worth only on the conceptual level of negating the basic requirement of semiotics—information: "The text is informative by being the negation of informativity itself" (Smirnov 2004b).

Smirnov is Sorokin's old friend. Usually, his conceptual and meta-literary interpretation of Sorokin's work was met by the author with tacit content. But this time Sorokin appeared unhappy with diagnoses of transinformative boredom. Replying to both Shevtsov and Smirnov in his article "Mea culpa" in the mainstream newspaper *Nezavisimaia gazeta* from April 14, 2005, Sorokin recommends not measuring his later texts by his early works and protests against meta-aesthetic interpretation:

> [...] I did not sit down to write the biography of Sasha Snegirev, who found the cosmic *lëd*, touched it, and was turned into a non-human, in order to merely laugh at consumerist society "in a boring and uninformed way." [...] Yes, once, in the novel *A Novel*, I did collide two styles like two monsters, for them to devour each other and exude that energy of annihilation and purification of language which gave me such enormous

pleasure. However, such experiments excited me in the 1980s. *Ice* and *Bro's Path* are constructed completely differently.

> [...] не для того я садился писать биографию Саши Снегирева, нашедшего космический Лёд, прикоснувшегося к нему и перероди́вшегося в нечеловека, чтобы всего лишь «зануд́но и неинформативно» посмеяться над консумирующим обществом. [...] Да, когда-то в романе *Роман* я столкнул два стиля, как два чудовища, дабы они пожрали друг друга и выделилась та самая энергия аннигиляции и очищения языка, доставившая мне колоссальное удовольствие. Но подобные эксперименты волновали меня в середине 80-х. *Лёд* и *Путь Бро* построены совсем по-другому. (Sorokin 2005c, 5)

The debate about *Ice* became so crucial for Sorokin scholarship in the 2000s that Boris Sokolov decided to reprint it in the appendix to his monograph *My Book on Sorokin* [*Moia kniga o Sorokine*] (2005, 191–212). Outside the Russian context, scholars have been less inclined to subscribe to one or the other interpretation. For them, the question as to whether Smirnov is right in seeing in *Bro's Path* a "destructive parody of literature," or whether the author is right in his denial, need not be solved one way or the other (Uffelmann 2006, 121; Rutten 2017, 155). The very *possibility* of both face-value reception and meta-literary interpretation remains. While for Mattias Ågren the trilogy boasts both "utopian and anti-utopian features" (Ågren 2014, 98, cf. Ågren 2008, 78) and for Russian-American scholar Mark Lipovetsky the postmodern myth set forth in the trilogy inevitably deconstructs itself, irrespective of any assumable or declared authorial intention (Lipovetskii 2008, 624, 633, 641), for Ellen Rutten and myself they coexist in conflict and the reader must decide which of them to prioritize.

Similar suggestions of openness to different interpretations subsequently seemed to be confirmed by the author in the form of ironic self-quotes. In a 2003 interview he replied to Elena Gribkova's question: "'what do you need then?'—'I miss global brotherhood.'—'And in earnest?'—'Also wings and gills" ["«в чем тогда вы нуждаетесь?»—«Мне не хватает всемирного братства.»—«Ну серьезно?»—«Еще крыльев и жабр»"] (Sorokin, Gribkova 2003). More importantly, in the third part of the *Trilogy* he provided a fictional confirmation of ambiguity. In B ́orn's and Ol ́ga's conversation from *23,000* quoted above, the author picked up on the critique of fascism advanced by his readers and reviewers and rendered it a part of his fictional world.

The result is an ambiguous (and thus structurally non-fascist) fictional answer to Sorokin's extra-fictional critics.

The heated debate came to a public end when *23,000* was about to be published together with the two preceding parts in December 2005. On the eve of the release Sorokin corrected his outraged reaction to his critics by returning to his customary restraint from self-interpretation: "[…] I would not want to go into self-interpretation—that's both immodest and unproductive … The author should better keep silent" ["(…) я бы не хотел заниматься самоинтерпретацией—это и нескромно и непродуктивно … Лучше автору помолчать"] (Sorokin, Kochetkova 2005). Despite this return to his previous abstinence from public polemics and the ambivalent moves made by Sorokin after his outburst from April 2005, it took almost eight years for the ultimate reconciliation between the former friends Sorokin and Smirnov, who had a falling out over *Bro's Path*. The reunion took place at the *Vladimir Sorokin's Languages* conference in Aarhus, Denmark (Roesen, Uffelmann 2013), on April 1, 2012.

Irrespective of scholarly struggles surrounding the trilogy, the mass-culture elements guaranteed the three *Ice* novels high sales: for both Russian first editions of *Ice* and *Bro's Path*, the initial print run was 30,000, and for the 2005 edition of the *Trilogy*, 15,000. For works by Sorokin, the novels were met with an unprecedented wave of book reviews, both professional and spontaneous, on- and offline (see Novokhatskii 2009, 42–63). Quantitative and not aesthetic considerations must also have been paramount to the American publishers. All three novels of the long, "transinformative" trilogy have been translated into English, while great conceptual books, above all *Marina's Thirtieth Love*, still await their turn.

CHAPTER 10

Day of the Oprichnik and Political (Anti-)Utopias

After his five-year long immersion in the *Ice Trilogy*, between 2000 and 2005, Vladimir Sorokin suddenly changed the main thematic vector of his fictional plots. Sorokin's works from 2006 stand in stark contrast to the metaphysical novels from 2002 to 2005. At first glance, politics seems to have replaced metaphysics. Does this mean that the first signal text of this period, the short novel [*povest'*] *Day of the Oprichnik* [*Den' oprichnika*] (2006), is Sorokin's third attempt at reforging himself? Does this novelette mark a third shift after Sorokin's turning away from Socialist Realism as his referential style to pulp fiction in *Blue Lard* and to esoteric metaphysics in the *Ice Trilogy*—now into a "socially engaged" writer (cf. Davidzon 2011)?

Such a paradigm shift would be fostered by Sorokin's public political statements. As he would recall in retrospect (Eng. Sorokin, Doerry, Schepp 2014, 280; Ger. Sorokin, Schepp, Doerry 2007, 107), the citizen awoke in Sorokin around his fiftieth birthday in 2005. Many commentators, reviewers, and scholars less acquainted with Sorokin's early works simply identify his personal civic views with the political motifs in the plots of *Day of the Oprichnik* and the subsequent filler stories of *Sugar Kremlin* [*Sakharnyi Kreml'*] (2008). As early as one and a half years after the Russian original of *Day of the Oprichnik* was released in August and September of 2006 (in Ekaterinburg and Moscow, respectively) with an initial print run of 15,000 copies, publishers in eleven countries took advantage of the international attention to the imminent Russian presidential elections in March 2008 and simultaneously released translations of the Russian bestseller (Jamey Gambrell's American edition was delayed by three years; Sorokin 2011a). On the rising wave of Sorokin scholarship that emerged after 2002, many unprepared readers wanted to read his short novel as pure political satire. This chapter will revisit such aesthetically insensitive reading by drawing attention to the meta-linguistic (socio- and psycho-linguistic) and meta-dystopian features in the *Oprichnik* narrative.

For most readers, the first linguistic observation about this text concerns the archaism in the title: its second noun points back to the historical *oprichnina*, a terror institution introduced by Tsar Ivan IV Groznyi (the Terrible) in the middle of the sixteenth century. From 1565 to 1572, the *oprichnina* terrorized Muscovy's princely elite, publicly executing thousands of noblemen, especially in the Suzdal´ and Novgorod regions, and confiscating their manors. Linked to this is the next paratext in Sorokin's short novel, the pseudo-dedication, which is presented from the point of view of the hero, not the author, "To Grigory Lukyanovich Skuratov-Belsky, nicknamed Malyuta" ["Григорию Лукьяновичу Скуратову-Бельскому, по прозвищу Малюта"] (Eng. Sorokin 2011a, 3; Russ. 2006b, 5). The name in the dedication calls to mind one of the most odious leaders of the *oprichnina* (d. 1573), who became infamous for strangling Filip, former Metropolitan of Moscow, with his bare hands.

On the first page the reader sees the fictitious protagonist-oprichnik of the near future, Andrei Danilovich Komiaga, wake up from a dream. Starting the day slowly, Komiaga takes the reader through his morning prayer, breakfast, jacuzzi, and shaving habits (Eng. Sorokin 2011a, 4–8; Russ. 2006b, 7–11) and then via a futurist double-store road (Eng. Sorokin 2011a, 11; Russ. 2006b, 15) to his first item of business, the lynching of a nobleman called Ivan Ivanovich Kunitsyn. In single combat with fists and knives, the oprichnik Pogoda kills Kunitsyn's representative, which is welcomed by the oprichniks with ritualized sadism:

> Pogoda puts his knife away and spits on the fallen servant. He winks at all the others:
> "Pah! His mug is bloody!"
> These are *famous* words. We always say them. That's the *custom*.
>
> Убирает нож Погода, сплевывает на поверженного, подмигивает челяди:
> — Тю! А морда-то в крови!
> Это—слова известные. Их завсегда наши говорят. Сложилось так.
> (Eng. Sorokin 2011a, 18; Russ. 2006b, 23, emphases in the originals)

The subsequent destruction and looting of the oligarch's house, the hanging of the aristocrat Kunitsyn, and the rape of his wife (Eng. Sorokin 2011a, 22;

Russ. 2006b, 29) are all presented in italics as ritual obligations in formulas affirming violence (cf. Roesen 2013, 269). The oprichniks implement the ordered repression with sadistic pleasure, often in the form of sexual violence: "How sweet to leave one's own seed in the womb of the wife of an enemy of the state" ["Сладко оставлять семя свое в лоне жены врага государства"] (Eng. Sorokin 2011a, 24; Russ. 2006b, 31). Rape serves as a means of "self-satisfying self-affirmation" of the enforcers' violent superiority (Höllwerth 2010, 81).

In his inner monologue Komiaga presents all this violence as good, joyful, and necessary (cf. Hodel 2013, 78–81). Like the second part of *Ice* and *Bro's Path*, *Day of the Oprichnik* employs a perpetrator's first-person perspective. In the 2006 short novel, the executioner's worldview amounts to closed totalitarian consciousness, making *Day of the Oprichnik* the most hermetic of all the hermetic plots in Sorokin's oeuvre. Many readers of the *Ice Trilogy* struggled with ascribing an ethical axiology to the inner perspective of the sectarians—should they believe in the claims of "sincere heart love" or be appalled by the serial murder and inhumaneness of the totalitarian sect? With *Day of the Oprichnik* the vast majority of readers (with the exception of some representatives of repressive institutions) had no doubt whatsoever that they were expected to disapprove of the corrupt hangman Komiaga's cynicism.

What Sorokin demonstrates in *Day of the Oprichnik* is the physical and psychological means by which repressive social standards are imposed in a neo-totalitarian society. While in his early *The Norm* Sorokin showed people's obedient and silent compliance with unquestioned norms, excluding any genealogical dimension, *Day of the Oprichnik*, on the contrary, depicts the actual process of imposing social standards by means of violence. The story takes place in the winter 2027/2028 (Sorokin himself mentions both years in interviews [Sorokin, Shirokova 2006; Sorokin, Bavil'skii 2006], the narrator refers to recent events of November 2027; Eng. Sorokin 2011a, 137 note 1; Russ. 2006b, 160, note 1). In the newly established fictional Russian monarchy, the social, juridical, and aesthetic norms are still young, not yet negotiated and have to be re-imposed again and again (cf. Uffelmann 2009). The oprichniks are representatives of the monarchy's repressive regime, but their inner monologue discloses that the new norms have only recently been imposed and still possess some relativity. As Tine Roesen notes, the oprichnik "over-identifies with the greater wisdom (by definition) of his superiors in the hierarchy" (Roesen 2013, 275). This over-identification leads to manifold comical collisions and contaminations (Danilkin 2006), although the first-person narrator Komiaga hardly seems to display any sense of humor.

Day of the Oprichnik is the most coherent "perpetrator text" in Sorokin's oeuvre (cf. Holm 2006), second only to the final part of *A Novel*, which depicts Roman's serial slaughtering of an entire village. The story is written exclusively from the perspective of the defender of a repressive system. For his victims, the oprichnik is the undisputed aggressor. The narrative covers twenty-four hours in the life of a leading enforcer in a futurist totalitarian state, one, as the first noun in the title suggests, representative *day*. The representativeness is fostered by the allusion to another day-long short novel, which also has strong political implications: Aleksandr Solzhenitsyn's *One Day in the Life of Ivan Denisovich* [*Odin den´ Ivana Denisovicha*] (1962). Obviously, the main difference is that Sorokin's short novel presents the perspective of an imposer of violence, while Solzhenitsyn's protagonist, Ivan Shukhov, is a victim of the totalitarian regime (cf. Obermayr 2013, 262). The only intertextual similarity between the camp inmate Shukhov and the guardsman Andrei Danilovich Komiaga is their love of accurately built walls (Eng. Sorokin 2011a, 19; Russ. 2006b, 24).

In contrast to almost all of Sorokin's previous novels, with the exception of *23,000*, *Day of the Oprichnik* is a piece of psychological literature, uncovering the thoughts and opinions of the perpetrator. Especially interesting is the oprichnik's attempt to internalize the righteousness of the repressive standards that he implements by murder, rape, and arson while extorting danegeld, exacting bribes, and expropriating drugs. Despite his attempts to "hide behind an armor" of "self-imposed insensitivity," Komiaga's monologue provides "hypocritical verbalization" ["verdruckste bis verschmockte Verbalisierung"] (Tretner 2007, 13–4) of violence with such imperatives as "If you raise the axe, let it fall!" ["А коли замахнулся—руби!"] (Eng. Sorokin 2011a, 14; Russ. 2006b, 18, a self-quotation from Sorokin's *A Novel*). The first-person narrative invites a psycho-linguistic reading, focusing on the repression of compassion and pangs of conscience.

In Sorokin's *Day* the repressed other is represented as a totalitarian personality's remembrance of liberal critique from the past. The oprichnik still recalls examples of anti-totalitarian critique, for example the poem "Arioso" ["Ariost"] (1933) by Osip Mandel´shtam, a victim of Stalinist repressions:

> [...] I disagree in principle with the cynic Mandelstam—the authorities are in no way "repellent, like the hands of a beard-cutter." They're lovely and appealing, like the womb of a virgin needleworker embroidering gold-threaded fancywork.

[…] я принципиально не согласен с циником Мандельштамом—
власть вовсе не «отвратительна, как руки брадобрея». Власть прелестна
и притягательна, как лоно нерожавшей златошвейки. (Eng. Sorokin
2011a, 7; Russ. 2006b, 9–10)

Driven by a need for self-justification, Komiaga and his fellow oprichniks hurry immediately after rape and murder to the Uspenskii cathedral, where Komiaga prays with special devotion (Eng. Sorokin 2011a, 29–31; Russ. 2006b, 37–9). Another important factor stabilizing the enforcers' psyche is the corporate identity within the group of oprichniks with their physical cult of Russian masculinity ("[…] they're made of the same Russian dough" ["(…) из одного русского теста слеплены"] (Eng. Sorokin 2011a, 16; Russ. 2006b, 21). This is actualized by their ritual formula "Hail! Hail! Hail!" ["Гойда! Гойда! Гойда!"], which they always shout three times (e.g. Eng. Sorokin 2011a, 15; Russ. 2006b, 19), their collective drug experiences, and their homosexual orgy called "oprichnik *caterpillar*" ["*гусеница опричная*"] (Eng. Sorokin 2011a, 170; Russ. 2006b, 200, emphasis in the original). These collective performances weld the oprichniks together in an overtly satirically imagined "nation body," filling their minds with the revered majesty (Gerasimov 2008, 406).

The emblems of the historical *oprichnina*, a dog's head and a broom, are fixed onto the protagonist's "Mercedov" ["мерин"] (Eng. Sorokin 2011a, 11; Russ. 2006b, 15). The oprichniks display blind subordination toward the ruler of their hereditary monarchy (Eng. Sorokin 2011a, 137; Russ. 2006b, 161): "[…] I am ready without hesitation to give my life for this [the ruler's] look" ["(…) за взгляд этот я готов не колеблясь отдать жизнь свою"] (Eng. Sorokin 2011a, 44; Russ. 2006b, 53). From the cult of the Tsar they derive a nationalist discourse: "[…] His Majesty is alive and well, and, most important of all: Russia is alive and well, rich, huge, united […] our Mother Russia […]" ["(…) Государь наш жив-здоров, а главное—Россия жива, здорова, богата, огромна, едина, (…) матушка (…)"] (Eng. Sorokin 2011a, 87; Russ. 2006b, 101). The joint devotion to the monarch and the totalitarian state implies pseudo-sacralization of the authorities (Höllwerth 2010), at times reminiscent of National Socialism (see the triple incantation of "Hail"), which posed a challenge for translation into German (Tretner, in Sorokin, Gambrell, Roesen, Tretner, Uffelmann 2013, 352). However, these allusions are by no means as dense as in the *Trilogy* and were never advocated by the author in his interviews. Quite the opposite: when speaking about *Day of the Oprichnik* in 2006 and 2007, Sorokin left no doubt about his civic disagreement with repressive state violence as enforced by his fictitious anti-hero Komiaga.

The Russia of 2027/2028 has insulated itself from the surrounding world by walls (Eng. Sorokin 2011a, 30; Russ. 2006b, 8, 38; cf. Lorková 2011c, 66). The citizens of this closed society have been forced to burn their travel passports (Eng. Sorokin 2011a, 116; Russ. 2006b, 137). International trade, at least with the West, has come to a halt. Komiaga does not even bother to praise the present Tsar's father for the closed economy that he introduced:

> His Majesty's father, the late Nikolai Platonovich, had a good idea: liquidate all the foreign supermarkets and replace them with Russian kiosks. And put two types of each thing in every kiosk, so the people have a choice. A wise decision, profound. Because our God-bearing people should choose from two things, not from three or thirty-three.

> Хороша была идея отца Государева, упокойного Николая Платоновича, по ликвидации всех иноземных супермаркетов и замены их на русские ларьки. И чтобы в каждом ларьке—по две вещи, для выбора народного. Мудро это и глубоко. Ибо народ наш, богоносец, выбирать из двух должен, а не из трех и не из тридцати трех. (Eng. Sorokin 2011a, 88; Russ. 2006b, 102–3)

But the temptation of the competing Western discourse remains: although afraid of anti-Russian propaganda, Komiaga listens to Voice of America out of curiosity (Eng. Sorokin 2011a, 65; Russ. 2006b, 78) but conscientiously refutes the radio's messages. One of the instruments with which he discards the voice of the other in him is a state-imposed anti-Semitism (Eng. Sorokin 2011a, 139–40; Russ. 2006b, 162, 164), which Komiaga redirects, for example, against a "narrow-chested, dour-eyed Judas" ["узкогрудый очкарик-иуда"] (Eng. Sorokin 2011a, 65; Sorokin 2006b, 78) from the German international broadcasting service Deutsche Welle.

If this psychology draws upon the totalitarian regimes of the twentieth century, other prophecies about the year 2027/2028 are made by extrapolating from discourses of the post-totalitarian Russia. Post-Soviet everyday life is resurrected in colloquially discussed motifs such as gated communities (Eng. Sorokin 2011a, 63; Russ. 2006b, 76), competing semi-administrative, semi-criminal clans (Eng. Sorokin 2011a, 98; Russ. 2006b, 114), or a strong anti-democratic mood (Eng. Sorokin 2011a, 181; Russ. 2006b, 213). Especially prominent is the Chinese trajectory: while the China policy of 2027/2028 Russia is much more cooperative than Russia's take on the West, *Day of the Oprichnik* reflects the Russian discourse of fear demonizing a "Chinese peril" (Gerasimov 2008, 411–2; Lorková 2011c, 69–70). In the short novel, the creeping occupation of Siberia by Chinese immigrants (Eng. Sorokin 2011a, 152; Russ. 2006b, 178) is transformed into twenty-eight million Chinese settlers in 2027/2028. The strong dependency of the future Russian economy on trade with China is envisaged as a kind of Chinese yoke, a fictional replica of the Golden Horde's rule over Russian territories from the thirteenth to the fifteenth century: "How long must our great Russia bow and cringe before China?!" ["Доколе России нашей великой гнуться-прогибаться перед Китаем?!"] (Eng. Sorokin 2011a, 156; Russ. 2006b, 183).

In contrast to the El´tsin period and the Putin era—with the exception of Berezovskii, Gusinskii, and Khodorkovskii—Russian oligarchs in 2027/2028, although dubbed as "untouchable" ["неприкосновенные"] (Eng. Sorokin 2011a, 162; Russ. 2006b, 190, emphasis in the Russian original), no longer find themselves immune to state prosecution. The oprichnik's negative delineation of a demonized alternative societal order is focused on a period of sixteen years, numerically more or less coincident with the period from the beginning of perestroika in 1985 to the end of the El´tsin era in 1999. Under the new, thus post-2000, regime, the legacy of El´tsin's chaotic democracy is doomed to go up in flames: "[…] to burn the legacy of the White Troubles" ["(…) сжечь наследие Белой Смуты"] (Eng. Sorokin 2011a, 116; Russ. 2006b, 137).

After the Troubles comes a less clearly dated neo-authoritarian "period of Holy Russia's Revival" ["период Возрождения Святой Руси"] (Eng. Sorokin 2011a, 30; Russ. 2006b, 38). Praised by Komiaga, it restored the lost superpower status by the "collecting" all Russians within a renewed empire (Eng. Sorokin 2011a, 165; Russ. 2006b, 193). This new state is entirely de-communized; the Kremlin has been re-painted in white (Eng. Sorokin 2011a, 93; Russ. 2006b, 107); the Lenin mausoleum has been closed; and Lenin's corpse has been buried (Eng. Sorokin 2011a, 35; Russ. 2006b, 43).

As far as cultural politics is concerned, the regime of 2027/2028 appears almost more repressive than Stalinism: the production of literature is restricted, centrally organized, and electronically controlled; all (!) 128 Russian writers can instantly receive the monarch's commands via digital circuit (Eng. Sorokin 2011a, 49; Russ. 2006b, 58–9). The ruler personally upholds the "purity" of Russian culture, in theaters and elsewhere: "And His Majesty [*Gosudar´*], as we all know, champions chastity and cleanliness on stage" ["Государь наш, как известно, борется за целомудрие и чистоту на сцене"] (Eng. Sorokin 2011a, 57; Russ. 2006b, 67). This can be read as an allusion to the State [*Gosudarstvennaia*] Duma's 2005 invective against *The Children of Rosenthal* (chapter Eight). Reacting to a malicious pasquil, the oprichniks obey a conditioned reflex: they anticipate a command to find and punish the poet (Eng. Sorokin 2011a, 44; Russ. 2006b, 52). Komiaga also justifies the burning of nineteenth-century classic works by Dostoevskii, Chekhov, and Tolstoi in terms of defending purity: "We burn only harmful books [...]. Obscene and subversive books" ["(...) у нас (...) токмо вредные книги жгут. Похабные да крамольные"] (Eng. Sorokin 2011a, 114; Russ. 2006b, 135). In this context, Komiaga inverts the famous quotation from Mikhail Bulgakov's *The Master and Margarita* [*Master i Margarita*] (1928–40): "In general, books burn well. Manuscripts go like gunpowder" ["Вообще, книги хорошо горят. А уж рукописи—как порох"] (Eng. Sorokin 2011a, 115; Russ. 2006b, 137; Eng. Bulgakov 1997, 406; Russ. Bulgakov 1968, 162). Here the reader familiar with recent Russian cultural history will also remember the scandal fabricated by the Putin youth organization *Walking Together* in 2002, when they tore copies of Sorokin's *Blue Lard* (cf. Andreeva, Bibergan 2012, 281–2 note 1). Whereas Komiaga allows himself no doubts about the efficacy of repressing free thoughts, the *Walking Together* rally against Sorokin's books obviously failed (see chapter Eight).

While in 2002 and 2005 Sorokin associated the attempts at censoring post-Soviet art with Stalinist politics, the centralization of culture in fictitious 2027/2028 Russia goes even further than in the Soviet 1930s. Here, the press is confined to three newspapers (Eng. Sorokin 2011a, 99; Russ. 2006b, 115) and smoking is officially a taboo (Eng. Sorokin 2011a, 27; Russ. 2006b, 34). In sharp contrast to the Soviet regime, but reminiscent of the new cooperation between the Russian authorities and the Russian Orthodox Church in the 2000s, the state takes care of pro-religious censorship ("Don't blaspheme!" ["Не богохульствуй!"]; Eng. Sorokin 2011a, 20; Russ. 2006b, 27). The dystopian world of 2027/2028 results from the successful implementation of Sergei Uvarov's nineteenth-century anti-revolutionary trinity of autocracy, Orthodoxy, and nationality [*samoderzhavie, pravoslavie, narodnost'*] (cf. Roesen 2013, 266).

Other details from the practical cultural life in 2027/28 that hint at discourses from the 2000s are nostalgia in cinematography and neo-monumentalism in choir music (Eng. Sorokin 2011a, 12; Russ. 2006b, 16). The mention of an archaism for "barber," *tsiriul'nik* (Eng. Sorokin 2011a, 6;

Russ. 2006b, 9) establishes nationalist film director Nikita Mikhalkov with his *Sibirskii tsiriul´nik* [*The Barber of Siberia*] (1998) as an agent of state nostalgia. A panegyrical poem devoted to the monarch's childhood (Eng. Sorokin 2011a, 89; Russ. 2006b, 105) is reminiscent of analogous books about Putin (cf. Goscilo 2013).

A problematic detail is a passage in which Komiaga listens to Western radio stations, which displays a strong satirical tendency—always from Komiaga's illiberal perspective—toward Sorokin's former co-conceptualist circles (Eng. Sorokin 2011a, 121–3; Russ. 2006b, 142–4). Komiaga distorts their artistic orientation with false etymology as "CON-SEP-CHEW-A-LISM" ["конь-сент-уализьм"] (Eng. Sorokin 2011a, 123; Russ. 2006b, 144). Komiaga's aggressive ridicule comprises an anti-Semitic allusion to Borukh Gross / Boris Groys (cf. Borenstein 2015, 101) and a mockery of Anna Al´chuk's tragic fate as a traumatized victim in the wake of the exhibition *Caution, Religion!* [*Ostorozhno, religiia!*], which was vandalized by Orthodox hooligans on January 18, 2003 ("the old bag [is] babbling on" / "бабуля [...] лепечет"]; Eng. Sorokin 2011a, 122; Russ. 2006b, 143), followed by criminal persecution and anonymous threats. This context was bound to create mixed feelings in most readers, even if Sorokin in 2006 could not foresee Al´chuk's suicide in March 2008.

The artistically successful narrow internal perspective of the apologist of repression is here stretched to its limits, leaving some interpreters puzzled about the author's actual sympathies—with liberals or with the authorities (Lipovetskii, in Etkind, Lipovetskii 2008, 192)? Is Sorokin using the totalitarian henchman Komiaga to voice some of his own arguments? This seems plausible if we consider Sorokin's polemical take on literary scholar-cum-philosopher Igor´ Smirnov. In the novel, he is mentioned in passing as Igor´ Pavlovich Tikhii, whose formal logic amuses Komiaga: "Negation of a Negation of Negation of a Negation" ["отрицания отрицания отрицания отрицания"] (Eng. Sorokin 2011a, 122; Russ. 2006b, 143). Komiaga's reaction is suspiciously similar to Sorokin's own protest against figures of negation in Smirnov's analysis of his *Ice Trilogy* (chapter Nine). However, when the Russian postmodernism expert Viacheslav Kuritsyn is evoked as the "enemy of the state" Ivan Kunitsyn (Andreeva, Bibergan 2012, 265 note 1), this cannot be read as the personal verdict of the postmodernist author. Rather, Sorokin uses Komiaga as a pointedly unclever prism, estranging the views he voices. This is an argument against identifying the author with the fictional protagonist, so it undermines and mitigates the polemic thrust against Smirnov from 2005 (chapter Nine). The pre-modern illiberal mentality of Komiaga clashes with (post-)modern theory while it aptly stabilizes the ideology of a futurist "high-tech empire" (Höllwerth 2010).

Combining heterogeneous elements from various periods of Russian history—from the sixteenth century through the ideology of Tsarism, Stalinism, and finally to the 1990s and 2000s, *Day of the Oprichnik* follows a classical pattern of literary dystopias. The short novel combines elements of futurist technology with archaic social mechanisms (Chantsev 2007), creating a sort of "futuristic archaism" (Trotman 2017, 134). In *Day of the Oprichnik* we find highways on two levels with ten lanes (Eng. Sorokin 2011a, 11; Russ. 2006b, 15), remote voice control of car radios (Eng. Sorokin 2011a, 11; Russ. 2006b, 15), three-dimensional video telephones (Eng. Sorokin 2011a, 12–3; Russ. 2006b, 16–7), and high-tech detectors (Eng. Sorokin 2011a, 21; Russ. 2006b, 27). The futurist gadgets are mostly used to implement an Orwellian surveillance state embodied in a single ruler: "But His Majesty sees everything, hears everything. He knows who needs what" ["А Государь все видит, все слышит. И знает—кому и что надобно"] (Eng. Sorokin 2011a, 88; Russ. 2006b, 103). Anti-state behavior detected by these technologies is prosecuted with pre-modern brutality. The intelligentsia, for example, is punished in the most traditional manner: "[…] they flog the intelligentsia" ["(…) секут интеллигенцию"] (Eng. Sorokin 2011a, 123; Russ. 2006b, 145).

The archaic-futurist paradox is most apparent in the way the dystopian regime and its guardsmen address language—especially since the fictitious spokesmen for the archaic purity of the great mighty Russian language appear in a text by an author who was hitherto notorious for violating every possible linguistic taboo. Once most productive in materializing vulgar phraseological metaphors, Sorokin in *Day of the Oprichnik* confines his linguistic innovations to the invention of lexemes reminiscent of a folkloristic old Russian which de facto spring from rather modern or, as Marina Aptekman points out, "Old New Russian" (Aptekman 2013, 287) etymologies. Although the politically repressive moment is obvious, Kerstin Holm's association of "Orwellian Newspeak" (Holm 2006) is hardly exhaustive as a means of describing the paradoxes of repressive purism which Sorokin lays bare in *Day of the Oprichnik*, a case-study in political-linguistic psychology. The most language-sensitive text since Sorokin's debut novel *The Queue*, *Day of the Oprichnik* is a meta-linguistic or meta-socio-linguistic text. In contrast to *The Queue*, oral discourse is not the main meta-linguistic vector of the 2006 short novel. Oral stylization and idiosyncrasies, the famous Gogolian *skaz* (Aptekman 2013, 290), play a role in Komiaga's stream of self-persuasion, but more importantly, the text focuses on the imagined purist and repressive language of a dystopian future.

In the closed society and economy of the dystopian Russian monarchy of the year 2027/2028, the linguistic culture is also closed, with walls protecting the language against "the filthy words that foreigners forced on them [Russian people] in bygone days" ["слова, навязанные ему в старину иноземцами"] (Eng. Sorokin 2011a, 67; Russ. 2006b, 80). In such a context of political hyper-caution toward everything foreign, even the use of a rather old-fashioned French loan-word such as "marquess" ["маркиза"] (Eng. Sorokin 2011a, 48; Russ. 2006b, 57) is viewed as an act of hatred against Russia. We learn nothing about the institutional context that guards the new Russian language, only that the monarch himself promotes its purity. Still, in the dystopian world of 2027/28 there seems to be a whole Foucauldian dispositif which promotes (pseudo-)old Russian equivalents for banned foreign words. The ineffectual purist lexical substitution produces the majority of the comical effects in this short novel. For example, on the very first page of *Day of the Oprichnik* Komiaga is woken up by the ring-tone of his "mobilov" ["мобило"] (Eng. Sorokin 2011a, 3; Russ. 2006b, 5) instead of "mobile" [*mobil'nik*]; to break into Kunitsyn's house, the oprichniks use a laser beam called "ray saw" ["резак лучевой"] (Eng. Sorokin 2011a, 19; Russ. 2006b, 25); by the time they have finished their murky business, waiting outside the burning villa are "messengers" ["вестники"] (Russ. Sorokin 2006b, 36) rather than "journalists" ["журналисты"] or "reporters" (Jamey Gambrell's translator solution; Eng. Sorokin 2011a, 28).

The purist control is not all-encompassing. Internationalisms like "Jacuzzi" ["джакузи"] (Eng. Sorokin 2011a, 5; Russ. 2006b, 8) or "minister" ["министр"] (Eng. Sorokin 2011a, 152; Russ. 2006b, 179) have escaped the cleansing impetus of Komiaga's self-censored inner monologue. The combination "intelligent machine" ["умная машина"] (Eng. Sorokin 2011a, 180; Russ. 2006b, 211) instead of "computer" [*компьютер*] merely replaces a newer foreign word with an older one. And purism is directed only against foreign words associated with the West. Chinese loan words are not purged and even viewed as stylish (Eng. Sorokin 2011a, 97; Russ. 2006b, 112), like in the 2068 part of Sorokin's *Blue Lard*. Tatiana Filimonova notices that in *Day of the Oprichnik* a more advanced China serves as a foil to the imagined neo-traditionalist neo-Russia (Filimonova 2014, 233). Indeed, Sorokin deconstructs the purported isolationism of 2027/2028 Russia by omnipresent dominance of China's economy and culture. However, Sorokin's emphasis is not on technology but rather on the archaist-futurist language associated with it.

In Komiaga's stream of consciousness even indisputably native Russian words are refashioned in an archaic manner, such as the vocative "Mamo" (Eng. Sorokin 2011a, 146; Russ. 2006b, 171). On the level of lexicology, the adverb "only" [*tol'ko*] is replaced by "токмо" (Eng. Sorokin 2011a, 33; Russ. 2006b, 40). The intelligence service KGB or FSB is renamed after the early-modern Muscovite "Secret Department" ["Тайный Приказ"] (Eng. Sorokin 2011a, 36; Russ. 2006b, 43). The archaisms have phonological and morphological features particular to specific dialects, such as the initial "в" in "умом востра" ["sharp"] (Eng. Sorokin 2011a, 155; Russ. 2006b, 182). The syntactical postposition of the adjective as in "для выбора народного" ["so the people have a choice"] (Eng. Sorokin 2011a, 88; Russ. 2006b, 103) can be associated with solemn classicist poetry. A simple alternative flexion ending is used in "в прошлом годе" ["last year"; Eng. Sorokin 2011a, 153; Russ. 2006b, 179, emphasis added]. The ancient Russian genre of *bylina* (heroic tale) is evoked in such phrases as "Grant victory over our foes …" ["Победу на супротивныя …"] (Eng. Sorokin 2011a, 8; Russ. 2006b, 12). Sometimes whole sentences are archaized for merely decorative purposes: "Склоняется Батя над руцею моею, яко Саваоф" ["Batya leans over my arm, like the Lord of the Hosts"] (Eng. Sorokin 2011a, 74; Russ. 2006b, 88, emphasis added). On pages 180–1 / 212–3 we find a digest of the Church Slavonic Nicene credo integrated into the text.

The main thrust of purist aggression is directed against the use of vulgar language. The West is blamed for the use of vulgar words in Russian: "And the loathsome West plays up to our underground foul-mouths" ["А Запад гниющий подыгрывает нашим подпольным матерщинникам"] (Eng. Sorokin 2011a, 67; Russ. 2006b, 81). The oprichniks try to substitute vulgar words with similar-sounding ones. For example, they use "уд" instead of "муде" ["member"] (Eng. Sorokin 2011a, 168; Russ. 2006b, 198). As this example shows, the oprichnik's purism is confined to the level of signifiers. It does not extend to decency on the level of signified or referents. This practical distinction is made clear by Komiaga's meta-linguistic and meta-literary discussion with his fellow oprichnik Posokha following a gang rape and Komiaga's praise for this "privilege" (Eng. Sorokin 2011a, 24; Russ. 2006b, 31). Posokha, the second to rape the hanged oligarch's wife in the oprichnina hierarchy after Komiaga, joins the latter in front of the door to smoke a cigarette. When Posokha fetches his cigarettes, a small book with Aleksandr Afanas'ev's ominous *Intimate Tales* [*Zavetnye skazki*] (published anonymously in Geneva in 1867) falls out of his pocket:

> I pick it up. I open it—Afanasev's *Secret Tale*. I read the epigraph:
> "In those far-off olden times,
>
> When Sacred Russia had no knives,
>
> Carving meat was done with pricks."
> […] "What are you reading, you impudent lout?" I slap Posokha on the forehead with the book. "If Batya sees it—he'll throw you out of the oprichnina!"
> […] "You're walking along a knife edge, you dimwit! This obscene stuff is subversive. There were purges in the Printing Department on account of these sorts of books."

> Поднимаю. Открываю — «Заветные сказки». Читаю зачин вступительный:
> В те стародавние времена
>
> на Руси Святой ножей не было,
>
> посему мужики говядину хуями разрубали.
> […]
> — Что ж ты читаешь, охальник? — шлепаю Посоху книгой по лбу. — Батя увидит—из опричнины турнет тебя!
> […]
> — По ножу ходишь, дура! Это ж похабень крамольная. За такие книжки Печатный Приказ чистили. (Eng. Sorokin 2011a, 25; Russ. 2006b, 32)

Komiaga's argument for disciplining his fellow oprichnik is the monarch's will: "His Majesty can't stand cusswords" ["Государь ведь слов бранных не терпит"] (Eng. Sorokin 2011a, 26; Russ. 2006b, 33). Lev Danilkin emphasizes that this imposition of purity from above via the agents of repression has bizarre and comical effects:

> The state regulation of speech activities […] is the main fantastic assumption of the *Oprichnik* and simultaneously the primary source for comical effects in the novel: the oprichniks zealously keep an eye on the observance of taboos which are violated above all by the enemies of Russia. (Danilkin 2006)

Komiaga conscientiously defends the newly imposed linguistic standard and imposes it on Posokha without the slightest attention to the outrageous contradiction between the oprichniks' excessive deeds and their measured words. But the contradiction between deeds and words is not the only inconsistency in official purism. The norm is hardly followed by all citizens. Understandably, the officially repressed vulgarisms serve as means of protest for the political opposition (Eng. Sorokin 2011a, 67; Russ. 2006b, 80–1). More importantly, the other person beyond control is the highest authority of the purist standard, the monarch, who freely uses vulgar words (but no *mat*) himself (Eng. Sorokin 2011a, 48; Russ. 2006b, 57). Some enforcers of the regime such as hangmen and army sergeant majors are also officially exempt from the purist norm (Eng. Sorokin 2011a, 125; Russ. 2006b, 147). Their linguistic behavior seems to take place in a gray zone. For example, the uneducated oprichnik Pravda whose name ironically means "truth" in Russian, exclaims: "'Komiaga's inventive! He studied at the university, fuckin' A!' Pravda grins" ["Комяга изобретательный! В университетах учился, еб твою!—усмехается Правда"] (Eng. Sorokin 2011a, 86; Russ. 2006b, 100). For this utterance he is immediately punished by Batia, the commander of the oprichnina, but not severely. The same happens to Komiaga (Eng. Sorokin 2011a, 161; Russ. 2006b, 189). The protagonist disciplines others for using vulgar language, but in his own speech practice he is no less hypocritical ("[…] traffic-fucking-jam, God forgive me" / "[…] пробище-уебище, прости Господи"; Eng. Sorokin 2011a, 132; Russ. 2006b, 155).

Hypocrisy is thus omnipresent; it even affects the discourse of the narrator. The translation of the Chinese vulgar expression "Diao," combined with an enigmatic "da liang!" ["Дяо да лян!"], is given in a footnote, so logically, it cannot be "authored" by a character. Still, the translation includes a vulgarism, too: "No fucking way! (Chin.)" ["Хуй на рыло! (кит.)"] (Eng. Sorokin 2011a, 121; Russ. 2006b, 142). Escaping the official purism, Chinese words allow the speakers to creatively negotiate the repressive standard. Thus, the ongoing process of norm implementation has failed to abolish alternative expressions (see Chantsev 2007, 286). If viewed meta-linguistically, *Day of the Oprichnik* can be seen as a not entirely "fatalistic" (Trotman 2017, 152) dystopia.

Even though Komiaga's behavior contradicts his own claims of a successfully closed despotic society, he hardly ever steps outside the internalized official worldview. This key feature of *Day of the Oprichnik* distinguishes Sorokin's short novel from literary dystopias such as Evgenii Zamiatin's classical *We* [*My*] (1920; cf. Gillespie 2016, 522) or Tat'iana Tolstaia's *The Slynx*

[*Kys'*] (2000; cf. Andreeva, Bibergan 2012, 290–4), with which it has many motifs in common. Sorokin's protagonist is not in conflict with the society of injustice but the instrument of injustice: "The novel is dystopian only for the reader; for Komyaga, life is precisely as it should be" (Borenstein 2015, 101; cf. Machoninová 2007). Sorokin's *Day* showcases the internal perspective of a defender of repression, which it shares with utopian texts written from a nationalist, imperialist, or authoritarian point of view.

Scholars have provided many comparable utopian narratives: Marina Aptekman reads *Day of the Oprichnik* as a commentary on neo-nationalist tendencies encapsulated in Pëtr Krasnov's 1927 utopian émigré novel *Behind the Thistle* [*Za chertopolokhom*], republished in post-Soviet Russia in 2000, 2002, and 2006, and calls Sorokin's text a "[p]ostmodern parody of recently reprinted nationalist literary work" (2009, 243). Barbara Kozak proposes metropolitan Ivan Snychev's sanctification of Ivan the Terrible and his idealization of *oprichnina* as defenders of Christian values in *Autocracy of the Spirit* [*Samoderzhavie dukha*] (1996) (Kozak 2016, 216). Marina Abasheva (2012, 204), Aleksandr Arkhangel′skii (2014), and Ulrich Schmid (2015, 133) are convinced that Mikhail Iur′ev's neo-imperialist and antidemocratic utopian novel *Third Empire: Russia as It Should Be* [*Tret′ia imperiia: Rossiia, kak ona dolzhna byt′*] (2006) served as Sorokin's blueprint, although Sorokin's short novel appeared in print three months before Iur′ev's text. However, Iur′ev's non-fictional project *Fortress Russia: Farewell to Liberalism* [*Krepost′ Rossiia: proshchanie s liberalizmom*] (2005), co-authored with Mikhail Leont′ev, Mikhail Khazin, and Anatolii Utkin, is certainly a part of the discursive field that Sorokin's novel meta-discursively evokes. Most extensively, Alexander Höllwerth demonstrates that the sacralization of repressive institutions such as the *oprichnina* in Sorokin's short novel may be related to the largely fascist vision of a future Eurasianist Russia proposed by Russian geopolitical philosopher Aleksandr G. Dugin (cf. Höllwerth 2015, 207–8). Höllwerth's suggestion is supported by the fact that a minor character of Sorokin's *Day of the Oprichnik*, "hairy Duga" ["волосатый Дуга"] (Eng. Sorokin 2011a, 146; Russ. 2006b, 171), unmistakably points to Dugin, who recognized himself in the "Eur-gasia, Eur-gasia, Eur-gasia!" ["Ев-газия, Ев-газия, Ев-газия!"]-babbling figure (cf. Gołąbek 2012, 189). The Eurasianist trace, however, leads further than to just Dugin. In *Day of the Oprichnik*, Sorokin continues the first trans-Eurasian fantasies from *Blue Lard* with his vision of a highway from Europe to China via Russia as propagated by Robert D. Kaplan (later visualized also in Zel′dovich's film *The Target* [*Mishen′*], 2011).

The internal perspective, which Sorokin's *Day of the Oprichnik* shares with other nationalist-imperialist justifications of repression, does not identify the foreign and the text's own discourse as suggested by Brigitte Obermayr ("Sorokin's 'new' texts [...] are *told* by their referential discourses"; Obermayr 2013, 251, emphasis in the original). Sorokin's fiction deconstructs the retrograde resurrection of a pre-modern feudal order by means of split psychology and linguistic inconsistencies as demonstrated above. It can therefore apply also to other utopian inspirations what Alexander Höllwerth states for Dugin's imperialism and Aleksandr Prokhanov's nationalism: *Day of the Oprichnik* can be viewed as

> [...] the deconstruction of the reconstruction of the neo-Eurasian ideology of Dugin and Prokhanov—with this it is also an examination of discourses and remains indebted to the conceptualist "disposition to discourse" while testing the (possible) relationship of the discourse to a (possible) future reality. (Höllwerth 2010, 74)

That is why the *Day of the Oprichnik*'s variety of the dystopian genre should be defined as "ironic dystopia" (Trotman 2017, 142) or, more precisely, meta-dystopia.

Still, Sorokin's meta-fictional work with straightforward discourses of apology of repression, dystopian prophecy, and direct political commitment lured many interpreters into attempting to recognize contemporary political reality in *Day of the Oprichnik* and ignore the intermediating discursive reference. Some of the *Oprichnik*-related press reviews (above all Vitukhnovskaia 2007; cf. the overview Kasper 2007, 115–7) betray a politicized direct referential reading of meta-discursive literature as a recognizable political satire on the present Putin regime (Hodel 2013, 84), a "gallery of Putinism" (Polonsky 2012, 29), or "Putinist dystopia" (Borenstein 2015, 102). Either these reviewers ignore the theoretical prehistory of Moscow Conceptualism, or they hastily intend to get rid of artistic complexity, attributing to a literary work of art the unsophisticated qualities of straightforward referentiality (see the one-to-one identifications of allusions in Bibergan 2014, 91–103, Kasper 2007b, 107–12 notes 25–58 or Kotkin 2011: "So it is in Putin's Russia"). Attempts to ascribe a fully engaged political impetus to the novel, calling it a "political pamphlet" (Nemzer 2006) or "attack" (Wood 2011, 33; cf. also Gillespie 2016, 522) were met with diametrically opposite evaluations by Sorokin scholars (Aptekman 2009, 241). Although the *lectio difficilior*, the more complex mode of reading, is traditionally preferred in literary criticism, the political-referential reading should nevertheless be taken as a symptom. A renewed "Mozartian simplicity," as we saw it in *The Queue*, now inherent in the inner monologue of a perpetrator, makes this third masterpiece by Sorokin prone to overly reductive readings.

With *Day of the Oprichnik* Sorokin either invites or at least embraces the possibility of double readability (cf. Kukushkin 2002, 250). Alongside the discourse-referential option, a reality-referential reading seems to be warranted. This non-exclusion of the political option means yet another "popular turn" in Sorokin's oeuvre after *Blue Lard*'s embrace of mass culture and the *Ice Trilogy*'s exploration of esotericism. Against this backdrop, scholars were again tempted to risk far-reaching diagnoses of yet another "new Sorokin," inscribing something like political "reality" into the "mainstream literature of representation" (Kustanovich 2004, 315).

In his own evaluation of the conceptualist or non-conceptualist character of his work, Sorokin is contradictory again. These recurring contradictions concern the topicality and satirical character of his *Day of the Oprichnik*. "In the last ten years Moscow has become the stronghold of 'new oprichniks'" ["Москва за последние 10 лет стала цитаделью «новых опричников»"], Sorokin says in his 2006 interview with Marina Suranova (Sorokin, Suranova 2006). Especially when talking to Western interviewers, Sorokin stresses the political vector: "Of course it's a book about the present. Unfortunately, the only way one can describe it is by using the tools of satire." ["Natürlich ist das ein Buch über die Gegenwart. Sie ist leider nur noch mit den Mitteln der Satire zu beschreiben."] But in the same *Spiegel* interview he refuses to call *Day of the Oprichnik* a satire on President Putin (Eng. Sorokin, Doerry, Schepp 2014, 278; Ger. Sorokin, Schepp, Doerry 2007, 106–7). In various other conversations, for example with Aleksandr Voznesenskii, he indefatigably denies the interpretation of his short novel as a "satire" ["не сатира"]: "One should not mix literature and life" ["Не надо смешивать литературу и жизнь"] (Sorokin, Voznesenskii 2006).

This also concerns the question of continuity or non-continuity between his early writings, the *Ice Trilogy*, and *Day of the Oprichnik*. Sorokin keeps stressing a form of continuity between his works, based on conceptualist writing from within foreign discourses. In his answer to Dmitrii Bavil´skii, Sorokin describes the development from the *Trilogy* to *Day of the Oprichnik* as a "return" to his early works, "to the author's free voice" ["возвращение к авторскому свободному языку"] (Sorokin, Bavil´skii 2006). Bavil´skii's evaluation of the *Trilogy* as a "deadlock" of conventional narrative (Bavil´skii 2006) is no less telling than his appreciation of *Day of the Oprichnik* as another "language 'trip' so typical for Sorokin, a product of self-sufficient, autonomous language reality" (Bavil'skii 2006), which applies to many early texts as well.

Could we then redirect Igor´ Smirnov's 2004 question about a "new Sorokin," raised in the discussion about *Ice* and *Bro's Path* (Smirnov 2004a), to the 2006 short novel *Day of the Oprichnik*? Perhaps the answer is implied in the second alternative of Ol´ga Bogdanova's reply to Smirnov, "A new Sorokin or a new conceptualist project by Sorokin?" [*Novyi Sorokin ili novyi kontseptual´nyi proekt Sorokina?*] (Bogdanova 2005, 44; cf. Uffelmann 2009, 166). Igor´ Smirnov observes a certain moment of self-negation in Sorokin's development after *Blue Lard* (Smirnov 2004a, 177), but his diagnosis is misleading. Sorokin moves in a pattern of contrary negations, not contradictory ones: "By announcing his departure from conceptualism Sorokin just continued the game he had already started" (Bogdanova 2005, 49–50).

This is true for both the *Trilogy* and the 2006 meta-dystopia. Sorokin changes the objects of his meta-discourses, including, among others, esotericism and political dystopia. However, the main vector remains the same: he continues to emulate other discourses and simulate foreign voices. Leaving Socialist Realism behind, Sorokin in his trilogy conceptualized the neo-esoteric tendencies of the post-Soviet society. In *Day of the Oprichnik* he continues in the same manner, with a conceptualization of satirical *discourses about* neo-authoritarian tendencies in the Putin era and an imitation of the ubiquitous post-Soviet dystopian historical novels (Lanin 2007; Chantsev 2007)—something which even Sorokin's long-term enemy Andrei Nemzer has acknowledged (Nemzer 2006).

Reductive interpretations based on political referentiality and "mainstream literature of representation" are downplayed by yet another referential reading: the interpretation of Sorokin's fictional meta-dystopia as a self-fulfilling prophecy that finds its references in political and societal reality only after publication. In 2008 Kerstin Holm reread the book as the blueprint for subsequent political murders (Holm 2008); for Aleksandr Arkhangel´skii the *oprichnina* metaphor anticipated the ongoing closure of Russian society after the attack on Ukrainian Donbas (Arkhangel´skii 2014); and Theodore Trotman stated that "[t]he function of the *oprichniki* has been adopted in real life by [Aleksandr] Zaldostanov [known as The Surgeon] and the [pro-Putin nationalist bike rocker gang] Night Wolves [*Nochnye volki*] [...]" (Trotman 2017, 133).

The last—and most problematic—political adoption of Sorokin's *Oprichnik* is the performative appropriation of Komiaga's apology of tyranny.

Advocates of a repressive regime see Sorokin's book as a positive utopia and a manual for further repressive actions (cf. Sokolov 2006; Franz 2013, 58). In 2008, Mikhail Leont'ev, co-author of *Fortress Russia*, opened a fashionable restaurant *Oprichnik* in Moscow (Schmid 2015, 134). When the restaurant's entrance was sealed with a metallic door by political performance artists of the *Voina* group, the mutual inspirations and borrowing back and forth came full circle. While Sorokin materialized a closing society in his *Oprichnik*, people like Leont'ev reappropriated his metaphor for commercial marketing; and the *Voina* activists rematerialized Karl Popper's classical political metaphor of a closed society by sealing the restaurant's door. With the commercial reappropriations of the oprichnik metaphor, Sorokin's fictional text has become part of everyday culture.

The sequel to *Day of the Oprichnik*, *Sugar Kremlin* [*Sakharnyi Kreml'*], came out in 2008 and consists of fifteen short stories. It explores everyday life in another version of dystopian "New Middle Ages," this time dated October 23, 2028. Only one of the stories, "Petrushka," is available in English translation (Sorokin 2014a; corresponding to Sorokin 2008b, 151–71). *Sugar Kremlin* focuses on the miserable poverty and daily suffering of the population, again in a despotic system of the near future, in which oil and gas have petered out (see Sokolov 2015, 254). Diverse perspectives of subaltern victims are added to supplement the one-sided monologue of the hangman (Sorokin, Żebrowska 2011). The eponymous Kremlin is not only a decommunized fetish, again repainted in white, but also candy given to the people for free as a kind of sub-cutaneous propaganda (cf. Naumann 2017, 97) and sacralized by its obedient consumers (Engel 2017). The contrast between the sacralization of power and the ways in which people live poorly under repressive standards "debunk Komiaga's image of [strong and prospering repressive] Russia as fiction" (Franz 2013, 60). Once more, the discourse of totalitarianism appears as a meta-dystopia and not as the historical "reality" of Putinism from before 2006.

CHAPTER 11

The Blizzard and Self-References of a Meta-Classic

Sorokin has never hesitated to use banal stereotypes about Russia (see Berg 2000, 108; Lunde 2009, 9; Artwińska 2017, 413–21), be it vodka and lightly salted cucumbers in *The Postnuptial Journey*, the provinces in *Into the Depth of Russia* [*V glub′ Rossii*] (Kulik, Sorokin 1994), or Siberian ice in the *Trilogy* (Sorokin, Dolin 2018). When Sorokin's short novel [*povest′*] *The Blizzard* [*Metel′*] was published in a 303-page pocket-size (13 × 17 cm) volume at the end of March 2010 and translated into English by Jamey Gambrell in 2015, its snowstorm metaphor tricked some readers into the assumption that Sorokin again employed Russian winter discourses (cf. Sorokin, Kochetkova 2010). There is at least one significant difference, however: the *lëd* of the Tunguska meteorite was attested to have magic revitalizing powers, but the blizzard of the eponymous short novel is unambiguously fatal for all the protagonists.

The topic of life-endangering snowstorms has obviously been highly visible in Russian literature before (see Wołodźko-Butkiewicz 2011, 3–8). Relevant texts have been listed in research about Sorokin's *The Blizzard*. Natal′ia Andreeva and Ekaterina Bibergan (2012, 395) support their enumeration of references in Sorokin's *The Blizzard* with a remark about the especially high degree of intertextuality: "The wealth of intertext ('foreign text') in Sorokin's [...] short novel is notable" (Andreeva, Bibergan 2012, 395). The Russian scholars mention mostly Russian pretexts—novels such as Aleksei Tolstoi's "The Garin Death Ray" ["Giperboloid inzhenera Garina"] (1927), short stories like Anton Chekhov's "Ionych" (1898), Aleksandr Pushkin's "The Snowstorm" ["Metel′"] (1831), Lev Tolstoi's short story of the same name (1856), various "Blizzard" poems by Iurii Lermontov, Sergei Esenin, and many other scattered references to classical Realist texts such as Ivan Turgenev's *Fathers and Sons* [*Ottsy i deti*] (1862) or Dostoevskii's *Humiliated and Insulted*

[*Unizhennye i oskorblënnye*] (1861), and so on and so forth. Although they do not claim their list to be exhaustive, it is astonishing that Andreeva and Bibergan omit one non-eponymous, but highly topical Russian short story: Lev Tolstoi's "Master and Man" ["Khoziain i rabotnik"] (1895). This chapter attempts to demonstrate that Sorokin's *The Blizzard*, while mesmerizing in its sheer number of various intertextual references, reads first and foremost as a rewriting of "Master and Man," and as a condensed version of Sorokin's take on Tolstoi's ethical claims.

As seen earlier in this Companion, the Realist novelist, moralist, and religious philosopher Lev Nikolaevich Tolstoi (1828–1910) has been a steady "competitor" for Sorokin. *Blue Lard* features a winter story written by the imperfect clone Tolstoi-4 (Sorokin 1999, 93–109) and contains a sex scene in which an underage peasant girl, Akulia, urinates on an old prince ["князь"] who resembles Count Tolstoi (Sorokin 1999, 106; cf. Leiderman, Lipovetskii 2001, 59). Referring to *Blue Lard*, Sorokin told Elena Kutlovskaia that "[i]n literature you can achieve a lot with the help of clones—become Tolstoi, for example. (Laughs)" ["При помощи клонов можно многое сделать в литературе—стать Толстым, например. (Смеется)"] (Sorokin, Kutlovskaia 2006). While this somewhat humorous statement focuses on fictional plots, Ekaterina Dëgot' has appropriated Sorokin's intertextual take on Tolstoi in order to acknowledge the increasingly comparable status of the two writers in the history of Russian literature: "As far as objective literary history is concerned, Sorokin has long since become Tolstoi" (Degot', Sal'nikov 2000). Before turning to the competition between the two writers for the status of classics in literary history, let us examine Sorokin's rewriting of Tolstoi's "Master and Man" in his *Blizzard* through a parallel reading.

By 1895, when he published "Master and Man," Tolstoi, had outlived his fellow Realist novelists Dostoevskii and Turgenev by more than ten years, and long since reached worldwide stardom as a Russian writer. In Tolstoi's winter story "Master and Man," the merchant Vasilii Andreich Brekhunov takes off on a sled together with his servant Nikita to visit a neighboring estate owner. The merchant hurries in order to leapfrog other prospective buyers of a forest the estate owner is selling. On their way, Brekhunov and Nikita are hit by a snowstorm. They stray over fields in the night and by chance arrive in a village where they receive shelter in a peasant's hut. Before dawn they depart from the village, again veering off of the road.

Not appropriately dressed for such a winter trip, Nikita is in jeopardy of freezing to death because Brekhunov hides from the wind and the cold alone in the cart (Eng. Tolstoi 1899, 35–6; Russ. 1954, 30). Guided by a selfish wish to survive, Brekhunov attempts riding off alone on their carriage horse, leaving the freezing Nikita behind in the cart. The horse flounders in the snow, Brekhunov descends, and the horse disappears in the snowfall. The merchant walks in circles in the dense snowfall, losing his way, and ends up returning to the cart where the horse has returned as well, while Nikita is already covered by snow.

Master and man are bound together without escape. In view of the deadly danger, the differences between the estates become blurred. In the end, the merchant saves the servant's life, lying down on Nikita and warming him with his own body. Nikita only loses several frostbitten toes on his feet, whereas Brekhunov expires. He dies touched by his own deed:

> He divines that this is death, and is not at all disturbed even by that. And he remembers that Nikita is lying under him, and that he has got warm, and is alive; and it seems to him that he is Nikita, and Nikita is he; that his life is not in himself, but in Nikita. [...]
> "Nikita is alive, and therefore I also am alive!" he says to himself, triumphantly.

> Он понимает, что это смерть, и нисколько не огорчается и этим. И он вспоминает, что Никита лежит под ним и что он угрелся и жив, и ему кажется, что он—Никита, а Никита—он, и что жизнь его не в нем самом, а в Никите. [...] «Жив Никита, значит жив и я»,—с торжеством говорит он себе. (Eng. Tolstoi 1899, 54; Russ. 1954, 43–4)

In this short story Tolstoi translates his own ideologeme of love for the ordinary people into the narcissistic sacrifice of a representative of the elite for the benefit of the common man (cf. Uffelmann 2012b).

In Sorokin's 2010 short novel *The Blizzard*, the plot-building snowstorm has been elevated to the title. Tolstoi's "master" is renamed "doctor" ["дохтур"] Platon Il´ich Garin, and the servant, Perkhusha (in the American translation this name is replaced with the onomatopoetic equivalent "Crouper"). Like Tolstoi's Nikita, he is servile and indulgent, naïve and tongue-tied. The original Russian first name of the servant in Sorokin, Perkhusha, is reminiscent of the last name of Tolstoi's merchant, Brekhunov—a first hint at a change of roles. The technical means have evolved as well: instead of Tolstoi's horse cart, Sorokin's Garin and Crouper travel on a self-driving "sledmobile" ["самокат"], which has 50 dwarf "horses" ["лошадки"] under its hood (Eng. Sorokin 2015a, 5; Russ. 2010a, 9).

In Sorokin's short novel the doctor is not driven by mercantile interest, but by a philanthropic mission: he is on his way to vaccinate villagers who are endangered by an epidemic imported from abroad. In the grandiloquent tonality of Tolstoi's moral-religious treatises, Sorokin's doctor proclaims the following about himself:

> For example, I, Dr. Garin, *Homo sapiens*, created in His image and likeness, am traveling along this field at night to a village, to sick people, in order to help them, to safeguard them from an epidemic.

> Например, я, доктор Гарин, Homo Sapiens, созданный по образу и подобию Божиему, сейчас еду по этому ночному полю в деревню, к больным людям, чтобы помочь им, чтобы уберечь их от эпидемии. (Eng. Sorokin 2015a, 128; Russ. 2010a, 215)

Garin's trip to a nearby village turns into an endless journey straying through the snowfall. It also entails slipping into the darkness of Garin's own consciousness because Sorokin's doctor is addicted to drugs, just like doctor Mikhail Poliakov in Mikhail Bulgakov's "Morphine" ["Morfii"] (1927), and suffers from hallucinations (Eng. Sorokin 2015a, 98–105; Russ. 2010a, 164–77; cf. on the different trips Glanc 2018, 213–4). It is entirely possible that the fantastic obstacles that Garin and Crouper face in *The Blizzard* are also related to the doctor's hallucinations and could therefore be open for a psycho-mimetic reading (cf. Andreeva, Bibergan 2012, 363, 369).

In the life-threatening cold, Sorokin's intellectual and the simple-minded servant begin to act in solidarity. Especially after the doctor's nightmarish drug trip, this sounds rhetorically hypertrophic: "All people are brothers, Kozma" ["Все люди братья, Козьма (…)"] (Eng. Sorokin 2015a, 109; Russ. 2010a, 183). But with the increasing desperation the extraordinary mutual solidarity starts to erode: the doctor several times commits violence against the common man (Eng. Sorokin 2015a, 131, 133, 144; Russ. 2010a, 220, 222, 240) and—just as Tolstoi's merchant—eventually leaves him behind in an open field (Eng. Sorokin 2015a, 160; Russ. 2010a, 267). It turns out that only the ordinary man displays convincing brotherly love (above all to his little horses), whereas the selfless mission of the doctor is questioned more and more, slowly becoming overshadowed by his selfish plans. Sorokin's story ends with Crouper's death; here the doctor survives, rescued by enigmatic Chinese traders and suffering from frostbite. In contrast to Tolstoi's Nikita, he loses not only several toes, but also his legs. That is why for Pavel Basinskii Sorokin's "*The Blizzard* is essentially Tolstoi's short novel 'Master and Man,' rewritten with a diametrically opposite ending" (Basinskii 2010), and Alicja Wołodźko-Butkiewicz places it squarely in the "genre of remakes of classics" (Wołodźko-Butkiewicz 2011, 8).

The intertextual relationship between the two texts is defined both by analogy and contrast (cf. Kuchina 2012, 248). Not only the plots are constructed along parallel lines (Danilenko 2012, 114), analogy is often additionally materialized in the narrative. For example, Tolstoi's doctor thinks: "'They say drunken men soon freeze to death'" ["Говорят, пьяные-то замерзают"] (Eng. Tolstoi 1899, 42; Russ. 1954, 35). Sorokin's protagonists both subscribe to this idea, and his plot additionally transposes the saying into the fictitious figure of a giant frozen with a three-liter bottle of vodka whom they meet later, materializing the colloquial hyperbole about Russian excessive drinking (Eng. Sorokin 2015a, 146; Russ. 2010a, 244).

The intersection of analogy and contrast obviously does not exhaust the construction of meaning through intertextual connections in Sorokin, the master of meta-literature. In 2000 Ekaterina Dëgot' approached this dimension of his texts from the side of scholarly readers:

> [Sorokin's] oeuvre is highly theoretical; he operates with premade models, both theoretical and literary; he has become accustomed to an enormous amount of quotes, among others from literary theory. That is why his texts are a paradise for the researcher, for the theoretician of literature, and a paradise for intertextuality. Philosophically oriented presenters have had the opportunity to compare him with Kant, literarily oriented lecturers could find literary examples. [...] with his all-embracing knowledge of literature, Igor' Smirnov [...] was simply unable to stop pointing to parallels either with Konstantin Leont'ev, with Vladimir Solov'ëv or with Andrei Belyi [...] (Degot', Sal'nikov 2000)

Does this mean that future academic editions of Sorokin's texts should be armed with abundant commentaries on all the diverse intertextual links? Sorokin himself, at the conference *Vladimir Sorokin's Languages* in Aarhus in 2012, did not generally disagree but expressed doubt about a detailed intertextual concordance to *The Blizzard*:

> Some of my things are rather hermetic, while others are really quite trans-
> parent, like, for example *The Snowstorm*. And in the latter case I would
> like the annotation [to a translation to another language] to be minimal.
> (Sorokin, Gambrell, Roesen, Tretner, Uffelmann 2013, 359)

Just as this authorial comment is critical of detective studies in intertextuality, *The Blizzard* does not give the impression of a complicated read that is doomed to fail without scrupulously deciphering all its allusions. Despite the potentially tragic plot, the narrative sounds light, serene, and playful. This compelled Andreeva and Bibergan to combine intertextuality and ludism:

> Similarly to the way in which Sorokin in his juvenile years *"played"*
> conceptual games together with conceptualist artists and "compiled"
> his artistic works from "parts" of other ("foreign") paintings, [...] thus
> Vladimir Sorokin, the follower of conceptual practices in literature, also
> piles up, unites, and makes use of "foreign" images, motifs, types, and
> characters. He creates almost a patchwork garment out of his prosaic
> text, assembled from micro-particles of Pushkin, Lermontov, Gogol',
> Ostrovskii, Goncharov, Turgenev, Dostoevskii, Chekhov, Bunin, Blok,
> and Platonov [...], in order to "illustrate" the programmatic formula of
> postmodern art—that there isn't anything new under the sun, that it is
> impossible to create *new* works of art [...] (Andreeva, Bibergan 2012,
> 395–6, emphasis added)

The idea that Sorokin merely "illustrates" the pre-formulated postmodern axiom claiming the impossibility of innovation clearly underestimates his efforts. Sorokin is an experimenting artist who has attempted to (partially) reinvent himself several times. Moreover, the notion that Sorokin generally works with *foreign* texts, styles, and discourses is correct, but it does not take into account the fact that Sorokin himself has been accumulating a growing artistic legacy over three decades, which allows him to allude to his own earlier texts as "semi-foreign." Whereas references to plainly foreign texts can be epitomized as "xenotextual" (Uffelmann 2010, 900–2), references which remain inside the same author's oeuvre can be called "autotextual" (cf. Uffelmann 2012a). For *The Blizzard*, the clash of the xenotextual and the autotextual vectors resembles a smooth linear plot disturbed by heterogeneous minor elements. Both types of references are varieties of intertextuality, and both comprise a certain playfulness. However, these two ludic modes are quite different.

The literary critics often state that autotextual qualities in Sorokin's *The Blizzard* are a drawback. On the other hand, comments such as Vladimir Bondarenko's verdict of Sorokin's "self-repetition" [*samopovtor*] (Bondarenko 2010) are descriptively quite fruitful. A third hint comes from scholarly opinions that ascribe a certain cyclicity to Sorokin's works. These scholars call *The Blizzard* "the third part of a cycle about the Russia of the future" (Andreeva, Bibergan 2012, 394) after *Day of the Oprichnik* and *Sugar Kremlin* (similarly Basinskii 2010; Bondarenko 2010; Pogorelaia 2012, 67). Brigitte Obermayr sticks to this suggestion despite Sorokin's insistence on the autonomy of *The Blizzard* in his reply to Marina Aptekman (in Sorokin, Gambrell, Roesen, Tretner, Uffelmann 2013, 361; Obermayr 2013, 246 note 5). Later Boris Sokolov (2015, 251) and Barbara Kozak (2016, 215) even postulated a tetralogy, encompassing also *Telluria* [*Telluriia*] (2013), a novel which, however, has more in common with the subsequent *Manaraga*. Although the cyclicity claims seem inconclusive, the majority of the self-quotes in *The Blizzard* indeed stem from the two preceding works, *Day of the Oprichnik* and *Sugar Kremlin*. They include toponyms such as Khropovo, the nickname Komiaga (cf. Andreeva, Bibergan 2012, 361), and a drug called "sphere" ["шар"] (Eng. Sorokin 2015a, 94; Russ. 2010a, 157).

Interestingly, the text of *The Blizzard* includes several derivatives of the word *soroka*, from which the author's name comes (for example "сорочья голова" [literally: "magpie's head," translated as "birdbrain" by Jamey Gambrell]; Eng. Sorokin 2015a, 48; Russ. 2010a, 79). As with Aptekman's suggestion of a winter trilogy, Vladimir Sorokin laughingly denied Tine Roesen's query whether these derivatives of *soroka* count as self-allusions (Sorokin, Gambrell, Roesen, Tretner, Uffelmann 2013, 357). Some of the attending discussants understood this as a playful affirmative answer.

In this context we can assume that the autotextual references are accompanied by an enhanced degree of playfulness. There might be some general reasons why autotextuality uses less serious means than xenotextuality. One might argue that the violation of standards of modesty can be compensated only by additional distance such as created by irony or playfulness. While xenotextual references are imbued with playful seriousness, autotextuality engages in a frank and open game, upon which the self-alluding author refuses to comment, insisting on the transparency of the short novel's textual world.

In the transparent and fundamentally tragic plot of *The Blizzard*, which to a high degree relies on the xenotextual rewriting of Tolstoi's *Master and Man*, the autotextual hints are clearly minor and dispersed throughout the text. Yet, these elements powerfully disturb the smooth, serious, and "sorrow-ful" surface (Basinskii 2010) of the snowstorm story. The autotextual connec-tors appear as material obstacles in the protagonists' way. The sled sometimes literally hits objects from different worlds that do not fit into the Tolstoian Realist rural setting of the late nineteenth century, such as the designer-drug "pyramids" of the Kazakh "vitaminders" (according to Sorokin's explanation in a personal conversation at the Aarhus conference, this word is a random result of internet research: the plural form of "vitamins" in Turkic languages is almost nonsensically appropriated for drug dealers; Eng. Sorokin 2015a, 112; Russ. 2010a, 188–9). The narrator inserts futurist devices like holographic radios in the pre-modern homes that Garin and Crouper visit (Eng. Sorokin 2015a, 60–3; Russ. 2010a, 100–4). He endows his protagonists with devia-tions which in the case of Garin advance to hallucinations, thus destroying the coherence of the closed xenotextual world of Tolstoi's rewritten story. At the end of the fragment that describes Garin's horrific trip on designer drugs, Sorokin uses his trademark dismembering the text by repetitions and word deformations, which reminds the reader of *The Norm, Marina's Thirtieth Love*, and *A Novel*:

> I'll die! [...] Isle-a-die! [...] Isled! Isled! Isled! Isled! Isled! Isled! Isled! Isled! Isled! Isled! Isled! Isled! Iled! Iled! Iled! Iled! Iled! Iled! I-l! I-l! I-l! I-l-! [sic] I-l! I-l! I-l! I-l! I-l! I-l! I-l! I-l! I-l! I-l!

> Я умру! [...] Ямру! [...] Ямр! Ямр! Ямр! Ямр! Ямр! Ямр! Ямр! Ямр! Ямр! Ямр! Ямр! Ямр! Ямр! Ямр! Ямр! Ямр! Ямр! Ям! Ям! Ям! Ям! Ям! Ям! Ям! Ям! Ям! Ям! Ям! Ям! Ям! Ям! (Eng. Sorokin 2015a, 105; Russ. 2010a, 176–7)

Most prominently, the coherence of the pseudo-Realist textual world is vio-lated by fantastic diminutions and enlargements—little horses and huge stallions, small men and the frozen colossus with his enormous snowmen (Eng. Sorokin 2015a, 179; Russ. 2010a, 37, 300). With the enlargements and the sexualization of the giant snowman, Sorokin establishes an auto-textual link to the giant baby Vil, a member of the earthfuckers' sect from *Blue Lard*. The frozen drunken giant, in whose nostril the sledmobile's blade eventually breaks (Eng. Sorokin 2015a, 144; Russ. 2010a, 241), provides a meta-textual rationale for Crouper's cold death. The autotextual deviation kills the xenotextual character.

Not by chance, directly before the accident with the giant in the snowstorm, the changes in sizes are explicitly connected with games: "They [the horses] looked just like toys" ["(лошадки) казались совсем игрушечными"] (Eng. Sorokin 2015a, 140; Russ. 2010a, 234). Given this meta-comment on plot-building playfulness, we may more precisely define what kind of game Sorokin is playing in *The Blizzard*. From the four varieties of games in Roger Caillois's seminal study *Games and People* [*Les Jeux et les Hommes*] (1958), mimicry (or simulation) comes closest to literary theory's notion of fictionality and thus to the xenotextual layer of *The Blizzard*, which creates a continuously developing plot. Another variety of games, "ilinx" (or vertigo), can "momentarily destroy the stability of perception and inflict a kind of voluptuous panic upon an otherwise lucid mind" (Eng. Caillois 1961, 23; French: Caillois 1977, 67). This kind of disturbance of the clear mind is exactly the cognitive effect of the autotextual references in Sorokin's short novel—among others, moments of inebriety—in relation to the xenotextual mimicking of Tolstoi's pretext. While the former is a forthright game, the latter performs a more ambiguous playful seriousness.

The most evident disturbance of the pseudo-Realist narrative comes from the confrontation between the epi-Tolstoian protagonists Garin and Crouper and what seem to be fantastic mutants of some kind. Straying in the snowstorm, the doctor finds himself under the colossal phallus of a snowman tall as a house (again, resembling the *Blue Lard*'s giant baby Vil with his huge genitals). As the doctor assumes, the snowman was built by the colossus whose nostril the sled had hit before:

> [...] at the top of the strange, vast, snowy shape, he made out the likeness of a human face. He realized that he was standing in front of a snowman of monstrous proportions, with a huge, erect phallus of snow.
> "Lord Almighty ...," the doctor mumbled, and crossed himself.
> The snowman was the height of a two-story building. Its phallus hung threateningly over Dr. Garin's head.

> [...] различив вверху непонятной снежной громадины подобие человеческого лица, [Гарин] понял, что перед ним чудовищных размеров снеговик с огромным, торчащим снежным фаллосом.
> — Господи ...—пробормотал доктор и перекрестился.
> Снеговик, ростом с двухэтажный дом, воздымался над ним. Фаллос его угрожающе нависал над головой доктора Гарина [...] (Eng. Sorokin 2015a, 162; Russ. 2010a, 271)

With regard to these sexualized horrors, Sorokin's short novel could inform investigations into masculinity in a most playful manner. The relevance to masculinity studies is confirmed early in the novel when Crouper, after only a brief acquaintance, outs himself as impotent (or so the doctor understands his utterance): "My fly got stuck" ["— Ускоп пристиг"] (Eng. Sorokin 2015a, 17; Russ. 2010a, 30). Because of his impotency, Crouper was abandoned by his wife. On the contrary, the doctor does not question his own prowess. At he first glance, he seems to deviate from a pattern of rather impotent intellectuals in Russian literature as diagnosed by Ellen Rutten (2010). Garin ungratefully uses the refuge provided to him by the miller and has sex with the miller's corpulent wife. But during their coitus, narrated in great physiological detail, Garin experiences an *ejaculatio praecox* (Eng. Sorokin 2015a, 61; Russ. 2010a, 101). And he degrades the miller, the rival of his lust, making him into a "little man" ["маленький человек"] (Eng. Sorokin 2015a, 41; Russ. 2010a, 68–9). It seems as if these divergent attestations of size depend on the doctor's perception. Of course, they are also made "real" in a feat of psycho-mimesis, following Sorokin's custom of materializing metaphors. Both the sexualization and fantastic changes in size are blatantly alien to Tolstoi's origin text where the merchant Brekhunov neither demeans the peasant nor desires the old peasant woman (Eng. Tolstoi 1899, 20; Russ. 1954, 20).

Sorokin's doctor, in stark deviation from the epi-Tolstoian snowstorm plot, repeatedly finds enlarged, but petrified figures of masculinity—the dead giant and his enormous snowman. Facing them, Garin feels helplessly tiny and—if read in a Freudian manner—threatened by castration:

> The doctor reached up and swung his hat, trying to reach the white phallus above. But he couldn't. The huge pole hung over him, aimed ominously at the darkness. [...] It stood with a sort of unflinching readiness to pierce the surrounding world with its phallus. The doctor met the gaze of the cobblestone eyes. The snowman looked at Garin. The hair on the doctor's head tingled. Terror seized him.

> Доктор поднял руку с малахаем, махнул им, пытаясь достать белеющий вверху фаллос. Но не достал. Орясина нависала над доктором, угрожающе целясь в темноту. [...] Тот стоял с неколебимой готовностью проткнуть своим фаллосом окружающий мир. Доктор встретился взглядом с глазами-булыжниками. Снеговик посмотрел на Гарина. Волосы зашевелились на голове у доктора. Ужас охватил его. (Eng. Sorokin 2015a, 163; Russ. 2010a, 272)

When reading this fragment as transposed from the psychology of the doctor, the imagined superiority of others tells something about Garin's own sexuality. This would mean that Sorokin—as before, for example in *A Month in Dachau*—deliberately plays with phallogocentrism and psychoanalytical templates. In *The Blizzard*, he addresses castration anxiety, in a rather transparent manner.

While the masculinity games of *The Blizzard* have not attracted much attention in Sorokin scholarship so far (Uffelmann 2012b), scholars have discussed another metaphorical reading of size mutations: political allegory. This, however, is far from being devoid of sexual implications. Sorokin's snowstorm, much alike Edgar Allan Poe's "A Descent into the Maelström" (1841), can be seen as symbolizing the metaphorical "whirlpool of history." Into this whirlpool the doctor is immersed in his contact with the provincial life of ordinary people, whom he, as he himself announces, wants to help. Do the gargantuan people and the snow-covered province which swallows the doctor jeopardize the superiority of the urban intellectual? Or is the seeming prowess and the revolutionary strength of the people, the "giant fool" from Heinrich Heine's *Germany: A Winter's Tale* [*Deutschland. Ein Wintermärchen*] (Caput I; Ger. Heine 1985, 91, trans. Joseph Massaad), no more than a harmless game, akin to the snowman? Sorokin's fantastic diminutions and enlargements seem to confirm the second political interpretation. The little miller can be regarded as the materialized metaphor of the conventional "small man" of Russian literature (see Genis 2011, 446), and his opposite, the giant—the materialized metaphor of the "great power of the people"—is dead. The miller's wife, who becomes sexually available to the doctor, would, as Mark Lipovetsky argues (Lipovetskii 2012, 809, 841) personify Russia. The common man (the miller) and the intellectual (the doctor) compete for this personification, bringing to mind Aleksandr Etkind's theory of Russia's internal colonization and its representation in gender triangles in nineteenth-century literature (Etkind 2003). This basic constellation of Russian cultural history from the times of Peter the Great to Stalinism becomes explicit when Crouper refuses to scourge his horses:

> He [Garin] suddenly realized that it was Crouper, this aimless man, lacking all ambition, with his disorganized slowness and centuries-old peasant reliance on "somehow or another" and "with luck, everything will turn out," who was preventing them from moving directly toward the doctor's goal.

> Он [доктор] вдруг понял, что Перхуша, этот бесцельный, никуда
> не стремящийся человечек, с его разболтанной неторопливостью, с
> извечной мужицкой надеждой на авось и есть то, что препятствует
> пути доктора, его прямому движению к цели. (Eng. Sorokin 2015a,
> 132; Russ. 2010a, 221)

Even this complaint is a remake of an inner monologue of Tolstoi's merchant Brekhunov: "Vasili Andreyitch shook his head disapprovingly at what Nikita was doing, as he usually found fault with the peasants' ignorance and stupidity [...]" ["Василий Андреич неодобрительно покачал головой на то, что делал Никита, как он вообще не одобрял необразованность и глупость мужицкую (...)"] (Eng. Tolstoi 1899, 36; Russ. Tolstoi 1954, 30).

In order to determine the possible political implications of Garin's hubris, one must know at which time the story is set. The village world of the Russian province seems to have fallen out of history. There, distances are still measured in "versts" ["версты"] (Eng. Sorokin 2015a, 22; Russ. 2010a, 34), people travel with stagecoaches (Eng. Sorokin 2015a, 3–4; Russ. 2010a, 6), and pay with "silver roubles" ["целковые"] (Eng. Sorokin 2015a, 10, without the precision "silver"; Russ. 2010a, 17). However, Sorokin adds scattered hints at post-Soviet social and technological conditions: quartz watches (Eng. Sorokin 2015a, 51; Russ. 2010a, 85), car fetishism (Eng. Sorokin 2015a, 13; Russ. 2010a, 22), the danger of being mugged on country roads (Eng. Sorokin 2015a, 19; Russ. 2010a, 33), a barter economy (Eng. Sorokin 2015a, 22; Russ. 2010a, 37), and improvised craftsmanship in the province (Eng. Sorokin 2015a, 27–8; Russ. 2010a, 46), as well as international migration and living-apart-together relationships (Eng. Sorokin 2015a, 31; Russ. 2010a, 52). Developments that are extrapolated from the situation in the 2000s, such as the impending exhaustion of mineral fuel resources, are anticipated in the fictional world of *The Blizzard*: the characters mention "precious gasoline" ["драгоценный бензин"] (Eng. Sorokin 2015a, 87; Russ. 2010a, 145). In this respect Sorokin's *Blizzard* is reminiscent of Tat'iana Tolstaia's post-apocalyptic dystopia *The Slynx* [*Kys'*] (2000).

Finally, the textual world of Sorokin's short novel contains elements of science fiction. For instance, the miller owns a "holografic radio" (Eng. Sorokin 2015a, 55–6; Russ. 2010a, 92). One of the Kazakh designer-drug dealers wears a "gold collar inset with sparkling superconductors" ["ошейник со светящимися вставками из сверхпроводников"] (Eng. Sorokin 2015a, 88; Russ. 2010a, 148), and the Kazakhs make a felt hut for Crouper and the "sledmobile" grow within minutes (Eng. Sorokin 2015a, 96; Russ. 2010a, 160–1). The plague which doctor Garin has been charged with tackling in the neighboring village of Dolgoe is said to have been imported from Bolivia. A half-frozen Garin is saved by traders with whom the doctor speaks a smattering of Chinese, an almost compulsory element in Sorokin's works since 1999 (Eng. Sorokin 2015a, 178–9; Russ. 2010a, 297–9).

This combination of old familiar and modern elements places the narrative in a sort of *"retrofuture"* [retrobudushchee] (Lipovetskii 2012, 839, emphasis in the original). From various hints in the text, the reader can conclude that the action takes place in the 2030s (see Wołodźko-Butkiewicz 2011, 10). *Day of the Oprichnik* and *Sugar Kremlin* are set around the same time. In these works, a pre-modern repressive order is kept up by a terror troupe named after the *oprichnina* of Ivan the Terrible from the mid-sixteenth century, for which purpose the oprichniks apply "mobilos" and three-dimensional "message bulbs." The ritually incanted title of His Majesty, "Gossudar" ["государь" or "sovereign"] (Eng. Sorokin 2015a, 40; Russ. 2010a, 66), reemerges in *The Blizzard*. These obvious autotextual hints have given rise to assumptions that the three texts are connected in a "second trilogy."

Even before these three retrofuturist books, *Blue Lard* already vacillated between a Stalinist past and a fantastic future. In its pulp-fiction-style narrative, a clone of Lev Tolstoi ("Tolstoi-4") is stimulated to produce a fantastic substance, the enigmatic blue lard, which Stalin eventually injects into his brain, attaining power over the universe. The vaccine "VISHNEVSKY OINTMENT + PROTOGEN 17W" ["Мазь Вишневского + PROTOGEN 17W"] (Eng. Sorokin 2015a, 27; Russ. 2010a, 45) from *The Blizzard* autotextually alludes to the "cloning science" of the 1999 novel. Later, *Manaraga* (2017) will continue with the futurist setting and the autotextual references (cf. Lipovetskii 2018, 643). Thus, *The Blizzard* joins a continuous chronotope of Sorokin's self-referential writing since 2006 and not a confined tri- or tetralogy.

How, ultimately, does the socio-political constellation of internal colonization and the triangular competition of the common man and the representative of the elite for a woman personifying Russia relate to Tolstoi, who provided the pretext for Sorokin's xenotextual rewriting? Sorokin repeatedly alludes to Tolstoi's moral and religious discourse in Garin's annoying announcements about humanism. The doctor's philanthropic mission and his sexual selfishness, which disillusions the reader, inspire a serious ethical reading of the xenotextual relation between Sorokin and Tolstoi in this otherwise playful autotextual short novel. If one reads the feigned seriousness of the Tolstoi xenotext in this vein, the sanctimony of Sorokin's doctor deconstructs Tolstoi's hypocritical love for the ordinary people.

On the autotextual level, Sorokin reinforces this effect of disillusionment through the doctor's phallic desire. It is well known that Tolstoi had a lot of sexual relationships with prostitutes, female servants, and serfs, for example with Aksin´ia Bazykina. Tolstoi's repeated sexual harassment of lower-class women was, however, camouflaged by his pedagogical mission (opening a school for village children). He even preached chastity in the afterword to "The Kreutzer Sonata" ["Kreitserova sonata"] (1889, six years before "Master and Man").

Sorokin's fictional doctor, much like Tolstoi, gets lost in magniloquent ruminations about supporting ordinary people. As the plot develops, his notions are debunked as empty declarations. Eventually in Sorokin's short novel, in contrast to Tolstoi's story, it is not the representative of the elite, Garin, who dies, touched by his own altruism, but Crouper, the common man. The doctor, who raves in phallogocentric hallucinations and phantasmas of masculinity ("fiery phallus" / "огненный фаллос"; Eng. Sorokin 2015a, 112; Russ. 2010a, 188), gets away with only being "castrated"—when his legs are frozen off.

This more serious interpretation of the playful short novel can be viewed as an ethical verdict. Moving in this direction without aesthetic meta-distance, Natal´ia Andreeva and Ekaterina Bibergan provide a detailed reading of Sorokin's *The Blizzard* as a moralizing text—in favor of the ingenious Crouper and to the detriment of hypocritical Garin (Andreeva, Bibergan 2012, 380). Such a moralizing reading has been rather hard to convincingly apply to other texts by Sorokin (as attempted in Dreyer 2011 or Lorková 2011b). But for *The Blizzard*, it seems relatively plausible. This must be valued as a symptom, disclosing the feigned seriousness of Sorokin's xenotextual rewriting and reevaluation of Tolstoi.

This meta-classical author of the early twenty-first century plays with the hypocrisy and the masculinity of the classical nineteenth-century author. Sorokin underpins Tolstoian allusions with materialized sexual metaphors from his own previous work. Since *Day of the Oprichnik*, Sorokin has been playing with allusions in such a way that Paul de Man's aporia of *either* referential *or* self-referential qualities of literary texts (de Man 1979) stopped working for him—in contrast to Sorokin's unambiguously meta-literary and thus discourse-referential early oeuvre. In *The Blizzard*, the references to Tolstoi's xenotext and the self-references to Sorokin's autotexts become as indistinguishable as playful seriousness and serious game.

CHAPTER 12

Manaraga and Reactionary Anti-Globalism

The utterly Russian scenery of *The Blizzard* changes dramatically with the following novels, *Telluria* [*Telluriia*] (2013) and *Manaraga* (2017). These texts open the fictional space of Sorokin's "heterotopic writing" (Chernetsky 2007, 87) further to include European and global settings (cf. Sorokin, Dolin 2017), prompting critics to comment on Sorokin's new "costume of European writer" (Sorokin, Shchulinskii 2018). While *Telluria* draws a panorama of post-apocalyptic sceneries both in Western Europe and in post-Russian micro-states, *Manaraga*'s protagonist, an international star in "grilling literature," jets around the entire Northern hemisphere. The modernity implied in the plots of these two books is, however, constantly challenged by various phobic, anti-modernist, anti-globalist, separatist, nationalist, and isolationist tendencies. In evoking this colorful array of retrograde discourses in the two mid-2010s novels, the customary meta-discursive outreach of Sorokin's writing takes on a kaleidoscopic dimension. This prompted Lev Danilkin to conceptualize the writer's head as a "tower of Babel" (Danilkin 2013) of existing discourses and Maiia Kucherskaia to speak of *Telluria* as "an inventory of existing cultural codes, predominantly those connected with national and cultural identity" (Kucherskaia 2013).

Published in mid-October of 2013, *Telluria* opens the international outreach with episodes set in Germany (V, XIII, XXXV), Spain (XV), France (XXI, XXXVIII), Switzerland (XLV), and tirades spanning Europe (VIII) and the world at large (XXVII). Western Europe is not separated from the approximately three fourths of *Telluria*'s fifty episodes that take place in a post-Russian setting. The space that occupies the former Russian-Federation and European-Union territories is rather presented as a splintered Eurasian totality—a ravaged plurality of post-war micro-states. The novel's title, which comes in the singular, supports the pan-Eurasian trace. *Telluria* is an unmistakable allusion to "tellurocracy" [*tellurokratiia*], a key concept of Dugin's neo-Eurasianist philosophy. It is part of what Dugin sells as the main "law" of geopolitical science, naturalizing and essentializing his own ideological dualism, from which he then draws his pre-conceived political and military conclusions:

> The main law of geopolitics is the assertion of the fundamental dualism which is reflected in the geographic nature of the planet and the historical typology of civilizations. This dualism manifests itself in the opposition of "tellurocracy" (land power) and "thalassocracy" (sea power). (Dugin 2000, 15)

As a counterweight to the accursed "thalassocracy" of the United States, "tellurocracy" is identified by Dugin with "the intracontinental spaces of North-East Eurasia (more or less coincident with the territories of Tsarist Russia and the USSR)" (Dugin 2000, 16)—the space that Sorokin's fictitious spatial entity Telluria also occupies.

Dugin, Eurasianism, and in a broader sense geopolitics have occasionally surfaced in Sorokin's works of the 2000s, in *Ice* (Menzel 2007, 13) and in *Day of the Oprichnik* (Höllwerth 2010; Abasheva 2012, 204; Gołąbek 2012, 189). While conservative (if not reactionary, revisionist, and proto-fascist) geopoliticians subscribe to President Putin's famous 2007 formulation that the dissolution of the Soviet Union was "the biggest geopolitical catastrophe of the twentieth century," Vladimir Sorokin, who likes to quote Putin's lament (Sorokin, Pavelka 2010), explicitly welcomes the dissolution of the Soviet empire (Sorokin, Ahrest-Korotkova 2010). Thus, the emergence of smaller states on the territory previously united by Russian and Soviet empires can be regarded as the historical basis for the fragmented chronotope and episodic narration of Sorokin's "novel."

Telluria consists of fifty largely autonomous episodes, tacked together—thus laying bare the literary mechanism that connects the heterogeneous novellas into a pseudo-novel—with telluric nails. These, if beaten directly into the brain, cause hallucinations, among other things. After the hallucinogenic pills of Sorokin's *Dostoevsky Trip* (1997) and the literary secretion called "blue lard" in *Goluboe salo*, this can be seen as yet another narcotic metaphor for fiction (see Glanc 2018, 214–5). Through the enigmatic substance tellurium, several of the episodes refer to a small Altaian state, the "Republic of Telluria" ["Республика Теллурия"], founded in 2028 (Sorokin 2013, 214). Apart from this spatially unifying factor, *Telluria*'s fifty episodes also share retrofuturist features (cf. Uffelmann 2017). They are all set in the near future, characterized by asynchronous contradictions. For instance, Moscow has a "nanomarket" ["нанорын(ок)"] (Sorokin 2013, 394) but the Great Muscovite Wall could never be finished because the pre-modern building material of bricks was stolen (Sorokin 2013, 261). The general impression is of a society thrown back into a "new Middle Ages" (Kasper 2014; Sokolov 2015, 258–9; Lipovetsky 2019, 305–7) but elderly people recall a Russian leader tenderly remembered as flying with cranes ("журавлик"; Sorokin 2013, 370): Vladimir Putin.

Several of *Telluria*'s episodes also deal with continental Western Europe, but they all are connected, in one way or another, to Russian (and / as Eurasian) discourses. With this in mind, Polina Ryzhova detects "manifold geopolitical insinuations" (Ryzhova 2013) in the novel. When it comes to the fictitious Eurasia of the near future, Sorokin has parcelled out the former Soviet territory into autonomous republics. This prompted Nastia Iarovaia to draw an "Alternative map of Russia and Western Europe according to Sorokin's *Telluria*" (Morozova, Iarovaia 2013), retranslating Sorokin's meta-geopolitical literature into a form of geopolitical map fetishism.

Retrofuturist elements can be found in almost all episodes of the novel, but chapter XXIII delves into Eurasianist concepts more intensely than the rest. It shows a small Altaian state, also called Telluria, from which the nails that tack the episodes together originate. In this chapter, the President of Telluria, the sportive and sun-tanned (Sorokin 2013, 214–5) Jean-François Trocart, flies on a microplane just as Russian President Vladimir Putin did on September 5, 2012, when he accompanied Siberian white (also called Eurasian) cranes allegedly for the sake of helping the local ecology (also referred to in Sorokin 2013, 231), while political self-marketing was obviously his main motivation. The Democratic Republic of Telluria has economically reoriented itself away from Western Europe and toward East Asia (Sorokin 2013, 224) as the Putin administration had already declared its intentions of doing before the Western sanctions of 2014 and the official establishment of the Eurasian Economic Union on January 1, 2015.

The cult of personality around Trocart is also reminiscent of Putin during his third presidential term. Sorokin renders it in a retrofuturistic way:

> In the valley [beneath the flying President] small peasant houses appeared—and smoke columns, rising smoke columns, smoke columns the meaning of which was just one: we await you, we love you [President].

В долине показались крестьянские домики и—дымы, дымы, восходящие кверху, дымы, смысл которых был один: мы ждем тебя, мы любим тебя. (Sorokin 2013, 228)

The compulsory panegyrics with pre-modern fireplace smoke and the alleged enthusiasm of every citizen meeting the President (Sorokin 2013, 230) evoke the historical prototype of the Putin hype—Stalin's cult of personality.

Characteristic of Sorokin's entire book, the post-apocalyptic coexistence of small states within the territory of the former Soviet Union affects Telluria as well. It is entrenched in a customs conflict with the Baikal Republic (Sorokin 2013, 221). The latter is especially a throwback to the political past: in Baikalia the communists have returned to power (Sorokin 2013, 222), opening the border for trade with the eponymous telluric nails. The "good old times" of borderless communication in the Soviet Union are back—now for the purpose of trading drugs.

The Soviet economy was never able to produce advanced technology. In the presidential Republic of Telluria, however, technological innovations are available to the elite. The President himself displays a boyish delight in advanced gadgets resembling James Bond's equipment: "The President was equipped in a black overalls, with a sophisticated backpack, a helmet with a respiratory apparatus on his head and ski boots on his feet" ["Президент был экипирован в черный комбинезон с замысловатым рюкзаком, на голове—шлем с кислородным респиратором, на ногах—горнолыжные ботинки"] (Sorokin 2013, 224). Like Bond actor Daniel Craig, he engages in "extreme downhill skiing" ["экстремальн(ый) спуск(...)"] (Sorokin 2013, 226). His flight downhill is also modeled according to retrofuturist visions. The President opens his mechanic wings, alluding to pre-Lindbergh enthusiasts' imaginings: "There was a snap in the backpack, narrow black wings emerged and opened, and two hard-firing propellers clapped and began to work" ["В рюкзаке щелкнуло, и плавно выдвинулись-раскрылись узкие черные крылья, хлопнули, заработав, два твердотопливных двигателя"] (Sorokin 2013, 227).

After his ski-flight ride, the President visits the Altaian peasants, who reside in small huts with bonfires. Their way of life points back to pre-modern agriculture, mostly unchanged since the Middle Ages. Another medievalesque detail are stone coins from Novgorod in the President's private collection (Sorokin 2013, 219–20). Directly after his high-tech flight he enjoys the pre-modern preparation of food by an Altaian traditional three-generation family (Sorokin 2013, 230).

The president's palace is situated on a slope of Kadyn-Bazhy (known in Russian as Belukha), the highest mountain in the Altai range (Sorokin 2013, 214). It is decorated with various objects of Altaian material culture: a "camel plaid," a "headboard from solid Altaian cedar," a "pillow filled with mountain herbs from the Altai" ["Верблюжье одеяло," "спинк(а) кровати из массива алтайского кедра," "подушк(а), набит(ая) горными травами Алтая"] (Sorokin 2013, 214). With these details, Sorokin once more (after *The Target*; cf. Kukulin 2013, 317–8) refers to the increasingly popular theory of the Altai as the "cradle" of Eurasian culture, advocated by Murad Adzhi, Andrei Ivanov, Pavel Zarifullin, and other Eurasianists. Sorokin also draws on Nikolai Trubetzkoy's Eurasianist theory of the Turanian language family. In episode XXIII, Sorokin uses the Kazakh expression "Mal aman! Mal aman!" ["Мал аман! Мал аман!"] (Sorokin 2013, 231), in episode XXII he indulges in non-Slavic Siberian toponyms (Sorokin 2013, 208), the pages 274–6 of episode XXVIII have so many various Kazakh and Altaian words that they are comprehensible only with the help of the glossary at the end of the book (Sorokin 2013, 445–6). Sorokin's exoticization of Asian facial features—of "an Altaian girl" ["алтайка"] with "a narrow-eyed face with high cheekbones" ["узкоглазое, широкоскулое лицо девушки"] (Sorokin 2013, 216)—evokes Lev Gumilёv's theory of fusion of Eastern Slavs with Turkic and other Asian peoples into a "superethnos." In episode XIV, the discussion as to why Batu Khan did not conquer all of Europe in the thirteenth century (Sorokin 2013, 116) alludes to the glorification of the Mongolian heritage by various Eurasianist authors, including Nikolai Trubetzkoy, and to Sergei Bodrov Sr.'s 2007 film *Mongol*. Episode XXIII contains explicit quotes from Petr Savitskii's Eurasianist "Exodus to the East" ["Исход к востоку"]: the phrase "way to the East" ["Путь на восток"] is repeated in this chapter three times (Sorokin 2013, 223, 233, 234). As shown before, the title of Sorokin's book hints at Aleksandr Dugin—a fact astonishingly not noticed by any of the reviewers (cf. Uffelmann 2017, 377). "Telluria" refers not just to the Latin word for "earth," *tellus*, as Alla Latynina argues (2014, 188), but also to Dugin's positive Eurasianist vision of *tellurokratiia*.

Sorokin's picture of a politically fragmented post-Soviet space alludes to Dugin's repeated call for a re-centralization of internal Russian geopolitics (2000, 302–3). The name of the fictitious Tellurian president Jean-François Trocart comes suspiciously close to that of the Belgian right-wing thinker Jean-François Thiriart, who coined the maximalist formula of a "Europe from Brest to Vladivostok." Dugin discusses and extensively quotes Thiriart in the appendix "Texts by the Classics of Geopolitics" ["Teksty klassikov geopolitiki"] of his

Principles of Geopolitics (Dugin 2000, 140–2, 515–25). Even when the figure of Trocart triggers associations with contemporary political leaders, they are evoked in a Duginian perspective: references to Putin resemble Dugin's occasional quasi-monarchic reverence for the Russian President (Dugin 2014, 83–5). This allows to claim that *Telluria*'s splintered narrative refers not simply to disparate phobias (Kurchatova 2013; Naval´nyi, Prokhorova, Krylov 2013). Sorokin's representation of neoconservative, authoritarian, anti-globalist, and retrofuturistic discourse prominently includes Eurasianist features, mostly structured and inspired by Dugin's writings.

The plot of *Manaraga*, Sorokin's second novel from the mid-2010s, released by AST Corpus on March 10, 2017, is also set in a world where big geopolitical units have been destroyed. *Manaraga* delves into the reactionary Russian discourses that call for revising the split-up of the Soviet Union. While in *Telluria* the Russian setting still made out more than three fourths of the episodes, *Manaraga*'s protagonist is a global jetsetter whose consciousness serves as a prism for global discourses such as Islamophobia and neo-nationalism.

In *Manaraga*'s post-catastrophic and—related to this—post-Islamist Europe of the year 2037, reactionary discourses are intermingled with meta-literature. Books are no longer produced, but only stored in archives and museums. A media-nostalgic mafia of book'n'grill chefs jet around the world in order to grill meat and fish for rich customers over flames fueled by stolen first editions of classical literature. The post-Russian hybrid protagonist Geza Iasnodvorskii sees his specialization—in his case Russian classics—jeopardized, first by transcultural world literature such as Nabokov's *Ada* (Sorokin 2017b, 119–20), and later by a "molecular" machine that clones books inside the eponymous Northern-Ural mountain Manaraga (Sorokin 2017b, 219). Representing mafiosi book grillers known as "The Kitchen" ["Kukhnia"], Geza opposes this looming threat, until he is captured at the Manaraga book-cloning plant and subjected to a complete brainwashing, also by technological means.

The 2037 world in which Geza defends his paradoxical book-loving and book-burning métier is post-apocalyptic, just as the retrofuturist micro-states of *Telluria*. The first-person narrator remembers the several waves of a "second Islamic revolution" ["Вторая исламская революция"] (Sorokin 2017b, 34), which affected his family and all of East Central Europe, using clichéd rhetoric to talk about sectarian terrorism:

> My parents had to flee: my father from the Orthodox fundamentalists, my mother from the Islamic. Both groups of long-bearded obscurantists

demanded love and understanding from the population and thus they bombed, burnt, slit people's throats, and shot them without mercy.

Родители мои бежали: отец от православных фундаменталистов, мать—от исламских. Те и другие бородатые мракобесы хотели от населения любви и понимания, поэтому бомбили, жгли, резали и расстреливали нещадно. (Sorokin 2017b, 34–5)

Sorokin's representation of Europe partially governed by Islamists alludes to zealous and best-selling Islamophobic dystopias such as Elena Chudinova's *Notre-Dame de Paris Mosque* [*Mechet' Parizhskoi Bogomateri*] from 2005 (see Lanin 2007, 379–80). A post-catastrophic world in which books are obsolete and rare is reminiscent of Tat'iana Tolstaia's novel *The Slynx* (2000). And a dystopian burning of books seems familiar from Ray Bradbury's classic dystopia *Fahrenheit 451* (1953; cf. Surkov 2017). This incomplete list calls for a reading of Sorokin's *Manaraga* as yet another cocktail of intertexts, much like *The Blizzard*.

Critical reviewers castigated *Manaraga* as a secondary text. Dmitrii Butrin only discerned in the novel a set of customary self-quotes (Butrin 2017). Lev Danilkin presented Sorokin as an antiquated classic, who abhorred what Danilkin, after his pro-imperialist turn, regarded as the only "true" contemporary literature: the nationalist works of Zakhar Prilepin, pro-Russian occupant in Eastern Ukraine. In Danilkin's view, Sorokin's anti-nationalist motifs bring nothing new to the table. Danilkin sarcastically rebukes Sorokin's

[…] fresh and original considerations about a deficit of democracy in Russia, consorted with an assortment of blood-curdling prophecies about a new *oprichnina*, centripetal tendencies, Sinicization, and Islamic revolutions. (Danilkin 2017)

Back in 1996, Danilkin worked as an aesthetically progressive literary scholar, who valued Sorokin's "meta-discourse." However, unlike Sorokin, Danilkin drastically changed his political orientation and aesthetic criteria. Now, Sorokin is criticized by Danilkin for the exact same things he would previously be praised for. Always picking up foreign discourses, Sorokin uses them in *Manaraga*, just as in *Telluria*, Sorokin to investigate reactionary political ideologies. This is especially dystopian, considering the recent proliferation of Islamophobic discourses by popular right-wing publicists such as Oriana

Fallaci (*The Rage and the Pride* / *La rabbia e l'orgoglio*, 2001) and Thilo Sarrazin (*Germany Abolishes Itself* / *Deutschland schafft sich ab*, 2010). Sorokin enters a discursive-literary field most prominently occupied by Michel Houellebecq, who in his 2015 novel *Submission* [*Soumission*]—before *Manaraga*, but after *Telluria*—claimed that the dystopian (for him) victory of a moderate Islamist in the French elections of 2022 was a likely outcome.

Fallaci, Sarrazin, Houellebecq, and Chudinova all differ from Sorokin's post-apocalyptic novels because they paint dystopian—and not post-dysto-pian—future. Sorokin's fictional meta-dystopias of 2013 and 2017 show the post-dystopian future perfect, a future world already after an Islamist revolution has played out and subsided, a *post*-Islamist Europe. In *Telluria* and *Manaraga* the Islamophobic dystopia of right-wing alarmists and cynical writers is notably nar-rated in the past tense. This aspect clearly separates Sorokin's post-Islamism as a meta-discourse and meta-dystopia from straightforward Islamophobic discourses.

In *Manaraga*, the temporal distance, which leaves the alarmist Islamophobia in the past, is reinforced by the narrator's anachronistic love for the printed word. This adds structural conservatism to post-Islamism, creating a complex picture of anti-globalist xenophobia. Islamophobia is de facto a cross-European phenomenon, but *Manaraga* uses Islamophobic discourse to highlight the reactionary ideology's opposition to transculturality. Sorokin demonstrates that Islamophobic dystopias are interconnected with negative perceptions of globalization and modernity and discontented with transcultural develop-ments. Much like Houellebecq, Sorokin deconstructs the anti-transcultural consciousness of his bibliophilic and structurally conservative first-person nar-rator, creating a transcultural world around Geza.

As researchers have argued (Lipovetskii 2012; Uffelmann 2017), in Sorokin's books spanning from 2006 (*Day of the Oprichnik*) to 2013 (*Telluria*), the dystopian near future is interspersed with anachronistic elements, mostly from the sixteenth and the nineteenth centuries. A comparative glance at *Telluria* and *Manaraga* shows that in both texts, the repercussions of the repres-sive past continue into the dystopian future. A period of post-imperial disinte-gration and rampant destruction has already taken place in the readers' future and the narrators' past. For the narrators, Islamist atrocities already became a part of the oral tradition, recounted either in reported speech (*Manaraga*) or in direct speech (*Telluria*), which is interrupted as an additional means of estrangement. Thus, any emotional affectation that the characters (or the readers) may feel regarding the Islamists is suppressed twice: first by the time distance, and second, by the interruptions.

In *Manaraga* the first-person narrator is deeply touched when a "young guy tells the heart-breaking history of his escape from Macedonian Salafists, who murdered his parents and chopped off his right hand for playing chess" ["Парень рассказал душераздирающую историю бегства от македонских салафитов, убивших его родителей, а ему отрубивших правую руку за игру в шахматы"] (Sorokin 2017b, 101). When the speaker reproduces an identical traumatized discourse a few minutes later, Geza perceives this as a provocation, and Sorokin undermines the emotional identification which his first-person narrator just experienced:

> [...] he showed his stump and started, as if nothing happened, to rattle off the same story of escape, parents, Salafists once again. I listened attentively until the very end. Then I turned around and smashed his mug in.

> [...] он показал свой обрубок и, [...] стал как ни в чем не бывало прогонять все ту же душераздирающую историю про бегство, родителей, салафитов и шахматы. Я внимательно прослушал ее до конца. Затем развернулся и заехал ему по морде [...] (Sorokin 2017b, 101)

Thus, in *Manaraga*, the repetition of the victim's discourse lets the emotions collapse. In episode V of *Telluria* Sorokin uses a media filter to present the suffering from atrocities as inauthentic. When the carnival in Cologne can be celebrated again for the first time after three years of Islamist terror, the narration jumps into a reporter's live coverage full of premade patterns of touching and imperative remembrance. The anti-Islamist pathos is disturbed by instructions which the reporter Richard receives through his ear-clip from the production director Samira:

> "Just today, on such a joyous day, I want to remind you and your children, so that you never forget it, of that quiet morning in May three years ago when in the dawn nineteen Hercules transporters from Bukhara dropped the paratrooper battalion *Taliban* in Cologne's suburb Leverkusen. Back then three dark years of occupation began. The Taliban occupied North-Rhine Westphalia." [...]
> "Richard, make it shorter!" Samira's voice sings in Richard's ear.
> "We all remember what followed: executions, torture, castigations, prohibition of alcohol, cinema, and theater, humiliation of women, depression, an oppressive atmosphere, inflation, collapse, and war." [...]

— […] Но я хочу напомнить вам именно сейчас, именно в этот радост-
ный день, напомню, чтобы вы и ваши дети никогда не забыли, как три
года назад девятнадцать транспортных «геркулесов», вылетевших
из Бухары, в тихое майское утро, на рассвете, высадили в пригороде
Кельна Леверкюзене десантную дивизию «Талибан». И начались три
года мрачной талибской оккупации Северного Рейна-Вестфалии. […]
— Рихард, короче!—поет в ухе голос Замиры.
— А что было потом—все мы помним: казни, пытки, телесные
наказания, запрет алкоголя, кино, театра, унижение женщин,
депрессия, гнетущая атмосфера, инфляция, коллапс, война. […]
(Sorokin 2013, 34)

With their post-dystopian future perfect, both narratorial situations refract
the dystopian discourse of the millennium and the 2000s (see Iur´eva 2005, 3,
8; Nikolenko, Kopach 2006, 192; Chantsev 2007, 28—6), which Sorokin has
repeatedly picked up since 2006. In *Telluria*, the single exception are Islamist
propagandistic imperatives that constitute episode VIII (Sorokin 2013, 72).
In *Manaraga*, the actual future domination of Salafists or Wahabis is never
shown. Instead, Sorokin presents the discourse of those traumatized after
their liberation from a short period of Islamist terror dominion.

Sorokin's post-dystopia is logically unthinkable without the literary
dystopian discourses such as Chudinova's or Houellebecq's, which he meta-
discursively evokes. The meta-dystopian subgenre, which he develops,
depends on the genre of dystopia. This fact should be considered alongside
Gary Saul Morson's definition of meta-utopia: "Meta-utopias are perhaps best
comprehended as examinations, rather than either endorsements or rejections,
of the presuppositions of utopian thinking and literature […]" (Morson 1981,
146). Transferring Morson's definition to meta-dystopias, it can be said that
Sorokin "examines" the dystopian discourse without unequivocally supporting
or refuting it, but instead by anatomizing it.

Both mid-2010s novels by Sorokin imagine dystopian Islamism as a
transnational phenomenon. However, for *Manaraga*'s first-person narrator,
transnationality appears not as transcultural reality, but as a problematic loss
of borders in a globalized world. As Sorokin stated in an interview (Sorokin,
Saprykin 2017), he sympathizes with Geza Iasnodvorskii, but only to a par-
tial extent. Not even the most critical reviewers have dared to attribute Geza's
views to the author himself. Sorokin scholarship has, with the exception of
the *Ice Trilogy*, routinely emphasized the non-congruity between the narrator

and the author, agreeing that it is impossible to ethically identify Sorokin with the violent excesses of his destructions of Socialist and classical Realism. In *Manaraga*, Sorokin draws on chimeras of Islamism with meta-discursive distance. His first-person narrator exhibits an Islamophobic discourse, but it is not evaluated as either good or bad, justified or xenophobic.

Geza is a globetrotter in the métier of book'n'grill and member of an international mafia. Nevertheless, he is afraid of Chinese influence on his bibliophilic enterprise (Sorokin 2017b, 219; cf. Narinskaia 2017) and comprehends organized crime as a negative collateral effect of globalization (Caucasians from Kansas; Sorokin 2017b, 113). Correspondingly, in the realm of literature, he regards Vladimir Nabokov's transcultural novel *Ada* as problematic, because the book's obscure national origin does not let him determine which chefs are supposed to burn it:

> There it is, the apple of discord by good old Nabokov: *Ada*, written in English by a Russian writer in Switzerland, in the francophone Canton of Vaud. [...] There's no monopoly on *reading*!

> Вот оно—яблочко раздора старика Набокова: Ада, написана по-английски русским автором в Швейцарии, во франкоязычном кантоне Во. [...] Эксклюзивных прав на *чтение* нет! (Sorokin 2017b, 119–20)

The verb *chitat'* ["read"] is emphasized in the original, because it has the metaphorical meaning of "use as combustible material." The plot-building metaphor for intertextuality—the illegal grilling with old editions of Russian classics—inscribes *Manaraga* into Sorokin's long series of explicitly meta-literary texts (cf. Sokolov 2017; Lipovetskii 2018). However, the self-referentiality of literature is here transported into in the political sphere and read as a critique of transculturalism. The media-anachronistic narrator abhors *Manaraga*'s cloning of books by "*graphomaniacs*" ["*графоманы*"] (Sorokin 2017b, 219, emphasis in the original) and dourly reflects on the "The Work of Art in the Age of Mechanical Reproduction" ["Das Kunstwerk im Zeitalter seiner technischen Reproduzierbarkeit"] (Walter Benjamin's famous essay from 1935). Geza's stale admiration of the printed book revolves precisely around Nabokov's most transcultural text, *Ada*: "One cubic meter of *Ada*! Of this and no other [book copy]" ["кубометр «Ады»! Той самой"] (Sorokin 2017b, 222). Geza laments that world literature can no longer be reserved for a single national cuisine. With transnational literature such as Nabokov, one could cook almost everything: "On *Ada* you can cook various things [...]" ["На «Аде» можно многое приготовить (...)"] (Sorokin 2017b, 224).

Geza is scared by the inflation of cheap, "graphomaniac" mass literature (Sorokin 2017b, 219, 231) and bases his bibliophilia on conservative idolatry of rare books. He also praises the cultural-memory capacity of forbidden literature: "[...] you cannot cook using manuscripts, they do not burn" ["(...) на рукописях нельзя жарить, они не горят"] (Sorokin 2017b, 169)—yet another reference to Bulgakov's meta-literary comment (Bulgakov 1968, 162) after *Day of the Oprichnik*. Geza prefers grilling on Russian classics, and he discards contemporary Russian literature such as the works of Zakhar Prilepin as "unburnable," that is, unreadable (Sorokin 2017b, 130–2).

Through the narratorial prism of *Manaraga*, Sorokin translates reactionary critiques of modernity, digitalization, transculturalism, and globalism into a paradoxical bibliophilic take on literary history and intertextuality. The protagonist's anti-globalist and anti-modernist worldview interlocks with the post-Islamist dystopia of the plot. However, he is defeated, together with the backward struggle of the international book-grilling mafia Kukhnia against technical reproduction and transculturalism. At the end of *Manaraga*, Geza undergoes a brainwashing by way of implanted Internet access, which inverts his previous literary axiology (Sorokin 2017b, 236). His bibliophilic resistance to modernity is ironically erased. Narrated from the point of view of the brainwashed Geza, the novel's end displays "narrative acrobatics: inserting a false happy end into the verbal continuum of the narrator" (Caramitti 2018).

But it is not only the pessimistic end which allows readers to distance themselves from the anti-transnational ideologies and phobias embodied in the narrator. The very plot of *Manaraga* refutes the narrator's ideological claims. Iasnodvorskii's intensive travel activities performatively illustrate the transnational and transcultural reality of the 2037 post-dystopian world. Like most other characters, Geza is a cyborg, and he makes extensive use of the implants that connect him to the Internet. The narrator is also a polyglot (Sorokin 2017b, 21) and nomad by profession (Sorokin 2017b, 33). He jets between various sites from Norway to Japan and displays an attitude reminiscent of a tourist flaneur (another allusion to Benjamin, this time to his unfinished *Arcades Project* [*Passagenwerk*]): "I am dressed like an old-fashioned tourist [...]" ["Я одет как старомодный турист (...)"] (Sorokin 2017b, 135). On Geza's path, Sorokin leaves bits and pieces of tourist information that he collected during his own tours, be this from a hotel on Hokkaido (Sorokin 2017b, 175), a lutefisk in Bergen, or the old cemetery of Passau (Sorokin

2017b, 40). The narrator also appropriates an autobiographical trace of his transcultural author, who commutes between his house in the Moscow region and his flat in Berlin. The text repeatedly hints at Sorokin's intimate knowledge of the Berlin district Charlottenburg (Sorokin 2017b, 13, 20–1, 32, 240).

The narrator's exclusivist thinking in terms of Russian culture and national literature is clearly misplaced in the post-dystopian world of 2037. In *Manaraga*, Russians have almost gone extinct after the loss of the Soviet empire and the disintegration of the post-Soviet space into a myriad of micro-states (very much like *Telluria*): "[…] when they had lost their world, Russians assimilated very quickly" ["(…) потеряв свой мір, русские быстро ассимилировались"] (Sorokin 2017b, 21). The atypical spelling of "мір" in this quote caustically alludes to Russkiy Mir, the Russian World Foundation founded in 2007, whose neo-imperialist aspirations crashed with the Ukrainian Euromaidan revolution of 2013/2014. In 2037, Russian is rarely heard and the so-called Russian book-grillers use non-Russian first names such as Alvizo and Beat (Sorokin 2017, 116). The only chef with the stereotypically Russian name Ivan is a Ukrainian from Québec (Sorokin 2017b, 117). For all his love of Russian literature, the ultra-hybrid (Caramitti 2018) Jewish-Lithuanian-Belarusian narrator Geza Iasnodvorskii has been born in Budapest (Sorokin 2017b, 35) and grew up in Passau.

At the international trade-union congress of Kukhnia, it turns out that German "chefs" only grill using French or Irish literature (Sorokin 2017b, 114). This discovery disproves Geza's nationalist prejudice that Russians must grill using Russian classics—even if they have long since ceased to be Russians in any linguistic, cultural, or ethnic sense of the word. Paradoxically, Sorokin in *Manaraga* uses the professional nomad and practical cosmopolite Geza Iasnodvorskii to show an utterly outdated and anti-transcultural worldview. This *makes Manaraga* a piece of paradoxical world literature. Moreover, Geza, a bibliophile, also burns and destroys books—a dimension that should not be dismissed for the sake of literature-centric interpretations (Lipovetskii 2018, 635). This allows Sorokin to debunk structural conservatism and media anachronism as "cyberfascism" (Surkov 2017; cf. Sorokin, Dolin 2017).

In *Manaraga*, Sorokin does not advocate for a naïve media anachronism as he did in his preface to a literary issue of the Russian *Esquire* in August 2016 (Sorokin 2016). In her interpretation of the 2017 novel, Galina Iuzefovich misleadingly used the *Esquire* piece to prove that Geza was Sorokin's mouthpiece. Geza is hardly even a "sad self-portrait of Sorokin himself" (Lipovetskii 2018, 645), and Sorokin is definitely not the "traditionalist" and "conservative" that

Danilkin finds in *Manaraga*, declaring him "worse than most alarmists that took to flooding literature with dystopias in the mid-2000s" (Danilkin 2017). Quite the contrary: Sorokin's cyberpunk fantasy of global jetset, transhuman cyborgs, and futurological machines represents an estranging antidote to political alarmism (like Sarrazin's) and the politically motivated fictional dystopias (as in Houellebecq).

An unbridgeable abyss remains between the private person, the essayist, and citizen of the world, Vladimir Sorokin, on the one hand, and the meta-discursive writer with the same name on the other. In Sorokin's post-Islamist meta-dystopia it is not obscurantist Islamists who burn books, but a bibliophilic conservative and outdated Russian cultural nationalist. As a result, Sorokin diagnoses the reactionary, anti-globalist, neo-nationalist, and Islamophobic psalmody of his first-person narrator as xenophobic, paradox, and self-destructive. It is not surprising that Sorokin, in an episode from *Telluria*, labeled the discourse of liberation from Islamism as "patriotic drivel" ["патриотическ(ая) чушь"] (Sorokin 2013, 47).

CHAPTER 13

Continuity in Discontinuity: Prospects

Scholarship on Sorokin has—when not distorted by polemical idiosyncrasies—over more than three decades relentlessly emphasized the relevance of his two statements: that his literary texts do not derive "from nature" ["не с натуры"] (Sorokin, Shapoval 1998, 17), and that his productions are "just letters on paper" ["просто буквы на бумаге"] (see the title quotes in Glanc 1995 and Dobrenko, Kalinin, Lipovetskii 2018). These formulaic truisms have been repeated to refute simplistic referential readings such as "satire on Putin regime" or "parody of new imperialism." Long-time Sorokin scholars insist that his "engagement with discourse" [*ustanovka na diskurs*, "Einstellung auf den Diskurs"] (Deutschmann 1999, 37) is the common thread of his oeuvre: "Once he began deconstructing Socialist Realist plots and characters, Sorokin soon realized that the same deconstruction was applicable to any other authoritative (and hence, sacralized) discourse" (Lipovetsky 2011, 188). Sure, much of the readers' increasing interest in Sorokin's works stems from referential concerns, but the object of reference in his fictional texts is not "reality" as such, whatever that might be. Rather, Sorokin is interested in different discursive modes of presenting reality (cf. Uffelmann 2017, 379–80).

As a result, the much-debated question whether there is a "new Sorokin"—emerging with the publication of *Blue Lard* in 1999, with *Ice* in 2002 or with *Day of the Oprichnik* in 2006—is better answered with caution. No doubt, Sorokin has exchanged the early sots-art variety of conceptualism, fascinated by Soviet discourses and the patterns of Socialist Realism, for other sources of inspiration—from classical Russian literature through pulp fiction, fantasy, and esotericism to dystopian modes of thinking, Eurasianism, and anti-globalism. Yet, despite these changing discursive objects, his meta-discursive poetics (Danilkin 1996; Deutschmann 1998) has been preserved (cf. Danilkin 2002; Bogdanova 2005; Uffelmann 2006). "I am a stylistic Proteus, therein lies my style" ["Я стилистический Протей, в этом и есть мой стиль"], Sorokin pointed out in 2004 (Sorokin, Bavil'skii 2004). After repeated insistence on changes in his poetics in the 2000s and 2010s, in 2017 Sorokin again acknowledged that he "has stayed faithful to the principles, which [he] developed in the Moscow underground of the 1970s and 1980s" ["я храню верность принципам, сложившимся у меня в московском андеграунде 70–80-х"] (Sorokin, Saprykin 2017).

The only exception were the years 2002–2005, when Sorokin was lured into partially identifying with the metaphysical claims of the totalitarian sect of his *Ice Trilogy*. Apart from that, the real-world author has maintained a safe distance from the hermetic fictional worlds of his prose, while the implied author has been sticking to the "device of positioning himself as 'I am not ...'" (Bogdanova 2005, 42). In sum, while it remains contested among researchers whether the thematic discontinuity allows to speak of a post-conceptualist Sorokin after 1999 or 2002 (when he certainly ceases to be a sots-artist), the meta-discursive poetics nevertheless forms a continuity in this apparent discontinuity. He "tried to say goodbye" to conceptualism without ever really leaving it, as Il´ia Kukulin splendidly remarked in 2002 [*proshchaetsia, no ne ukhodit*] (Kukulin 2002, 258).

The author's turn to popular discourses and genres such as pulp fiction or fantasy paved the way for a second, popular reception of the hitherto hardly-accessible underground author. The popularity of Sorokin, which began to rise in the 2000s, is ironically due, in part, to a referential miscomprehension. As he became a bestselling classic of contemporary Russian literature, unprepared reviewers and scholars from comparative literature were baffled by his popular genre emulation. Starting with *Blue Lard*, the misinterpretations opted for straightforward referentiality in a way that simplifies Paul de Man's aporia of either choosing a referential or self-referential reading of literature (de Man 1979).

When Sorokin ceased to be just an insider among fellow underground artists and specialized scholars of neo-avant-garde art, this second, increasingly wider and more international reception has considerably contributed to his canonization. Together with the world-famous artist Il´ia Kabakov his theoretician Boris Groys, who moved to New York, and the hyperactive multi-talent Dmitrii Prigov, Vladimir Sorokin, the most successful prose writer emerging from the Moscow Conceptualist circle, became a classic of late and post-Soviet art.

Sorokin's books have been translated into tens of languages, albeit very unevenly. While his oeuvre is almost completely available in German translation, only four of his books—*The Queue*, the *Ice Trilogy*, *Day of the Oprichnik*, and *The Blizzard*—and a number of smaller texts (*A Month in Dachau*, *Dostoevsky-trip*, as well as several short stories; Sorokin 1986a; 1994a; 1995a; 2000; 2003b; 2011c; 2017a) and excerpts from novels (Sorokin 1991b; 2003a; 2004a; 2005a; 2014a) have been translated into English. Despite the heroic efforts of translators like Jamey Gambrell, American publishers have remained rather hesitant when it comes to popularizing Sorokin's oeuvre for a North American public (Barry 2011).

Given the challenges that readers face when digesting Sorokin's early texts, academic research has been paramount in canonizing Sorokin as a living classic. This ongoing process is marked by collective efforts such as two exclusively "Sorokinist" conference volumes, one predominantly in German (Burkhart 1999), and one in English (Roesen, Uffelmann 2013). There are also a Dutch, rather essayistic special issue ("Vladimir Sorokin" 2006), a Slovakia-centered volume (Lorková 2011a), a short Russian thematic cluster ("Prostranstvo" 2012), and three sections in the leading Russian journal for literary studies, *Novoe literaturnoe obozrenie* (issues 56, 2002, and 119 and 120, 2013). As a clear signal of proceeding secondary canonization, there also exist two impressive collections of previously published articles (Lawrence 2015, 153 pp. letter-size; Dobrenko, Kalinin, Lipovetskii 2018, 711 pp.). A telling symptom of academic appraisal is specialized research articles devoted to the process of canonizing Sorokin (Glanc 2014, 64; Stryjakowska 2017b). Sorokin already showed self-glorifying autotextual references in such works as *The Blizzard*, and now scholarly scrutiny goes the same way.

Quite naturally, scholarship on Sorokin is predominantly available in Russian, featuring pioneering essays by Boris Groys (1979), Sven Gundlakh (1985), Mikhail Ryklin (1992, 185–221), and abiding critics such as Mikhail Ephstein, Aleksandr Genis, Mark Lipovetskii, and Igor´ Smirnov. Monographs in Russian appeared much later: first thin booklets (Bogdanova 2005; Giliarov 2008), then single-authored books drawing on rather narrow selections of primary texts (Andreeva and Bibergan 2012; Bibergan 2014, practically no more than a revised edition of the previous volume) and PhD theses (Pozdniakov 2003; Umbrashko 2004; Kiun 2005; Novokhatskii 2009; Marusenkov 2012), often with virtually monolingual bibliographies.

Less natural than the Russian dominance in writing on a Russian writer is the German contribution. The earliest conference volume by Burkhart from 1999 essentially started the canonization process abroad (Uffelmann 2000, 279). In Germany Sorokin has been an object of several PhD dissertations

(Deutschmann 2003, 286–358; Sasse 2003, 189–292; Vassilieva 2014, 133–184; Naumann 2016, 50–167), though it remains an unsubstantiated polemical myth that thirty-five PhD theses alone were prepared at German universities in the early 1990s (Levshin 1993, 283). English-language research can only boast some early articles (Porter 1994, 38–42; Gillespie 1997; Roll 1998; Vladiv-Glover 1999b), of which just a few were congenial (Genis 1999; Lipovetsky 2000) and paved the long way for an English-language edited volume (Roesen, Uffelmann 2013), a collection of previously published articles (Lawrence 2015), and some segments of English-language PhD dissertations (Paulsen 2009, 122–34; Dreyer 2011, 189–225; Douzjian 2013, 143–70; Ågren 2014, 95–117; Trotman 2017, 72–104, 128–53). Thus, it may be no coincidence that the author of the current Companion has a German background as well. Drawing on my continuous preoccupation with Sorokin's work for more than two decades, *Vladimir Sorokin's Discourses* is the first attempt at a comprehensive overview of the entire oeuvre with exemplary readings of long-prose texts from all periods of his work.

Since the focus in this Companion has been on Sorokin's longer prose texts, other facets of his oeuvre could not be scrutinized in the same degree of depth. Sorokin as a master of the short story, as a script writer and playwright, and more recently his renewed activities as a painter (see this book's cover)—all his artistic hypostases deserve separate book-length studies. Research into Sorokin's short prose can draw on early studies (Witte 1989, 150–6; Porter 1994, 39–41; Burkhart 1997; Kuznitsin 1999; Lipovetsky 2000, 171–8; Strätling 2000, 164–71; Leiderman, Lipovetskii 2001, 54–8), but also on more recent research (Kiun 2005; Langeveld, Weststeijn 2005, 369–72; Morelli 2006; Marusenkov 2012, 185–94; Lunde 2013). Film script studies can continue threads laid in several articles (Flickinger 1997; Degot´ 1999; Hänsgen 1999; Kononova 2006; Kukulin 2013; Kostiukov 2016). Most remains to be done for theater after the seminal chapter in Beumers's and Lipovetsky's 2009 book (90–101) and the sections of Marusenkov's (2012, 218–36) and Douzjian's (2013, 143–70) PhD dissertations, for his work as a book designer (Sorokin, Schwarzstein 2019) as well as for the librettos after a few rather contextualizing essays (Gustiakova 2006; Engel 2009). Specific challenges for Sorokin studies consist in scrutinizing the genre poetics of his book-length prose works compiled of heterogeneous short stories (*Sugar Kremlin* and *Telluria*) and the juxtaposition of different genres, which appears not only in the pseudo-novel *The Norm*, but also in collections such as *The Feast, Monoclone,* and *White Square*. The East Asian elements in Sorokin's works from 1999 onward deserve a separate investigation that adds a reading from within Chinese and Japanese cultural history to the existing Euro-American research (Pogorelaia 2012; Uffelmann 2013b; Filimonova 2014).

While first steps in these directions have already been taken in scholarly articles and academic book chapters, one segment in the process of canonization has—symptomatically—so far remained in the shadows. Given his neo-avant-garde poetics and violation of every possible taboo—from linguistic, aesthetic and sexual to political and ideological—Sorokin was only recently awarded literary prizes in Russia and abroad. He was shortlisted for the Russian Booker Prize in 1992. Not until 2001 did he obtain the prestigious but merely symbolic Andrei Belyi Prize. In the 2000s, international literary prizes followed, among them the American Liberty Prize (2005) and the Italian-Russian Gor´kii Prize (2010), before he eventually came in second for the Russian Bol´shaia kniga award in 2011 and 2014 and received the NOS prize in 2010 and 2017.

This list is not especially impressive, in contrast to Sorokin's recognition as a "classic in his own lifetime" [*prizhiznennyi klassik*], which has become a topos in introductions and book reviews (for example Kurchatova 2013). The reviewers even developed a habit of comparing Sorokin to nineteenth-century novelist Lev Tolstoi to characterize his high status in Russian literary history (cf. chapter Eleven). With Lev Tolstoi, Sorokin shares the dubious honor of contested fame. Tolstoi survived his fellow Realists by almost three decades, eventually reaching the status of an international star, corresponded with leading intellectuals from all over the world such as Mahatma Gandhi, and was venerated by Russian sectarians as a prophet. But he was excommunicated by the Russian Orthodox Church, ostracized by the Tsarist elites, and never received the prize which no other living writer at the beginning of the twentieth century would have deserved more than he: the Nobel Prize for Literature. Similarly, Sorokin scholars have long envisaged him receiving the Nobel (for example Sokolov 2005, 134) and each of his four masterpieces thus far—*The Queue, Marina's Thirtieth Love, Day of the Oprichnik*, and *The Blizzard*—alone might justify this choice. Still, it is utopian to believe that this controversial author will ever live to receive the prize, just as we cannot right the wrongs that were done to Tolstoi in the 1900s.

Bibliography

Sorokin's Works in English translation

Sorokin, Vladimir. 1986a. "Start of the Season" [Short story "Otkrytie sezona"]. Trans. Sally Laird. *Index on Censorship* 15.9: 43–6.

_____. 1988a. *The Queue* [Novel *Ochered'*]. Trans. Sally Laird. New York, London: Readers International.

_____. 1991a. "A Business Proposition" [Short story "Delovoe predlozhenie"]. Trans. Jamey Gambrell. In *Glas*. Vol. 2. *Soviet Grotesque*. 9–15. Moscow: Russlit.

_____. 1991b. "Four Stout Hearts" [Excerpt from the novel *Serdtsa chetyrëkh*]. Trans. Jamey Gambrell. In *Glas*. Vol. 2. *Soviet Grotesque*. 15–48. Moscow: Russlit.

_____. 1994a. "A Month in Dachau" [Short story "Mesiats v Dakhau"]. Trans. Jamey Gambrell. *Grand Street Magazine* 48: 233–53.

_____. 1995a. "Next Item on the Agenda" [Short story "Zasedanie zavkoma"]. Trans. Andrew Reynolds. In Victor Erofeyev, Andrew Reynolds (eds.). *New Russian Writing: Russia's Fleurs du Mal*, 321–44. London: Penguin.

_____. 2000. "Dostoevsky-trip" [Play *Dostoevsky-trip*]. Trans. Mikhail Magazinnik. *Koja Magazine* 3: 33–53.

_____. 2003a. "Trick Lard" [Excerpt from the novel *Goluboe salo*]. Trans. Arch Tait. *Index on Censorship* 2: 204–13.

_____. 2003b. "Hiroshima" [Short story "Khirosima"]. Trans. Jamey Gambrell. *Grand Street Magazine* 71: 48–56.

_____. 2004a. "The Norm" [Excerpt from the novel *Norma*]. Trans. Keith Gessen. *n+1* 1: 75–95.

_____. 2005a. "Ice" [Excerpt from the Novel *Lëd*]. Trans. Andrew Bromfield. *Index on Censorship* 4: 83–91.

_____. 2007a. *Ice* [Novel *Lëd*]. Trans. Jamey Gambrell. New York: New York Review Books.

_____. 2008a. "Afterword: Farewell to the Queue." Trans. Jamey Gambrell. In Vladimir Sorokin. *The Queue*, 253–63. New York: New York Review Books.

_____. 2011a. *Day of the Oprichnik* [Short novel *Den' oprichnika*]. Trans. Jamey Gambrell. New York: Farrar, Straus and Giroux.

_____. 2011b. *Ice Trilogy* [Three novels *Lëd*, *Put' Bro*, and *23,000*]. Trans. Jamey Gambrell. New York: New York Review Books.

_____. 2011c. "Passing Through" [Short story "Proezdom"]. Trans. Valentina Brougher and Frank Miller with Mark Lipovetsky. In Mark Lipovetsky, Valentina Brougher (eds.). *50 Writers: An Anthology of 20th Century Russian Short Stories*, 604–10. Boston (MA): Academic Studies Press.

_____. 2014a. "Petrushka" [Excerpt from the short novel *Sakharnyi Kreml'*]. Trans. Boris Dralyuk. In Mark Lipovetsky, Lisa Ryoko Wakamiya (eds.). *Late and Post-Soviet Russian Literature: A Reader*. Vol. 1, 285–95. Boston (MA): Academic Studies Press.

_____. 2014b. "Let the Past Collapse on Time!" *The New York Review of Books* May 8. https://www.nybooks.com/articles/2014/05/08/let-the-past-collapse-on-time/, accessed January 7, 2019.

_____. 2014c. "Russia Is Pregnant with Ukraine." Trans. Jamey Gambrell. *The New York Review of Books* July 24. https://www.nybooks.com/daily/2014/07/24/russia-pregnant-with-ukraine/, accessed January 7, 2019.

_____. 2015a. *The Blizzard* [Short novel *Metel'*]. Trans. Jamey Gambrell. New York: Farrar, Straus and Giroux.

_____. 2017a. "The Swim / Zaplyv." Trans. Brian James Baer. In Brian James Baer (ed.). *New Penguin Parallel Text: Short Stories in Russian / Rasskazy na russkom iazyke*, 177–97. New York: Penguin.

Sorokin, Vladimir; Doerry, Martin; Schepp, Matthias. 2014. [Interview] "Russia Is Slipping Back into an Authoritarian Empire." Trans. from the German: Christopher Sultan. In Mark Lipovetsky, Lisa Ryoko Wakamiya (eds.). *Late and Post-Soviet Russian Literature: A Reader*. Vol. 1, 278–84. Boston (MA): Academic Studies Press.

Sorokin, Vladimir; Gambrell, Jamey; Roesen, Tine; Tretner, Andreas; Uffelmann, Dirk, et al. 2013. [Roundtable discussion] "Translating Sorokin / Translated Sorokin." In Tine Roesen, Dirk Uffelmann (eds.). *Vladimir Sorokin's Languages*, 345–66. Bergen: University of Bergen. Also online: http://boap.uib.no/books/sb/catalog/book/9, accessed January 7, 2019.

Sorokin, Vladimir; Laird, Sally. 1999. [Interview] "Vladimir Sorokin (b. 1955)." Trans. Sally Laird. In Sally Laird. *Voices of Russian Literature: Interviews with Ten Contemporary Writers*, 143–62. Oxford: Oxford University Press.

Sorokin, Vladimir; Roll, Serafima. 1998. [Interview] "Literature as a Cemetery of Stylistic Finds." Trans. Serafima Roll. In Serafima Roll (ed.). *Contextualizing Transition: Interviews with Contemporary Russian Writers and Critics*, 77–83. New York et al.: Lang.

Sorokin's Works in Russian

Erofeev, Viktor; Prigov, Dmitrii; Sorokin, Vladimir. 2002. *ëps*. Moscow: Zebra E.

Kulik, Oleg; Sorokin, Vladimir. 1994. *V glub' Rossii* [*Into the Depths of Russia*]. Moscow: Institut sovremennogo iskusstva.

Sorokin, Vladimir. 1985a. *Ochered': roman* [*The Queue: A Novel*]. Paris: Sintaksis.

_____. 1985b. "Otkrytie sezona" ["Start of the Season"]. *A–Ia: literaturnoe izdanie / A–Ya: Literary Issue* 1: 60–2.

_____. 1985c. "Geologi" ["Geologists"]. *A–Ia: literaturnoe izdanie / A–Ya: Literary Issue* 1: 62–4.

_____. 1985d. "Proshchanie" ["The Farewell"]. *A–Ia: literaturnoe izdanie / A–Ya: Literary Issue* 1: 64–5.

_____. 1985e. "Proezdom" ["Passing Through"]. *A–Ia: literaturnoe izdanie / A–Ya: Literary Issue* 1: 65–7.

_____. 1985f. "Liubov'" ["Love"]. *A–Ia: literaturnoe izdanie / A–Ya: Literary Issue* 1: 67–8.

_____. 1985g. "Ochered'" [Excerpt from the novel *The Queue*]. *A–Ia: literaturnoe izdanie / A–Ya: Literary Issue* 1: 69–74.

_____. 1986b. "Kiset" ["The Tobacco Pouch"]. *Mitin zhurnal* 11. Also online: http://kolonna.mitin.com/archive.php?number=11/, accessed January 7, 2019.

_____. 1986c. "Dorozhnoe proisshestvie" ["The Road Accident"]. *Mitin zhurnal* 11. Also online: http://kolonna.mitin.com/archive.php?number=11/, full text not accessible on August 28, 2018.

_____. 1987a. "Zemlianka" [Play "The Ditch"]. *Mitin zhurnal* 17. http://kolonna.mitin.com/archive.php?number=17/, accessed on August 28, 2018.

_____. 1987b. "Pel'meni" [Play "Pelmeni"]. *Mitin zhurnal* 18. http://kolonna.mitin.com/archive.php?number=18/, full text not accessible on August 28, 2018.

_____. 1989. "Otkrytie sezona" ["Start of the Season"]. *Rodnik* 11 (35): 23–9.

_____. 1990. "Pel'meni" [Play "Pelmeni"]. *Iskusstvo kino* 6: 158–71.

_____. 1991c. "Ochered'" [Excerpt from the novel *The Queue*]. *Ogonek* 46: 10–2.

_____. 1991d. "Padëzh" ["The Cattle Plague," excerpt from the novel *The Norm*]. *Volga* 9: 10–29.

_____. 1991e. "Zasedanie zavkoma" ["Next Item on the Agenda"]. *Strelets* 3: 122–35.

_____. 1991f. "Dorozhnoe proisshestvie" ["The Road Accident"]. *Vestnik novoi literatury* 3: 131–46.

_____. 1991g. "Kiset" ["The Tobacco Pouch"]. In Oleg Berg (ed.). *Vidimost' nas: sbornik*, 28–36. Moscow: Vsesoiuznyi Gumanitarnyi Fond im. A.S. Pushkina.

_____. 1991h. "Otkrytie sezona" ["Start of the Season"]. In Oleg Berg (ed.). *Vidimost' nas: sbornik prozy*, 37–43. Moscow: Vsesoiuznyi Gumanitarnyi Fond im. A.S. Pushkina.

_____. 1991i. "Doverie" ["Trust"]. In *Al'manakh LIA R. Elinina*, vyp. 4, 76–116. Moscow: Literaturno-izdatel'skoe agentstvo R. Elinina.

_____. 1992a. *Sbornik rasskazov* [*Collected Stories*]. Moscow: Russlit.

_____. 1992b. "Zabintovannyi shtyr'" ["The Bandaged Dowel"]. *Wiener Slawistischer Almanach Sonderband* 31: 565–8.

_____. [1992]c. *Mesiats v Dakhau* [*A Month in Dachau*]. Cologne: M A.

_____. 1994b. *Norma* [*The Norm*]. Moscow: Obscuri Viri, Tri kita.

_____. 1994c. *Roman* [*A Novel*]. Moscow: Obscuri Viri, Tri kita.

_____. 1994d. "Serdtsa chetyrëkh" ["Four Stout Hearts"]. *Konets veka* 1994: 4–116.

————. 1995b. *Tridtsataia liubov′ Mariny* [*Marina's Thirtieth Love*]. Moscow: Elinin.

————. 1996. "Hochzeitsreise: vodevil′ v piati aktakh" ["The Postnuptial Journey: A Vaudeville in Five Acts"]. *Mesto pechati* 8: 90–137.

————. 1997a. *Dostoevsky-trip*. Moscow: Obscuri Viri.

————. 1998. *Sobranie sochinenii v dvukh tomakh* [*Collected Works in Two Volumes*]. Moscow: Ad Marginem.

————. 1999. *Goluboe salo* [*Blue Lard*]. Moscow: Ad Marginem.

————. 2001a. *Pervyi subbotnik: rasskazy* [*The First Volunteer Saturday Workday: Short Stories*]. Moscow: Ad Marginem.

————. 2001b. *Pir* [*The Feast*]. Moscow: Ad Marginem.

————. 2001c. *Moskva* [*Moscow*]. Moscow: Ad Marginem.

————. 2002a. *Sobranie sochinenii v trekh tomakh* [*Collected Works in Three Volumes*]. Moscow: Ad Marginem.

————. 2002b. *Lëd* [*Ice*]. Moscow: Ad Marginem.

————. 2002c. *Utro snaipera* [*Morning of a Sniper*]. Moscow: Ad Marginem.

————. 2004b. *Put′ Bro* [*Bro's Path*]. Moscow: Zakharov.

————. 2005b. *4*. Moscow: Zakharov.

————. 2005c. "Mea culpa? 'Ia nedostatochno izvrashchen dlia podobnykh eksperimentov'" ["Mea culpa? 'I Am not Perverse enough for Such Experiments'"]. *Nezavisimaia gazeta Exlibris* April 14. Repr. in Boris Sokolov. *Moia kniga o Vladimire Sorokine*, 194–200. Moscow: AIRO-XXI, Probel-2000.

————. 2006a. *Put′ Bro. Lëd. 23 000: Trilogiia* [*Bro's Path. Ice. 23,000: A Trilogy*]. Moscow: Zakharov.

————. 2006b. *Den′ oprichnika* [*Day of the Oprichnik*]. Moscow: Zakharov.

————. 2007b. *Kapital: polnoe sobranie p′es* [*The Capital: Complete Plays*]. Moscow: Zakharov.

————. 2007c. *Loshadinyi sup* [*Horse Soup*]. Moscow: Zakharov.

————. 2008b. *Sakharnyi Kreml′* [*Sugar Kremlin*]. Moscow: Astrel′, AST.

————. 2008c. *Zaplyv: rannie rasskazy i povesti* [*The Swim: Early Stories and Short Novels*]. Moscow: Astrel′, AST, Khranitel′.

————. 2009a. *Ledianaia trilogiia* [*Ice Trilogy*]. Moscow: Astrel′, AST.

————. 2009b. "Kushat′ podano!" ["The Meal Has Been Served"]. *Snob* May 25. www.snob.ru/selected/entry/3245, accessed January 7, 2019.

————. 2010a. *Metel′: povest′* [*The Blizzard: A Short Novel*]. Moscow: Astrel′, AST.

————. 2010b. *Monoklon* [*Monoclone*]. Moscow: Astrel′, AST.

————. 2013. *Telluriia: roman* [*Telluria: A Novel*]. Moscow: AST.

———— (ed.). 2014d. *Russkii zhestokii rasskaz* [*The Russian Cruel Story*]. Moscow: AST.

————. 2016. "Predislovie" ["Preface"]. *Esquire Russkoe Izdanie* August: 14.

————. 2017b. *Manaraga: roman* [*Manaraga: A Novel*]. Moscow: AST.

————. 2018a. *Belyi kvadrat: sbornik korotkoi prozy* [*The White Square: Short Prose Collection*]. Moscow: AST Corpus.

_____. 2018b. *Triumf Vremeni i Beschuvstviia: sbornik libretto* [*Triumph of Time and Insensitivity: A Volume of Libretti*]: Moscow: AST Corpus.

Sorokin, Vladimir; Schwarzstein, Yaroslav. 2019. *Oprichnaia kniga / Das Buch der Opritschniks* [*The Book of the Oprichniks*]. Berlin: ciconia ciconia.

Sorokin, Vladimir; Alekseev, Nikita. 2002. [Interview] *"Lëd, a Lëd, ty kto?"* ["Ice, hey, Ice, Who Are You?"]. *Inostranets*. www.inostranets.ru/cgi-bin/materials.cgi?id=3653&chapter=20, accessed July 4, 2005.

Sorokin, Vladimir; Arkhangel′skii, Andrei. 2003. [Interview] "Na khvoste u Sorokina" ["Tailing Sorokin"]. *Ogonek* 34: 48–50. www.ogoniok.com/win/200334/34-48-50.html, accessed July 4, 2005.

Sorokin, Vladimir; Bavil′skii, Dmitrii. 2004. [Interview] "Komu by Sorokin Nobelevskuiu premiiu dal ..." ["The One to Whom Sorokin Would Award the Nobel Prize ..."]. *Topos* March 11. www.topos.ru/article/3358, accessed January 7, 2019.

_____. 2006. [Interview] "Perestroika u nas eshche ne nachinalas′" ["Perestroika Has Not Started in Russia yet"]. *Vzgliad* August 29 and 30. https://vz.ru/culture/2006/8/29/46870.html and https://vz.ru/culture/2006/8/30/47115.html, accessed January 7, 2019.

Sorokin, Vladimir; Dolin, Anton. 2013. [Interview] "Vladimir Sorokin, pisatel′" ["The Writer Vladimir Sorokin"]. *Vedomosti* October 11. https://www.vedomosti.ru/library/articles/2013/10/11/intervyu-vladimir-sorokin-pisatel, accessed January 7, 2019.

_____. 2017. [Interview] "V Rossii nastoiashchee stalo budushchim, a budushchee slilos′ s proshlym" ["In Russia the Present Has Become the Future, and the Future Has Merged with the Past"]. *Meduza* March 10. https://meduza.io/feature/2017/03/10/v-rossii-nastoyaschee-stalo-buduschim-a-buduschee-slilos-s-proshlym, accessed January 7, 2019.

_____. 2018. [Interview] "Tukhliatina v zamorozhennom vide kak by i ne pakhnet" ["In Frozen Form Rotten Meat Seems Not to Smell"]. *Meduza* August 22. https://meduza.io/feature/2018/08/22/tuhlyatina-v-zamorozhennom-vide-kak-by-i-ne-pahnet, accessed January 7, 2019.

Sorokin, Vladimir; Genis, Aleksandr; Vail′, Petr. 1992. [Interview] "Vesti iz onkologicheskoi kliniki" ["News from the Oncology Hospital"]. *Sintaksis* 32: 138–43.

Sorokin, Vladimir; Gribkova, Elena. 2003. [Interview] "'V 14 let ia napisal eroticheskii rasskaz'" ["'At the Age of Fourteen I Wrote an Erotic Tale'"]. *Moskovskii komsomolets* September 22. www.mk.ru/numbers/577/article17339.htm, accessed May 4, 2005.

Sorokin, Vladimir; Khvors, Liza. 2008. [Interview] "Volodymyr Sorokin pro fantomni boli Bat′kivshchyny" [Ukrainian title and introduction, interview in Russian: "Vladimir Sorokin on the Motherland's Phantom Pains"]. *Pravda* September 12. http://life.pravda.com.ua/surprising/48ca64520f788/, accessed August 27, 2018.

Sorokin, Vladimir; Klimova, Marusia. 1997. [Interview] "Prozaik Vladimir Sorokin zhelaet piterskim chitateliam i pisateliam pobol′she khodit′ v kino" ["The Prose Writer Vladimir Sorokin Recommends that the Readers and Writers of St. Petersburg Go to Cinema More Often"]. *Mitin zhurnal*. http://www.mitin.com/people/klimova/sorokin.shtml, accessed January 7, 2019.

Sorokin, Vladimir; km.ru. 2001. [Interview] "Vladimir Sorokin". *km.ru* December 6. http://www.km.ru/glavnoe/2001/12/06/intervyu-s-izdatelem/vladimir-sorokin, accessed January 7, 2019.

Sorokin, Vladimir; Kochetkova, Natal´ia. 2004. [Interview] "'Ia literaturnyi narkoman, no ia eshche umeiu izgotovliat´ eti narkotiki'" ["I Am a Literary Drug Addict, but I Also Know how to Prepare These Drugs"]. *Izvestiia* September 5: 14, 16.

——. 2005. [Interview] "Mne nado sogret´sia posle *L´da*" ["I Have to Warm Up after *Ice*"]. *Izvestiia* December 14. https://iz.ru/446837/pisatel-vladimir-sorokin-mne-nado-sogret-sia-posle-lda, accessed January 7, 2019.

——. 2010. [Interview] "Obniat´ Metel´" ["Embracing the Blizzard"]. *Izvestiia* April 2. https://srkn.ru/interview/obnyat-metel.html, accessed January 7, 2019.

Sorokin, Vladimir; Kucherskaia, Maiia. 2005. [Interview] "Mnogie budut plakat´" ["Many Will Cry"]. *Polit.ru* March 9. www.polit.ru/culture/2005/03/09/sorokin, accessed August 27, 2018.

Sorokin, Vladimir; Kutlovskaia, Elena. 2005. [Interview] "Spiashchii v nochi: vol´nye zaplyvy Vladimira Sorokina" ["The One Sleeping at Night: Vladimir Sorokin's Free Swims"]. *Nezavisimaia gazeta* September 16. http://www.ng.ru/saturday/2005-09-16/13_sorokin. html, accessed January 7, 2019.

Sorokin, Vladimir; Neverov, Aleksandr. 2002. [Interview] "Proshchai, kontseptualizm!" ["Goodbye, Conceptualism!"]. *Itogi* March 18. http://www.itogi.ru/archive/2002/11/94751.html, accessed January 7, 2019.

Sorokin, Vladimir; Rasskazova, Tat´iana. 1992. [Interview] "Tekst kak narkotik" ["The Text as a Drug"]. In Vladimir Sorokin. *Sbornik rasskazov*, 119–26. Moscow: Russlit.

Sorokin, Vladimir; Reshetnikov, Kirill. 2004. [Interview] "Ia—ne brat Sveta, ia skoree miasnaia mashina" ["I Am not a Brother of the Light, I Am rather a Machine Made of Meat"]. *Gazeta. py*. http://gzt.ru/rub.gzt?rubric=reviu&id=64050700000029002, accessed July 4, 2005.

Sorokin, Vladimir; Roll, Serafima. 1996. [Interview] "Literatura ili kladbishche stilisti-cheskikh nakhodok" ["Literature or a Cemetery of Stylistic Finds"]. In Serafima Roll (ed.). *Postmodernisty o postkul´ture: interv´iu s sovremennymi pisateliami i kritikami*, 123–30. Moscow: Elinin.

Sorokin, Vladimir; Samoilenko, Sergei. 2003. [Interview] "Ia ne tsinik i ne provokator" ["I Am neither a Cynic nor a Provocateur"]. *Novaia Sibir´*. www.newsib.cis.ru/2003/2003_41/artss_1.htm, accessed July 4, 2005.

Sorokin, Vladimir; Saprykin, Iurii. 2017. [Interview] "Ia—beznadezhnoe literaturnoe zhivot-noe" ["I Am an Irredeemable Literary Animal"]. *Gor´kii* March 11. http://gorky.media/context/ya-beznadezhnoe-literaturnoe-zhivotnoe, accessed January 7, 2019.

Sorokin, Vladimir; [Schepp, Matthias; Doerry, Martin]. 2007a. [Interview] "Temnaia energiia obshchestva" ["The Sinister Energy of Society"]. http://www.srkn.ru/interview/spiegel.shtml, accessed January 7, 2019.

Sorokin, Vladimir; Semenova, Oksana. 2002. [Interview] "'Ia khotel napolnit´ russkuiu literaturu govnom'" ["'I Wanted to Fill Russian Literature with Shit'"]. *Moskovskii Komsomolets* July 21. http://laertsky.com/sk/sk_037.htm, accessed January 7, 2019.

Sorokin, Vladimir; Shapoval, Sergei. 1998. [Interview] "'V kul´ture dlia menia net tabu': Vladimir Sorokin otvechaet na voprosy Sergeia Shapovala" ["'In Culture There Are no

Taboos for Me': Vladimir Sorokin Answers the Questions of Sergei Shapoval"]. In Vladimir Sorokin. *Sobranie sochinenii v dvukh tomakh.* Vol. 1, 7–20. Moscow: Ad Marginem.

Sorokin, Vladimir; Shirokova, Sof′ia. 2006. [Interview] "Pisatel′ Vladimir Sorokin: moi *Den′ oprichnika*—eto kupanie avtorskogo krasnogo konia" ["The Writer Vladimir Sorokin Says: My *Day of the Oprichnik* Is an Anti-Soviet Authorial Statement"]. *Izvestiia* August 25. http://izvestia.ru/news/316688, accessed August 24, 2008.

Sorokin, Vladimir; Sokolov, Boris. 2005. [Interview] "Vladimir Sorokin: Rossiia ostaetsia liubovnitsei totalitarizma" ["Vladimir Sorokin: Russia Remains the Concubine of Totalitarianism"]. *Grani* March 23. http://grani.ru/Culture/Literature/m.86612.html, accessed January 7, 2019.

Sorokin, Vladimir; Sobchak, Kseniia. 2017. [Interview] "Ia by pokazal Tolstomu aifon" ["I Would Show Tolstoi the iPhone"]. *L'Officiel* June 21. https://www.lofficielrussia.ru/art/vladimir-sorokin, accessed January 7, 2019.

Sorokin, Vladimir; Suranova, Marina. 2006. [Interview] "Luchshe sobaki druga net" ["There Is no Better Friend than a Dog"]. *Sobesednik* 35: 28.

Sorokin, Vladimir; V.B. 2004. "My vse otravleny literaturoi" ["We Are All Poisoned by Literature"]. *Arba* January. http://www.arba.ru/art/849/7, accessed January 7, 2019.

Sorokin, Vladimir; Voznesenskii, Aleksandr. 2006. [Interview] "Zakony russkoi metafiziki" ["The Laws of Russian Metaphysics"]. October 26. www.srkn.ru/interview/voznesenski.shtml, accessed January 7, 2019.

Significant Texts in Other Languages

Sorokin, Vladimir. 1991j. "Mit Solschenizyn auf die Straße" [German: "Onto the Street with Solzhenitsyn"]. Trans. Peter Urban. *die tageszeitung* November 15: 25–6.

―――. 1992d. *Ein Monat in Dachau* [German: *A Month in Dachau*]. Trans. Peter Urban. Zurich: Haffmans.

―――. 1997b. *Pelmeni. Hochzeitsreise: Zwei Stücke* [German: *Pelmeni. The Postnuptial Journey: Two Plays*]. Trans. Barbara Lehmann. Frankfurt/Main: Verlag der Autoren.

―――. 2014d. "Die Ukraine ist in uns eingedrungen" [German: "Ukraine Has Penetrated Us"]. Trans. Kerstin Holm. *Frankfurter Allgemeine Zeitung* July 24.

―――. 2015b. "Putins Zeitmaschine" [German: "Putin's Time Machine"]. Trans. Dorothea Trottenberg. *Die Zeit* March 10: 41–2.

Sorokin, Vladimir; Ahrest-Korotkova, Svitlana. 2010. "Volodymyr Sorokin: Problema v tomu, shcho Rosiia ne pokhovala 'sovok'" [Ukrainian: "Vladimir Sorokin: The Problem Is that Russia Has Not Buried the 'Soviet Union'"]. *Den′* November 5. https://day.kyiv.ua/print/116203, accessed January 7, 2019.

Sorokin, Vladimir; Bonet, Pilar; Fernandez, Rodrigo. 2002. "'El totalitarismo es una planta exótica y venenosa, sumamente rara y peligrosa'" [Spanish: "'Totalitarianism Is an Exotic, Poisonous, Extremely Rare and Dangerous Plant'"]. https://elpais.com/diario/2002/09/22/domingo/1032666757_850215.html, accessed January 7, 2019.

Sorokin, Vladimir; Drubek-Meyer, Natascha. 1995. [Interview] "Russland und Deutschland: Eine missglückte Romanze" [German: "Russia and Germany: A Failed Romance"]. *Via Regia* May/June: 67–71.

Sorokin, <Vladimir> Vladimír; Pavelka, Zdenko. 2010. "Opričníci přesedlali na mercedesy, říká ruský spisovatel Vladimír Sorokin" [Czech: "The Oprichniks Have Switched to Mercedes, Says the Russian Writer Vladimir Sorokin"]. *Novinky.cz* April 21. https://www.novinky.cz/kultura/salon/197631-opricnici-presedlali-na-mercedesy-rika-rusky-spisovatel-vladimir-sorokin.html, accessed January 7, 2019.

Sorokin, <Vladimir> Władimir; Piotrowska, Agnieszka L.; Sobolewska, Justyna. 2014. [Interview] "Organizm w agonii" [Polish: "Organism in Agony"]. Trans. Agnieszka L. Piotrowska. *Polityka* September 3–9: 77–9.

Sorokin, Vladimir; Schepp, Matthias; Doerry, Martin. 2007b. [Interview] "Die finstere Energie unseres Landes" [German: "The Sinister Energy of Our Country"]. *Der Spiegel* 5: 106–8.

Sorokin, Vladimir; Shchulinskii, Igor´. 2018. [Interview] "Kak chitat´ moi rasskaz? Vstat´ s voskhodom solntsa, napolnit´ vedro vodoi, razdet´sia dogola ..." ["How to Read My Short Story? Get up with the Sunrise, Fill a Bucket of Water, and Strip Naked ..."]. *Moskvich MAG.* https://moskvichmag.ru/владимир-сорокин-как-читать-мой-расс/, accessed January 7, 2019.

Sorokin, Vladimir; Tetzlaff, Marie. 2009. "Forfatter: Rusland er atter blevet en politistat" [Danish: "The Author Says: Russia Is and Remains a Police State"]. *Politiken* December 10. https://politiken.dk/kultur/boger/interview_boger/art5385229/Forfatter-Rusland-er-atter-blevet-en-politistat, accessed January 7, 2019.

Sorokin, Vladimir; Thumann, Michael. 2014. "Auch Stalin wäre schockiert" [German: "Stalin Would Be Shocked as Well"]. *Die Zeit* October 30: 47.

Sorokin, Vladimir; Żebrowska, Anna. 2011. "Średniowiecze w mercedesie" [Polish: "The Middle Ages in a Mercedes"]. *Gazeta Wyborcza* February 6. http://wyborcza.pl/1,75410,9069228,Sredniowiecze_w_mercedesie.html, accessed January 7, 2019.

Research and Other Literature

Abasheva, Marina P. 2012. "Sorokin nulevykh: v prostranstve mifov o natsional´noi identichnosti" [Russian: "The Sorokin of the 2000s: In the Realm of Myths about National Identity"]. *Vestnik Permskogo universiteta: rossiiskaia i zarubezhnaia filologiia* 1: 202–9.

Ågren, Mattias. 2008. "Den totalitära myten: Vladimir Sorokins *Trilogija*" [Swedish: "The Totalitarian Myth: Vladimir Sorokin's *Trilogy*"]. In Ingunn Lunde, Sanna Witt (eds.). *Terminal Øst: Totalitære og posttotalitære diskurser*, 75–87. Oslo: Spartacus.

————. 2014. *Phantoms of a Future Past: A Study of Contemporary Russian Anti-Utopian Novels.* PhD dissertation. Stockholm University.

Akinsha, Konstantin (ed.). 2011. "Between Lent and Carnival: Moscow Conceptualism and Sots Art (Differences, Similarities, Interconnections): A Series of Interviews." Trans. Konstantin Akinsha. In Alla Rosenfeld (ed.). *Moscow Conceptualism in Context*, 24–47. Munich et al.: Prestel.

"Aktivisty." 2016. "Aktivisty potrebovali zapretit´ rasskaz Sorokina 'Nastia'" [Russian: "Activists Demanded the Prohibition of Sorokin's Short Story 'Nastia'"]. *Novaia Gazeta* August 23. https://www.novayagazeta.ru/news/2016/08/23/124370-aktivisty-potrebovali-zapretit-rasskaz-sorokina-nastya, accessed January 7, 2019.

Alaniz, José. 2013. "The Writer's Speech: Stuttering, Glossolalia and the Body in Sorokin's *A Month in Dachau*." In Tine Roesen, Dirk Uffelmann (eds.). *Vladimir Sorokin's Languages*, 209–29. Bergen: University of Bergen. Also online: http://boap.uib.no/books/sb/catalog/book/9, accessed January 7, 2019.

Andreeva, Natal´ia N.; Bibergan, Ekaterina S. 2012. *Igry i teksty Vladimira Sorokina* [Russian: *Vladimir Sorokin's Games and Texts*]. St. Petersburg: Petropolis.

Anninskii, Lev. 2001. "Pesn´ pepsi v utrobe pokoleniia, kotoroe smeias´ rasstalos´ so svoim budushchim" [Russian: *"Pepsi Song in the Womb of a Generation Which Laughingly Said Goodbye to Its Future"*]. *Dvadtsat´ dva* 120: 110–24.

Aptekman, Marina. 2006. "Kabbalah, Judeo-Masonic Myth, and Post-Soviet Literary Discourse: From Political Tool to Virtual Parody." *The Russian Review* 65.4: 657–81.

———. 2009. "Forward to the Past, or Two Radical Views on the Russian Nationalist Future: Pyotr Krasnov's *Behind the Thistle* and Vladimir Sorokin's *Day of an Oprichnik*." *Slavic and East European Journal* 53.2: 241–60.

———. 2013. "The Old New Russian: The Dual Nature of Style and Language in *Day of the Oprichnik* and *Sugar Kremlin*." In Tine Roesen, Dirk Uffelmann (eds.). *Vladimir Sorokin's Languages*, 282–97. Bergen: University of Bergen. Also online: http://boap.uib.no/books/sb/catalog/book/9, accessed January 7, 2019.

Arkhangel´skii, Aleksandr. 2014. "Oprichnina vmesto elity" [Russian: "An Oprichnina instead of an Elite"]. *Republic.ru* June 11. https://republic.ru/world/peis_gology-1112166.xhtml, accessed January 7, 2019.

Artwińska, Anna. 2017. "The (Post-)Communist Orient: History, Self-Orientalization and Subversion by Michał Witkowski and Vladimir Sorokin." *Zeitschrift für Slawistik* 62.3: 404–26.

Bakshtein, Iosif. 1993. "Zametki o literaturnom kontseptualizme / Bemerkungen zum literarischen Konzeptualismus" [Russian and German: "Remarks on Conceptualism in Literature"]. In Il´ia Kabakov. *NOMA ili Moskovskii kontseptual´nyi krug / NOMA oder Der Kreis der Moskauer Konzeptualisten*. 61–5. Stuttgart: Cantz.

Barabanov, Yevgeny. 2011. "Moscow Conceptualism: Between Self-Definition and Doctrine." Trans. Lynn Visson. In Alla Rosenfeld (ed.). *Moscow Conceptualism in Context*, 48–99. Munich et al.: Prestel.

Barry, Ellen. 2011. "From a Novelist, Shock Treatment for Mother Russia." *The New York Times* April 29.

Basinskii, Pavel. 2010. "Otmetelilsia: vyshla novaia kniga Vladimira Sorokina" [Russian: "He Snow Stormed off: New Book by Vladimir Sorokin Released"]. *Rossiiskaia gazeta* April 13. http://www.rg.ru/2010/04/13/metel.html, accessed January 7, 2019.

Bavil'skii, Dmitrii V. 2006. "*Mertvye dushi* na novorusskii lad" [Russian: "*Dead Souls* à la nouveau russe"]. *Vzgliad* August 29. https://vz.ru/columns/2006/8/29/46871.html, accessed January 7, 2019.

Belovinskii, Leonid V. 2017. *Povsednevnaia zhizn' cheloveka sovetskoi epokhi: predmetnyi mir i sotsial'noe prostranstvo* [Russian: *Everyday Life in the Soviet Period: The World of Objects and the Social Realm*]. Moscow: Akademicheskii proekt, Triksta.

Berg, Mikhail. 2000. *Literaturokratiia: problema prisvoeniia i pererpredeleniia vlasti v literature* [Russian: *Literaturocracy: The Appropriation and Redistribution of Power in Literature*]. Moscow: Novoe literaturnoe obozrenie.

Beumers, Birgit; Lipovetsky, Mark. 2009. *Performing Violence: Literary and Theatrical Experiments of New Russian Drama*. Bristol, Chicago (IL).

Bibergan, Ekaterina S. 2014. *Rytsar' bez strakha i upreka: khudozhestvennoe svoeobrazie prozy Vladimira Sorokina* [Russian: *A Knight without Fear and beyond Reproach: The Artistic Diversity of Vladimir Sorokin's Prose*]. 2nd edition. St. Petersburg: Petropolis.

Bibergan, Ekaterina S.; Bogdanova, Ol'ga V. 2014. "Ideino-khudozhestvennoe svoeobrazie romana Vladimira Sorokina *Roman*" [Russian: "The Conceptual and Artistic Diversity of Vladimir Sorokin's Novel *A Novel*"]. In Ekaterina S. Bibergan. *Rytsar' bez strakha i upreka: khudozhestvennoe svoeobrazie prozy Vladimira Sorokina*, 228–313. St. Petersburg: Petropolis.

Blair, Elaine. 2009. "The Wait: On Vladimir Sorokin." *The Nation* March 25. https://www.thenation.com/article/wait-vladimir-sorokin/, accessed January 7, 2019.

Bogdanova, Ol'ga V. 2005. *Kontseptualist, pisatel' i khudozhnik Vladimir Sorokin* [Russian: *The Conceptualist Writer and Artist Vladimir Sorokin*]. St. Petersburg: Filologicheskii fakul'tet Sankt-Peterburgskogo gosudarstvennogo universiteta.

Bondarenko, Maria. 2002. "Roman-attraktsion i katastroficheskaia dekonstruktsiia" [Russian: "The Novel as a Joy Ride and Catastrophic Deconstruction"]. *Novoe literaturnoe obozrenie* 56: 241–8.

Bondarenko, Vladimir. 1995. "Fekal'naia proza Sorokina Vovy" [Russian: "Vova Sorokin's Fecal Prose"]. In *Krakh intelligentsii: zlye zametki Zoila*, 147–9. Moscow: Paleia.

———. 2010. "Vladimir Sorokin teper' v Meteli" [Russian: "Vladimir Sorokin, now in a Blizzard"]. *Proza.ru* April 22. http://www.proza.ru/2010/04/22/978, accessed January 7, 2019.

Borenstein, Eliot. 2005. "Stripping the Nation Bare: Russian Pornography and the Insistence on Meaning." In Lisa Z. Sigel (ed.). *International Exposure: Perspectives on Modern European Pornography, 1800–2000*, 232–54. New Brunswick (NJ): Rutgers University Press.

Borenstein, Eliot. 2019. *Plots against Russia: Conspiracy and Fantasy after Socialism*. Ithaca (NY), London: Cornell University Press.

———. 2015. "Dystopias and Catastrophe Tales after Chernobyl." In Evgeny Dobrenko, Mark Lipovetsky (eds.). *Russian Literature since 1991*, 86–103. Cambridge: Cambridge University Press.

Boym, Svetlana. 1994. *Common Places: Mythologies of Everyday Life in Russia*. Cambridge (MA), London: Harvard University Press.

Breslauer, George W. 2002. *Gorbachev and Yeltsin as Leaders*. Cambridge: Cambridge University Press.

Brockhoff, Annette. 1992. "Schießt meine körper dicke bertha im himmel groß Deutschland. Versuch über Vladimir Sorokin" [German: "Shoot my bodies big bertha in the sky great Germany: An Essay into Vladimir Sorokin"]. *Schreibheft* 40: 136–43.

Brougher, Valentina. 1998. "Demythologising Socialist Realism: Vladimir Sorokin's *Marina's Thirtieth Love*." *Australian Slavonic and East European Studies* 12.1: 97–113.

Brouwer, Sander. 2006. "Sorokins IJs-Trilogie" [Dutch: "Sorokin's *Ice Trilogy*"]. *Tijdschrift voor Slavische Literatuur* 45: 59–63.

Brouwer, Sander; Noordenbos, Boris. 2006. "Vladimir Sorokins Blauw spek—een shot voor literaire junkies" [Dutch: "Vladimir Sorokin's *Blue Lard*—a Shot for Literary Junkies"]. *Tijdschrift voor Slavische Literatuur* 45: 35–41.

Buida, Iurii. 1994. "'Nechto nichto' Vladimira Sorokina" [Russian: "Vladimir Sorokin's Some Sort of Nothing"]. *Nezavisimaia gazeta* April 5: 7.

Bulgakov, Mikhail. 1968. *Master i Margarita: roman* [Russian: *The Master and Margarita: A Novel*]. Paris: YMCA-Press.

———. 1997. *The Master and Margarita*. Trans. Richard Pevear, Larissa Volokhonsky. London et al.: Penguin.

Burkhart, Dagmar. 1997. "Intertextualität und Ästhetik des Häßlichen: Zu Vladimir Sorokins Erzählung 'Obelisk'" [German: "Intertextuality and the Aesthetics of the Nasty: On Vladimir Sorokin's Short Story 'Obelisk'"]. In Elisabeth Cheauré (ed.). *Kultur und Krise: Rußland 1987–1997*, 253–66. Berlin: Spitz.

——— (ed.). 1999. *Poetik der Metadiskursivität: Zum postmodernen Prosa-, Film- und Dramenwerk von Vladimir Sorokin* [German: *Poetics of Metadiscursivity: On Vladimir Sorokin's Postmodern Prose, Film, and Drama Oeuvre*]. Munich: Otto Sagner.

Butrin, Dmitrii. 2017. "Samoszhigaiushcheesia prorochestvo: novyi roman *Manaraga* Vladimira Sorokina—o budushchikh nas vnutri Evropy" [Russian: "Self-Inflaming Prophecy: Vladimir Sorokin's New Novel about Future Us in Europe, *Manaraga*"]. *Kommersant.ru* March 13. https://www.kommersant.ru/doc/3240558, accessed January 7, 2019.

Caillois, Roger. 1961. *Man, Play, and Games*. Trans. Meyer Barash. New York: Free Press of Glencoe.

———. 1977. *Les Jeux et les Hommes* [French: *Games and People*]. Paris: Gallimard.

Caramitti, Mario. 2018. "Il neo-medioevo di Sorokin" [Italian: "Sorokin's New Middle Ages"]. *Il manifesto* July 1. https://ilmanifesto.it/il-neo-medioevo-di-sorokin/, accessed January 7, 2019.

Caryl, Christian. 2007. "Ice Capades." *The New York Review of Books* September 27: 60–3.

Chantsev, Aleksandr. 2007. "Fabrika antiutopii: sotsial´nye fobii v sovremennom russkom romane" [Russian: "Dystopia Factory: Social Phobias in Russian Contemporary Novels"]. *Novoe literaturnoe obozrenie* 86: 269–301.

Chernetsky, Vitaly. 2007. *Mapping Postcommunist Cultures: Russia and Ukraine in the Context of Globalization*. Montreal et al.: McGill-Queen's University Press.

Chitnis, Rajendra A. 2005. *Literature in Post-Communist Russia and Eastern Europe: The Russian, Czech and Slovak Fiction of the Changes, 1988–1998.* London, New York: RoutledgeCurzon.

Clark, Katerina. 2000. *The Soviet Novel: History as Ritual.* 3rd edition. Bloomington (IN), Indianapolis: Indiana University Press.

Danilenko, Iuliia. 2012. "Reministsentsii klassiki v sovremennom tekste (na materiale povesti *Metel'* Vladimira Sorokina)" [Russian: "Reminiscences of the Classics in a Contemporary Text (on the material of Vladimir Sorokin's Short Novel *The Blizzard*"]. *Filologicheskii klass* 28.2: 113–6.

Danilkin, Lev. 1996. "Modelirovanie diskursa (po romanu Vladimira Sorokina *Roman*)" [Russian: "The Modeling of Discourse (on the Example of Vladimir Sorokin's *A Novel*"]. In Ol'ga M. Goncharova (ed.). *Literaturovedenie XXI veka. Analiz teksta: metod i rezul'tat. Materialy mezhdunarodnoi konferentsii studentov-filologov, Sankt-Peterburg, 19–21 aprelia 1996 goda,* 155–9. St. Petersburg: Rossiiskii gosudarstvennyi pedagogicheskii universitet imeni A. I. Gertsena.

———. 2002. "Serdtse Sorokina" [Russian: "Sorokin's Heart"]. *Afisha* April 29. https://daily. afisha.ru/archive/gorod/archive/vladimir_sorokin/, accessed January 7, 2019.

———. 2006. "Vladimir Sorokin: *Den' oprichnika*" [Russian: "Vladimir Sorokin: *Day of the Oprichnik*"]. September 9. http://www.srkn.ru/criticism/ldanilkin.shtml, accessed January 7, 2019.

———. 2013. "*Telluriia* kak entsiklopediia russkoi rechi" [Russian: "*Telluria* as an Encyclopedia of Russian Speech"]. *Afisha Vozdukh* October 17. http://www.srkn.ru/criticism/telluri-ya-kak-entsiklopediya-russkoi-rechi.html, accessed January 7, 2019.

———. 2017. "O chem na samom dele *Manaraga* Vladimira Sorokina" [Russian: "What Vladimir Sorokin's *Manaraga* Is Really About"]. *Afisha* March 14. https://daily.afisha. ru/brain/4792-o-chem-na-samom-dele-manaraga-vladimira-sorokina-obyasnyaet-lev-danilkin/, accessed Dezember 19, 2017.

Davidzon, Vladislav. 2011. "Russia's Enfant Terrible: On Vladimir Sorokin." *Bookforum* August 8. https://www.bookforum.com/review/8142, accessed January 7, 2019.

Degot', Ekaterina. 1991. "Priiatnye zaniatiia" [Russian: "Pleasant Preoccupations"]. *Tvorchestvo* 11: 16–8.

———. 1999. "Kinostsenarii Vladimira Sorokina *Moskva* v novorusskom i postavangardnom kontekstakh" [Russian: "Vladimir Sorokin's Film Script *Moscow* in the New-Russian and Post-Avant-Garde Context"]. In Dagmar Burkhart (ed.). *Poetik der Metadiskursivität: Zum postmodernen Prosa-, Film- und Dramenwerk von Vladimir Sorokin,* 223–8. Munich: Sagner.

Degot', Ekaterina; Sal'nikov, Vladimir. 2000. "Retsept dekonstruktsii" [Russian: "Recipe for Deconstruction"]. *Pushkin* 4. http://klinamen.comli.com/read2.html, accessed January 7, 2019.

de Man, Paul. 1979. *Allegories of Reading,* New Haven (CT): Yale University Press.

Deutschmann, Peter. 1998. "Dialog der Texte und Folter: Vladimir Sorokins *Mesjac v Dachau*" [German: "Dialogue of Texts and Torture: Vladimir Sorokin's *A Month in Dachau*"]. In Christine Gölz, Anja Otto, Reinhold Vogt (eds.). *Romantik–Moderne–Postmoderne: Beiträge zum ersten Kolloquium des Jungen Forums Slavistische Literaturwissenschaft, Hamburg 1996*, 324–51. Frankfurt/Main et al.: Lang.

———. 1999. "Der Begriff der Norm bei Sorokin" [German: "The Notion of the Norm in Sorokin"]. In Dagmar Burkhart (ed.). *Poetik der Metadiskursivität: Zum postmodernen Prosa-, Film- und Dramenwerk von Vladimir Sorokin*, 37–52. Munich: Sagner.

———. 2003. *Intersubjektivität und Narration: Gogol´, Erofeev, Sorokin, Mamleev* [German: *Intersubjectivity and Narration: Gogol´, Erofeev, Sorokin, Mamleev*]. Frankfurt/Main et al.: Lang.

———. 2009. "Der Text als Droge: Glosse zu einem metaliterarischen Vergleich" [German: "The Text as a Drug: A Gloss on a Meta-Literary Comparison"]. *Plurale* 8: 145–74.

Dobrenko, Evgenii. 1990. "Preodolenie ideologii: zametki o sots-arte" [Russian: "Overcoming Ideology: Remarks on Sots-Art"]. *Volga* 11: 164–84.

———. 1999. *Formovka sovetskogo pisatelia: sotsial´nye i esteticheskie istoki sovetskoi literaturnoi kul´tury* [Russian: *The Formation of the Soviet Writer: The Social and Aesthetic Origins of the Soviet Literary Culture*]. St. Petersburg: Akademicheskii proekt.

——— (Dobrenko, Evgeny). 2011. "Socialist Realism." In Evgeny Dobrenko, Marina Balina (eds.). *The Cambridge Companion to Twentieth-Century Russian Literature*, 97–114. Cambridge: Cambridge University Press.

Dobrenko, Evgenii; Kalinin, Il´ia; Lipovetskii, Mark (eds.). 2018. *"Eto prosto bukvy na bumage…" Vladimir Sorokin: posle literatury* [Russian: *"It Is just Letters on Paper …" Vladimir Sorokin: After Literature*]. Moscow: Novoe literaturnoe obozrenie.

Döring-Smirnov, Johanna R. 1992. "Gender Shifts in der russischen Postmoderne" [German: "Gender Shifts in Russian Postmodernism"]. In Aage A. Hansen-Löve (ed.). *Psychopoetik: Beiträge zur Tagung Psychologie und Literatur. München 1991*, 557–63. Vienna: Gesellschaft zur Förderung Slawistischer Studien.

———. 1995. "Eine Axt für die Idylle: Sorokins Roman *Roman*—wieder das 'Ende der Literatur' oder Literatur nach ihrem Ende?" [German: "An Axe for the Idyll: Sorokin's Novel *A Novel*—the 'End of Literature' again or Literature after Its End?"]. *Süddeutsche Zeitung* November 4/5: Literatur iv.

Douzjian, Myrna A. 2013. *Resistant Postmodernisms: Writing Postcommunism in Armenia and Russia*. PhD dissertation. University of California Los Angeles.

Dreyer, Nicolas. 2011. *"Post-Soviet Neo-Modernism": An Approach to "Postmodernism" and Humour in the Post-Soviet Russian Fiction of Vladimir Sorokin, Vladimir Tuchkov and Aleksandr Khurgin*. PhD dissertation. University of St Andrews.

Dugin, Aleksandr G. 2000. *Osnovy geopolitiki: geopoliticheskoe budushchee Rossii: myslit´ prostranstvom* [Russian: *Principles of Geopolitics: The Geopolitical Future of Russia: Considering Space*]. 4th edition. Moscow: Arktogeia-Tsentr.

Dugin, Alexander. 2014. *Putin vs. Putin: Vladimir Putin Viewed from the Right*. Trans. Gustaf Nielsen. London: Arktos.

Engel, Alexander. 2017. "The Presence of Sacralization: The Configuration of Presence in Vladimir Sorokin's *Kremlin Made of Sugar*." In Markus Gottwald, Kay Kirchmann, Heike Paul (eds.). *(Extra) Ordinary Presence: Social Configurations and Cultural Repertoires*, 137–56. Bielefeld: Transcript.

Engel, Christine. 1997. "Sorokin im Kontext der russischen Postmoderne: Problem der Wirklichkeitskonstruktion" [German: "Sorokin in the Context of Russian Postmodernism: The Problem of Constructing Reality"]. *Wiener Slavistisches Jahrbuch* 43: 53–66.

———. 1999. "Sorokins allesverschlingendes Unbewußtes: Inkorporation als kannibalischer Akt" ["Sorokin's All-Swallowing Unconscious: Incorporation as a Cannibalistic Act"]. In Dagmar Burkhart (ed.). *Poetik der Metadiskursivität: Zum postmodernen Prosa-, Film- und Dramenwerk von Vladimir Sorokin*, 139–49. Munich: Sagner.

———. 2009. "Der Kampf um Deutungsmacht als inszenierter Skandal: Vladimir Sorokin im Bol´šoj-Theater" [German: "The Struggle for the Power of Interpretation as a Staged Scandal: Vladimir Sorokin at Bol´shoi Theater"]. 2nd edition. In Stefan Neuhaus, Johann Holzner (eds.). *Literatur als Skandal: Fälle—Funktionen—Folgen*, 707–17. Gottingen: Vandenhoeck & Ruprecht.

Epshtein, Mikhail. 1989. "Iskusstvo avangarda i religioznoe soznanie" [Russian: "Avant-Garde Art and Religious Consciousness"]. *Novyi mir* 12: 222–35.

———. 1990. "Katalog novykh poezii" [Russian: "A Catalog of New Poetries"]. In Walter Thümler (ed.). *Moderne russische Poesie seit 1966: Eine Anthologie*, 359–63. Berlin: Oberbaum.

——— (Epstein). 1995. *After the Future: The Paradoxes of Postmodernism and Contemporary Russian Culture*. Trans. Anesa Miller-Pogacar. Amherst (MA): The University of Massachusetts Press.

———. 2018. "Norma u Platona i Vladimira Sorokina" [Russian: "The Norm in Plato and Vladimir Sorokin"]. In Evgenii Dobrenko, Il´ia Kalinin, Mark Lipovetskii (eds.). *"Eto prosto bukvy na bumage …" Vladimir Sorokin: posle literatury*, 327–31. Moscow: Novoe literaturnoe obozrenie.

Ermolin, Evgenii. 2003. "Pis´mo ot Vovochki" [Russian: "Letter from Vovochka Sorokin"]. *Kontinent* 115: 402–18.

Erofeyev, Victor. 1995. "Russia's *Fleurs du Mal*." Trans. Andrew Reynolds. In Victor Erofeyev, Andrew Reynolds (eds.). *New Russian Writing: Russia's Fleurs du Mal*, ix–xxx. London et al.: Penguin.

Erofeev, Viktor. 1997. "Russkie tsvety zla" [Russian: "Russian Flowers of Evil"]. In Viktor Erofeev (ed.). *Russkie tsvety zla: Sbornik*, 7–30. Moscow: Podkova.

Eşanu, Octavian. 2013. *Transition in Post-Soviet Art: The Collective Actions Group Before and After 1989*. Budapest, New York: Central European University Press.

Etkind, Aleksandr. 2003. "Russkaia literatura, XIX vek: roman vnutrennei kolonizatsii" [Russian: "Russian Literature, Nineteenth Century: The Novel of Internal Colonization"]. *Novoe literaturnoe obozrenie* 59: 103–24.

———<Etkind, Alexander>. 2009. "Stories of the Undead in the Land of the Unburied: Magical Historicism in Contemporary Russian Fiction." *Slavic Review* 68.3: 631–58.

Etkind, Aleksandr; Lipovetskii, Mark. 2008. "Vozvrashchenie tritona: sovetskaia katastrofa i postsovetskii roman" [Russian: "Triton's Return: The Soviet Catastrophy and the Post-Soviet Novel"]. *Novoe literaturnoe obozrenie* 94: 174–206.

Filimonova, Tatiana. 2014. "Chinese Russia: Imperial Consciousness in Vladimir Sorokin's Writing." *Region* 3.2: 219–44.

Firsov, Boris M. 2008. *Raznomyslie v SSSR: 1940–1960-e gody. Istoriia, teoriia i praktika* [Russian: *Diversity of Thinking in the USSR: 1940s–1960s: History, Theory and Practices*]. St. Petersburg: Izdatel´stvo Evropeiskogo universiteta v Sankt-Peterburge.

Flickinger, Brigitte. 1997. "Dismorphie: Gestaltverlust als Merkmal postsowjetischer Mentalität (am Beispiel der Prosa Vladimir Sorokins)" [German: "Dysmorphy: The Loss of Gestalt as a Feature of Post-Soviet Mentality (on the Example of Vladimir Sorokin's Prose"]. In Elisabeth Cheauré (ed.). *Kultur und Krise: Rußland 1987–1997*, 243–51. Berlin: Spitz.

Franz, Norbert. 2013. "Der Opričnik" [German: "The Oprichnik"]. In Laura Burlon, Nina Frieß, Irina Gradinari, Katarzyna Różańska, Peter Salden (eds.). *Verbrechen—Fiktion—Vermarktung: Gewalt in den zeitgenössischen slavischen Literaturen*. 45–63. Potsdam: Universitäts-Verlag.

Gabowitsch, Mischa. 2017. *Protest in Putin's Russia*. Trans. from German and Russian: Mischa Gabowitsch. Cambridge, Malden (MA): Polity.

Gambrell, Jamey. 2015. "Russia's New Vigilantes." In Lawrence J. Trudeau (ed.). *Contemporary Literary Criticism: Criticism of the Works of Today's Novelists, Poets, Playwrights, Short-Story Writers, Scriptwriters, and Other Creative Writers*. Vol. 374, 209–14. Farmington Hills (MI): Gale.

Gambrell, Jamey; Rudick, Nicole. 2011. [Interview] "Jamey Gambrell on Vladimir Sorokin." *The Paris Review* June 23. https://www.theparisreview.org/blog/2011/06/23/jamey-gambrell-on-vladimir-sorokin/, accessed January 7, 2019.

Genis, Aleksandr A. 1997. "'Chyzn´ i zhido': Vladimir Sorokin" [Russian: "Mirfe and Liacle: Vladimir Sorokin"]. *Zvezda* 10: 222–5.

———— (Genis, Alexander). 1999. "Postmodernism and *Sots-Realism*: From Andrei Sinyavsky to Vladimir Sorokin." In Mikhail Epstein, Alexander Genis, Slobodanka Vladiv-Glover (eds.). *Russian Postmodernism: New Perspectives on Post-Soviet Culture*, 197–211. Oxford, New York: Berghahn.

————. 2011. *Dovlatov i okrestnosti* [Russian: *Around Dovlatov*]. Moscow: Astrel´, Corpus.

Gerasimov, Il´ia. 2008. "'Pravda russkogo tela i sladostnoe nasilie voobrazhaemogo soobshchestva'" [Russian: "The Truth of the Russian Body and the Delightful Seduction of Violence in the Imagined Community"]. *Ab Imperio* 3: 401–16.

Gessen, Masha. 2017. *The Future Is History: How Totalitarianism Reclaimed Russia*. London Granta.

Gierzinger, Georg. 2008. "Neues Bewusstsein durch schwule Sexualität: Funktion und Konstruktion homosexueller Männlichkeit bei Vladimir Sorokin und Viktor Erofeev" [German: "New Consciousness through Gay Sexuality: The Function and Construction of Homosexual Masculinity in Vladimir Sorokin and Viktor Erofeev"]. In Miranda Jakiša, Thomas Skowronek (eds.). *Osteuropäische Lektüren II: Texte zum 8. Treffen des Jungen Forums Slavistische Literaturwissenschaft*, 53–62. Frankfurt/M. et al.: Lang.

Giliarov, Kirill. 2008. *Rasshifrovannyi Sorokin* [Russian: *Deciphered Sorokin*]. Moscow: Pallada.

Gillespie, David. 1997. "Sex, Violence and the Video Nasty: The Ferocious Prose of Vladimir Sorokin." *The Journal of the British Neo-Formalist Circle* 22: 158–75.

————. 1998. "Vladimir Georgievich Sorokin 1955–: Prose Writer." In Neil Cornwell, Nicole Christian (eds.). *Reference Guide to Russian Literature*, 779–81. London, Chicago (IL): Fitzroy Dearborn Publishers.

———. 2000. "Vladimir Sorokin and the Norm." In Arnold McMillin (ed.). *Reconstructing the Canon: Russian Writing in the 1980s*, 299–309. Amsterdam: Harwood.

———. 2016. "Vladimir Sorokin and the Return of History." In Olga Tabachnikova (ed.). *Facets of Russian Irrationalism between Art and Life: Mystery inside Enigma*, 519–30. Leiden, Boston (MA): Brill Rodopi.

Glanc, Tomáš. 1995. "Papír pokrytý tiskařskou barvou" [Czech: "Paper Covered with Printer's Ink"]. In Vladimir Sorokin. *Třicátá Marinina láska*, 9–14. Prague: Český spisovatel.

———. 2003. "'Trvá to celou věčnost!' Fronta Vladimira Sorokina 2003: souvislosti tvorby" [Czech: "'This Takes an Eternity!' Vladimir Sorokin's *The Queue* in 2003: Continuities in His Oeuvre"]. In Vladimir Sorokin. *Fronta*. Trans. Jakub Šedivý, 5–19. Prague: Malá Skála.

———. 2005. "Narkotická literatura podle Sorokina" [Czech: "Narcotic Literature according to Sorokin"]. *Revolver Revue* 58: 135–6.

———. 2014. "The Process of Canonisation in Russian Literature in the Late Twentieth and Early Twenty-First Century: Theses for Analysis." In Yordan Lyutskanov, Hristo Manolakev, Radostin Rusev (eds.). *Russian Classical Literature Today: The Challenges / Trials of Messianism and Mass Culture*, 58–70. Cambridge: Cambridge Scholars Publishing.

———. 2017. *Autoren im Ausnahmezustand: Die tschechische und russische Parallelkultur* [German: *Writers in a State of Emergency: Czech and Russian Parallel Cultures*]. Münster: LIT.

———. 2018. "Antropologicheskie narkotiki Sorokina" [Russian: "Sorokin's Anthropological Drugs"]. In Evgenii Dobrenko, Il´ia Kalinin, Mark Lipovetskii (eds.). *"Eto prosto bukvy na bumage…" Vladimir Sorokin: posle literatury*, 204–18. Moscow: Novoe literaturnoe obozrenie.

Goehrke, Carsten. 2003–2005. *Russischer Alltag* [German: *Russian Everyday Life*]. 3 vols. Zurich: Chronos.

Gołąbek, Bartosz. 2012. *Lew Gumilow i Aleksander Dugin: o dwóch obliczach eurazjatyzmu w Rosji po 1991 roku* [Polish: *Lev Gumilev and Aleksandr Dugin: Two Faces of Eurasianism in Russia after 1991*]. Cracow: Wydawnictwo Uniwersytetu Jagiellońskiego.

Gorokhov, Andrei; Shevtsov, Vasilii. 2004. "Dal´neishee raschlenenie Sorokina" [Russian: "Sorokin's Ongoing Mutilation"]. *Topos* September 30. www.topos.ru/article/2828, accessed January 7, 2019.

Goscilo, Helena. 2013 (ed.). *Putin as Celebrity and Cultural Icon*. London, New York: Routledge.

Grigoryeva, Nadezhda. 2013. "Speak, Heart …: Vladimir Sorokin's Mystical Language." In Tine Roesen, Dirk Uffelmann (eds.). *Vladimir Sorokin's Languages*, 108–27. Bergen: University of Bergen. Also online: http://boap.uib.no/books/sb/catalog/book/9, accessed January 7, 2019.

Groys, Boris E. 1979. "Moskovskii romanticheskii kontseptualizm / Moscow Romantic Conceptualism." *A–Ia / A–Ya* 1: 3–11.

———. 1992. *The Total Art of Stalinism: Avant-Garde, Aesthetic Dictatorship, and Beyond*. Trans. Charles Rougle. Princeton (NJ): Princeton University Press.

———. 1997. "O nashem kruge" [Russian: "About Our Circle"]. *Wiener Slawistischer Almanach* 44: 414–21.

_____. 2000a. "The Russian Novel as a Serial Murder or The Poetics of Bureaucracy." In Willem van Reijen, Willem G. Weststeijn (eds.). *Subjectivity*, 235–54. Amsterdam, Atlanta (GA): Rodopi.

_____. 2000b. "Polutornyi stil´: sotsrealizm mezhdu modernizmom i postmodernizmom" [Russian: "One and a Half Styles: Sots-Realism between Modernism and Postmodernism"]. In <Hans Günther> Khans Giunter, Evgenii Dobrenko (eds.). *Sotsrealisticheskii kanon*, 109–18. St. Petersburg: Akademicheskii proekt.

_____. 2010. *History Becomes Form: Moscow Conceptualism*. Cambridge (MA), London: MIT Press.

Groys, Boris E.; Kabakov, Il´ia. 1993. "Beseda o Nome. Gespräch über Noma" [Russian and German: "Conversation about Noma"]. In Il´ia Kabakov. *NOMA ili Moskovskii kontseptual´nyi krug / NOMA oder Der Kreis der Moskauer Konzeptualisten*, 19–40. Stuttgart: Cantz.

Gundlakh, Sven. 1985. "Personazhnyi avtor" [Russian: "The Author-Character"]. *A–Ia: literaturnoe izdanie / A–Ya: Literary Issue* 1: 76–7.

Günther, Hans. 1984. *Die Verstaatlichung der Literatur: Entstehung und Funktionsweise des sozialistisch-realistischen Kanons in der sowjetischen Literatur der 30er Jahre* [German: *Communization of Literature: Emergence and Function of the Socialist-Realist Canon in 1930s Soviet Literature*]. Stuttgart: Metzler.

Gustiakova, Dar´ia Iu. 2006. "Rossiiskii opernyi teatr v kontekste massovoi kul´tury" [Russian: "The Russian Opera Theater in the Context of Mass Culture"]. *Vestnik Pomorskogo universiteta: seriia "Gumanitarnye i sotsial´nye nauki"* 6: 123–6.

Hansen-Löve, Aage A. (ed.). 1992. *Psychopoetik: Beiträge zur Tagung Psychologie und Literatur. München 1991* [German: *Psychopoetics: Contributions to the Conference Psychology and Literature, Munich 1991*]. Vienna: Gesellschaft zur Förderung Slawistischer Studien.

Hänsgen, Sabine. 1999. "Das Medium des Massenmediums: Michail Romms *Obyknovennyj fašizm* und Vladimir Sorokins *Bezumnyj Fritz*" [German: "Medium of Mass Media: Michail Romm's *Ordinary Fascism* and Vladimir Sorokin's *Mad Fritz*"]. In Dagmar Burkhart (ed.). *Poetik der Metadiskursivität: Zum postmodernen Prosa-, Film- und Dramenwerk von Vladimir Sorokin*, 213–22. Munich: Sagner.

Heine, Heinrich. 1985. "Deutschland. Ein Wintermährchen" [German: "Germany: A Winter's Tale"]. In *Historisch-kritische Gesamtausgabe der Werke*. Vol. 4, 89–157. Hamburg: Hoffmann und Campe.

Hillings, Valerie L. 2011. "Where Is the Line Between Us?: Moscow and Western Conceptualism in the 1970s." In Alla Rosenfeld (ed.). *Moscow Conceptualism in Context*, 260–83. Munich et al.: Prestel.

Hodel, Robert. 2013. "Der Gewaltdiskurs der Politik als literarische Vorlage bei Andrej Platonov und Vladimir Sorokin" [German: "The Political Discourse of Violence as a Literary Template in Andrei Platonov and Vladimir Sorokin"]. In Laura Burlon, Nina Frieß, Irina Gradinari, Katarzyna Różańska, Peter Salden (eds.). *Verbrechen—Fiktion—Vermarktung: Gewalt in den zeitgenössischen slavischen Literaturen*. 65–85. Potsdam: Universitätsverlag.

Hoffman, Deborah; Korchagina, Nadezhda. 2006. "Notes toward a Postmodern Translation: 'Translating' Sorokin's *Goluboe salo*." *Ohio Slavic Papers* 8: 131–48.

Höllwerth, Alexander. 2010. *"Den' Opričnika*—die Vision eines pseudosakralen, totalitären *High-Tech*-Imperiums zwischen Rekonstruktion und Dekonstruktion" [German: "*Day of the Oprichnik*—the Vision of a Pseudo-Sacred, Totalitarian *High-Tech* Empire between Reconstruction and Deconstruction"]. *Anzeiger für Slavische Philologie* 37: 55–97.

————. 2015. "V impériu 'posthumanismu'? Zamyšlení nad četbou románů Vladimira Sorokina *Ljod* a *Deň opričnika*: Konec sovětské ideokracie a specifika postmoderního prožívání světa v Rusku" [Czech: "In an Empire of 'Post-Humanism'? Reflections on Vladimir Sorokin's Novels *Ice* and *Day of the Oprichnik*: The End of Soviet Ideocracy and the Peculiarities of the Postmodern World Experience in Russia"]. In Helena Ulbrechtová (ed.). *Ruské imperiální myšlení v historii, literatuře a umění: Tradice a transformace. Kolektivní monografie*, 191–210. Prague: Slovanský ústav AV ČR.

Holm, Kerstin. 2006. "Iwans Rückkehr: Wladimir Sorokins neuer Roman: Rußland im Jahr 2027" [German: "Ivan Returns: Vladimir Sorokin's New Novel: Russia in 2027"]. *Frankfurter Allgemeine Zeitung* October 11: 35.

————. 2008. "Wladimir Sorokins düstere Russland-Vision: Die Monstersklaven sind unter uns" [German: "Vladimir Sorokin's Sinister Vision of Russia: The Monster Slaves Are among Us"]. *Frankfurter Allgemeine Zeitung* December 9. http://www.faz.net/aktuell/feuilleton/buecher/autoren/wladimir-sorokins-duestere-russland-vision-die-monstersklaven-sind-unter-uns-1742272.html, accessed January 7, 2019.

Howanitz, Gernot. 2014. "(Selbst-)Inszenierung im Netz: Neue Strategien russischer AutorInnen" [German: "(Self-)Staging on the Web: New Strategies of Russian Authors"]. In Anja Tippner, Christopher Laferl (eds.). *Künstlerinszenierungen: Performatives Selbst und biographische Narration im 20. und 21. Jahrhundert*, 191–219. Bielefeld: transcript.

Isakova, Ol'ga. S. 2003. "Telo teksta: zametki o proze Vladimira Sorokina" [Russian: "The Body of the Text: Remarks on Vladimir Sorokin's Prose"]. In *Almanakh "Vita Cogitans,"* 156–65. St. Petersburg: Sankt-Peterburgskoe filosofskoe obshchestvo. Also online: http://anthropology.ru/ru/text/isakova-os/telo-teksta-zametki-o-proze-vladimira-sorokina, accessed January 7, 2019.

Iur'eva, Lidiia M. 2005. *Russkaia antiutopiia v kontekste mirovoi literatury* [Russian: *The Russian Dystopia in the Context of World Literature*]. Moscow: IMLI RAN.

Iuzefovich, Galina. 2017. "*Manaraga* Vladimira Sorokina: kak pravil'no zhech' knigi" ["Vladimir Sorokin's *Manaraga*: How to Correctly Burn Books"]. *Meduza* March 4. https://meduza.io/feature/2017/03/04/manaraga-vladimira-sorokina, accessed January 7, 2019.

Jackson, Matthew J. (ed.). 2010. *The Experimental Group: Ilya Kabakov, Moscow Conceptualism, Soviet Avant-Gardes*. Chicago (IL), London: The University of Chicago Press.

<Janaszek-Ivaničková, Halina> Ianashek-Ivanichkova, Khalina. 2003. "Metafizika i seks v postmodernistskoi proze (Manuela Gretkovskaia. *Metafizicheskoe kabare*; Kristina Kofta. *Nich'ë telo*; Vladimir Sorokin. *Tridtsataia liubov' Mariny*" [Russian: "Metaphysics and Sex in Postmodern Prose (Manuela Gretkowska. *Metaphysical Cabaret*; Krystyna Kofta. *Nobody's Body*; Vladimir Sorokin. *Marina's Thirtieth Love*"]. In Viktor A. Khorev (ed.). *Studia Polonorossica: k 80-letiiu Eleny Zakharovny Tsybenko: sbornik statei*, 540–60. Moscow: Izdatel'stvo Moskovskogo universiteta.

Kabakov, Il´ia 1993. *NOMA ili Moskovskii kontseptual´nyi krug / NOMA oder Der Kreis der Moskauer Konzeptualisten. Instaliatsiia / Installation* [Russian and German: *NOMA or the Moscow Conceptualist Circle: An Installation*]. Ostfildern: Cantz.

———. 1999. *60-e–70-e. Zapiski o neofitsial´noi zhizni v Moskve* [Russian: *Notes about Unofficial Life in Moscow*]. Vienna: Gesellschaft zur Förderung Slawistischer Studien.

Kagarlitsky, Boris. 2002. *Russia under Yeltsin and Putin: Neo-Liberal Autocracy.* London, Sterling (VA): Pluto.

Kalfus, Ken. 2007. "They Had a Hammer." *The New York Times* April 15. https://www.nytimes.com/2007/04/15/books/review/Kalfus.t.html, accessed January 7, 2019.

Kalinin, Ilya. 2013. "The Blue Lard of Language: Vladimir Sorokin's Metalingual Utopia." In Tine Roesen, Dirk Uffelmann (eds.). *Vladimir Sorokin's Languages*, 128–47. Bergen: University of Bergen. Also online: http://boap.uib.no/books/sb/catalog/book/9, accessed January 7, 2019.

———. 2017. "Why 'Two Russias' Are Less than 'United Russia': Cultural Distinctions and Political Similarities: Dialectics of the Defeat." In Birgit Beumers, Alexander Etkind, Olga Gurova, Sanna Turoma (eds.). *The Shrew Untamed: Cultural Forms of Political Protest in Russia*, 48–67. London: Routledge.

Kasper, Karlheinz. 1999. "Das Glöckchen und die Axt in Sorokins *Roman*" [German: "The Bell and the Axe in Sorokin's *A Novel*"]. In Dagmar Burkhart (ed.). *Poetik der Metadiskursivität: Zum postmodernen Prosa-, Film- und Dramenwerk von Vladimir Sorokin*, 103–14. Munich: Sagner.

———. 2007a. "Vladimir Sorokin: Roman" [German: "Vladimir Sorokin: A Novel"]. In Bodo Zelinsky (ed.). *Der russische Roman*, 472–87. Cologne et al: Böhlau.

———. 2007b. "Terror der Opričnina oder Dikatur der Vampire? Vladimir Sorokin und Viktor Pelevin warnen vor Russlands Zukunft" [German: "Terror of the Oprichnina or Dictatorship of Vampires? Vladimir Sorokin and Viktor Pelevin Warn of Russia's Future"]. *Osteuropa* 57.10: 103–25.

———. 2014. "Die Zukunft der Vergangenheit: Das 'Neue Mittelalter' im russischen Gegenwartsroman" [German: "The Future of the Past: The 'New Middle Ages' in Russian Contemporary Novels"]. *Osteuropa* 64.7: 121–39.

Kenzheev, Bakhyt. 1995. "Antisovetchik Vladimir Sorokin" [Russian: "The Anti-Soviet Vladimir Sorokin"]. *Znamia* 4: 202–5.

Kharkhordin, Oleg. 1999. *The Collective and the Individual in Russia: A Study of Practices.* Berkeley (CA) et al.: University of California Press.

Kholmogorova, Ol'ga (ed.). 1994. *Sots-art.* Moscow: Galart

Kiem, Elizabeth. 2007. "Ice by Vladimir Sorokin." *Bookslut* February. http://www.bookslut.com/fiction/2007_02_010611.php, accessed January 7, 2019.

Kiun, Kim Yn. 2005. *Malaia proza V.G. Sorokina v kontekste modernistskikh i postmodernistskikh tendentsii sovremennoi russkoi literatury* [Russian: *Vladimir Sorokin's Short Prose in the Context of Modernist and Postmodernist Tendencies in Contemporary Russian Literature*]. PhD dissertation. Lonomosov Moscow State University.

Klepikova, Tatiana. 2018. *Crossing Soviet Thresholds: Privacy, Literature, and Politics in Late Soviet Russia.* PhD dissertation. University of Passau.

Kononova, Viktoriia. 2006. "Svoboda i smysl v literature postmodernizma: analiz interteksta v p´ese Vladimira Sorokina *Dostoevsky-trip*" [Russian: "Freedom and Meaning in Postmodern Literature: An Analysis of Vladimir Sorokin's Play *Dostoevsky-trip*"]. In Vladimir B. Kataev, <Andrew Wachtel> Endriu Vakhtel´ (eds.). *Ot Igrokov do Dostoevsky-trip: intertekstual´nost´ v russkoi dramaturgii XIX–XX vekov*, 209–19. Moscow: Izdatel´stvo Moskovskogo universiteta.

Koschmal, Walter. 1996. "Ende der Verantwortungsästhetik?" [German: "The End of the Aesthetics of Responsiblity?"]. In Jochen-Ulrich Peters, German Ritz (eds.). *Enttabuisierung: Essays zur russischen und polnischen Gegenwartsliteratur*, 19–43. Bern et al.: Lang.

Kostiukov, Leonid. 2016. "Moskva (2000)" [Russian: "Moscow (2000)"]. In *Kino stolitsa: Moskva v zerkale kinematografa* [Russian: *Cinema Capital City: Moscow in the Mirror of the Cinematograph*], 307–14. Moscow: B.S.G.-Press.

Kotkin, Stephen. 2011. "A Dystopian Tale of Russia's Future." *The New York Times* March 11. https://www.nytimes.com/2011/03/13/books/review/book-review-day-of-the-oprichnik-by-vladimir-sorokin.html, accessed January 7, 2019.

Kovalev, Manuela. 2013. "Empty Words? The Function of Obscene Language(s) in Vladimir Sorokin's *Blue Lard*." In Tine Roesen, Dirk Uffelmann (eds.). *Vladimir Sorokin's Languages*, 148–69. Bergen: University of Bergen. Also online: http://boap.uib.no/books/sb/catalog/book/9, accessed January 7, 2019.

Kozak, Barbara. 2016. "Rosja za kamiennym murem: Nowe średniowiecze w twórczości Władimira Sorokina (na przykładzie powieści *Dzień opricznika*)" [Polish: "Russia behind a Stone Wall: The New Middle Ages in Vladimir Sorokin's Oeuvre (on the Example of His Novel *Day of the Oprichnik*")]. *Acta Neophilologica* 18: 213–21. Olsztyn: Wydawnictwo Uniwersytetu Warmińsko-Mazurskiego.

Kozlov, Dmitrii. 2018. "Fartsovshchiki, bitlomany, pepsi-kola: sovetskaia molodezh´ i Zapad" [Russian: "Illegal Traders, Beatlemaniacs, and Pepsi-Cola: Soviet Youth and the West"]. *Arzamas.academy: istoriia russkoi kul´tury*. http://arzamas.academy/materials/1485, accessed January 7, 2019.

Kubasov, Aleksandr V. 2012. "Politicheskii diskurs v khudozhestvennom elektronnom tekste" [Russian: "Political Discourse in a Belles-Lettres Electronic Text"]. *Politicheskaia lingvistika* 42.4: 201–4.

Kucherskaia, Maiia. 2013. "*Telluria*: Vladimir Sorokin opisal postapokalipticheskii mir" [Russian: "*Telluria*: Vladimir Sorokin Has Described a Post-Apocalyptic World"]. *Vedomosti* October 21. http://www.srkn.ru/criticism/telluriya-vladimir-sorokin-opisal-postapokaliptich.html, accessed January 7, 2019.

Kuchina, Tat´iana G. 2012. "Zimniaia doroga: stilevaia rekonstruktsiia metasiuzheta v povesti *Metel´* Vladimira Sorokina" [Russian: "Winter Road: Stylistic Reconstruction of the Snowstorm Plot in Vladimir Sorokin's novelette *The Blizzard*"]. *Iaroslavskii pedagogicheskii vestnik*. Tom 1: *Gumanitarnye nauki* 1: 246–9.

Kukulin, Il´ia. 2002. "Every Trend Makes a Brand" [Russian text with English title]. *Novoe literaturnoe obozrenie* 56: 253–68.

_____. 2013. "From History as Language to the Language of History: Notes on *The Target*." In Tine Roesen, Dirk Uffelmann (eds.). *Vladimir Sorokin's Languages*, 314–44. Bergen: University of Bergen. Also online: http://boap.uib.no/books/sb/catalog/book/9, accessed January 7, 2019.

Kukushkin, Vladimir. 2002. "Mudrost' Sorokina" [Russian: "Sorokin's Wisdom"]. *Novoe literaturnoe obozrenie* 56: 249–52.

Kurchatova, Natal'ia. 2013. "Vladimir Sorokin napisal roman o raspade Rossii i Evropy: *Telluriia* okazalas' blistatel'noi poemoi o sovremennykh mediafobiiakh" [Russian: "Vladimir Sorokin Has Written a Novel about the Disintegration of Russia and Europe: *Telluria* Turned out to Be a Splendid Poem about Contemporary Media Phobias"]. *Izvestiia* October 20. https://iz.ru/news/559153, accessed January 7, 2019.

Kuritsyn, Viacheslav. 2001. *Russkii literaturnyi postmodernizm* [Russian: *Russian Literary Postmodernism*]. Moscow: OGI.

Kustanovich, Konstantin V. 2004. "Vladimir Georgievich Sorokin (7 August 1955–)." In *Dictionary of Literary Biography*. Vol. 285. *Russian Writers since 1980*, 301–15. Farmington Hills (MI): Gale.

Kuz'min, Dmitrii. 2001. "Postkontseptualizm: kak by nabroski k monografii" [Russian: "Post-Conceptualism: A Kind of Outline for a Monograph"]. *Novoe literaturnoe obozrenie* 50: 459–76.

_____. 2002. "Posle kontseptualizma" [Russian: "After Conceptualism"]. *Arion* 1. Also online: http://magazines.russ.ru/arion/2002/1/ku1.html, accessed January 7, 2019.

Kuz'min, Dmitrii. 2019. "Post-Conceptualism." *Russian Studies in Literature* 54.1/3: 7–31.

Kuznitsin, Oleg. 1999. "Posle smerti on obradovalsia (Opyt postteoreticheskogo kommentariia k 'Zasedaniiu zavkoma' V. Sorokina)" [Russian: "After His Death He Rejoiced (an Attempt at a Post-Theoretical Comment on Vladimir Sorokin's 'Next Item on the Agenda')"]. *Novoe literaturnoe obozrenie* 39: 280–5.

Lachmann, Renate. 2004. "Der Bachtinsche Groteskebegriff und die postsowjetische Literatur (das Beispiel Vladimir Sorokin)" [German: "Bakhtin's Notion of the Grotesque and Post-Soviet Literature (the Example of Vladimir Sorokin)"]. *kultuRRevolution* 48.2: 44–51.

Laird, Sally. 2008. "Preface." In Vladimir Sorokin. *The Queue*. Trans. Sally Laird, vii–x. New York: New York Review Books.

Langeveld, Arthur; Weststeijn, Willem G. 2005. *Moderne Russische literatuur: Van Poesjkin tot heden* [Dutch: *Modern Russian Literature: From Pushkin to the Present Day*]. Amsterdam: Pegasus.

Lanin, Boris A. 2007. "Voobrazhaemaia Rossiia v sovremennoi russkoi antiutopii" [Russian: "Imagined Russia in Contemporary Russian Dystopias"]. *Slavic Eurasian Studies* 17: 375–90.

Latynina, Alla. 2006. "Sverkhchelovek ili neliud'?" [Russian: "Superhuman or Inhuman?"]. *Novyi mir* 4: 136–42.

_____. 2014. "Crazy Quilt Vladimira Sorokina: loskutnoe odeialo *Tellurii* sshito masterom po unikal'noi tekhnologii: povtorit' nevozmozhno" [Russian: "Vladimir Sorokin's Crazy Quilt: The Patchwork Blanket of *Telluriia* Was Sewn by the Master in a Unique Technique: Unrepeatable!"]. *Novyi mir* 3: 182–9.

Lawrence, Adam. 2015. "Vladimir Sorokin 1955–." In Lawrence J. Trudeau (ed.). *Contemporary Literary Criticism: Criticism of the Works of Today's Novelists, Poets, Playwrights, Short-Story Writers, Scriptwriters, and Other Creative Writers.* Vol. 374, 167–320. Farmington Hills (MI): Gale.

Leiderman, Naum L.; Lipovetskii, Mark N. 2001. *Sovremennaia russkaia literatura.* Kn. 3: *V kontse veka (1986–1990-e gody)* [Russian: *Contemporary Russian Literature.* Vol. 3. *Toward the End of the Century (1986–1999s)*]. Moscow: URSS.

Ledeneva, Alena V. 1998. *Russia's Economy of Favours: Blat, Networking and Informal Exchange.* Cambridge: Cambridge University Press.

Leitner, Andreas. 1999. "Der Absturz ins Glück: *Tridcataja ljubov' Mariny* von Vladimir Sorokin" [German: "The Crash into Happiness: Vladimir Sorokin's *Marina's Thirtieth Love*"]. In Dagmar Burkhart (ed.). *Poetik der Metadiskursivität: Zum postmodernen Prosa-, Film- und Dramenwerk von Vladimir Sorokin,* 95–101. Munich: Sagner.

Levshin, Igor' 1993. "Etiko-esteticheskoe prostranstvo Kurnosova-Sorokina" [Russian: "The Ethical-Aesthetic Space of Kurnosov-Sorokin"]. *Novoe literaturnoe obozrenie* 3: 283–8.

Lichina, Natalia. 2000. "Ochered' kak kontsept zhizni v tekste V. Sorokina *Ochered'*" [Russian: "The Queue as a Life Concept in Vladimir Sorokin's Text *The Queue*"]. *Acta Neophilologica* 2: 155–63. Olsztyn: Wydawnictwo Uniwersytetu Warmińsko-Mazurskiego.

Lipovetskii, Mark. 1999. "Goluboe salo pokoleniia, ili Dva mifa ob odnom krizise" [Russian: "The Blue Lard of a Generation, or Two Myths about One Crisis"]. *Znamia* 11: 207–15.

———. (Lipovetsky). 2000. "Vladimir Sorokin's 'Theater of Cruelty.'" In Marina Balina, Nancy Condee, Evgeny Dobrenko (eds.). *Endquote: Sots-Art Literature and Soviet Grand Style,* 167–92. Evanston (IL): Northwestern University Press.

———. 2008. *Paralogii: transformatsii (post)modernistskogo diskursa v russkoi kul'ture 1920–2000-kh godov* [Russian: *Paralogies: Transformations of the (Post-)Modernist Discourse in Russian Culture from the 1920s to the 2000s*]. Moscow: Novoe literaturnoe obozrenie.

———. (Lipovetsky). 2011. "Post-Soviet Literature between Realism and Postmodernism." In Evgeny Dobrenko, Marina Balina (eds.). *The Cambridge Companion to Twentieth Century Russian Literature,* 175–93. Cambridge: Cambridge University Press.

———. 2012. "Sovetskie i postsovetskie transformatsii siuzheta vnutrennei kolonizatsii" [Russian: "Soviet and Post-Soviet Transformations of the Inner Colonization Plot"]. In Aleksandr Etkind, Dirk Uffelmann, Il'ia Kukulin (eds.). *Tam, vnutri: praktiki vnutrennei kolonizatsii v kul'turnoi istorii Rossii,* 809–45. Moscow: Novoe literaturnoe obozrenie.

———. (Lipovetsky). 2013. "Fleshing / Flashing Discourse: Sorokin's Master Trope." In Tine Roesen, Dirk Uffelmann (eds.). *Vladimir Sorokin's Languages,* 25–47. Bergen: University of Bergen. Also online: http://boap.uib.no/books/sb/catalog/book/9, accessed January 7, 2019.

———. (Lipovetsky). 2015. "Postmodernist Novel." In Evgeny Dobrenko, Mark Lipovetsky (eds.). *Russian Literature since 1991,* 145–66. Cambridge: Cambridge University Press.

———. 2018. "Avtoportret khudozhnika s grilem: *Manaraga* i literaturotsentrizm" [Russian: "Self-Portrait of the Artist with a Grill: *Manaraga* and Literature-Centrism"]. In Evgenii Dobrenko, Il'ia Kalinin, Mark Lipovetskii (eds.). *"Eto prosto bukvy na bumage …" Vladimir Sorokin: posle literatury,* 634–46. Moscow: Novoe literaturnoe obozrenie.

_____. (Lipovetsky). 2019. "The New 'Norma': Vladimir Sorokin's *Telluria* and Post-Utopian Science Fiction." In Mikhail Suslov, Per-Arne Bodin (eds.). *Utopian Worlds in Post-Soviet Russia: Politics, Fiction and Fantasy*, 301–14. London et al.: I.B. Tauris.

Lorková, Zuzana (ed.). 2011a. *Vladimír Sorokin: Tvorca mnohých tvárí. Interpretačné podoby v slovenskom kultúrnom priestore* [Slovak: *Vladimir Sorokin, Many-Faced Creator: Interpretative Forms in Slovak Cultural Space*]. Bratislava: Stimul. http://stella.uniba.sk/texty/ZL_sorokin. pdf, accessed January 7, 2019.

_____. 2011b. "Tragédia ruského človeka v tvorbe V. Sorokina" [Slovak: "The Tragedy of Russian Man in Vladimir Sorokin's Oeuvre"]. In Zuzana Lorková (ed.). *Vladimír Sorokin: Tvorca mnohých tvárí. Interpretačné podoby v slovenskom kultúrnom priestore*, 39–47. Bratislava: Stimul. http://stella.uniba.sk/texty/ZL_sorokin.pdf, accessed January 7, 2019.

_____. 2011c. "Východ verzus Západ v diele Opričníkov deň" [Slovak: "East vs. West in *Day of the Oprichnik*"]. In Zuzana Lorková (ed.). *Vladimír Sorokin: Tvorca mnohých tvárí. Interpretačné podoby v slovenskom kultúrnom priestore*, 64–72. Bratislava: Stimul. http://stella. uniba.sk/texty/ZL_sorokin.pdf, accessed January 7, 2019.

Lunde, Ingunn. 2009. "Køen som språkrom" [Norwegian: "The Queue as a Linguistic Space"]. In Vladimir Sorokin: *Køen*, 9–13. Oslo: Flamme.

_____. 2013. "Simultaneity of the Non-Simultaneous: On the Diachronic Dimensions of Language in Sorokin." In Tine Roesen, Dirk Uffelmann (eds.). *Vladimir Sorokin's Languages*, 298–313. Bergen: University of Bergen. Also online: http://boap.uib.no/books/sb/catalog/ book/9, accessed January 7, 2019.

Machoninová, Alena. 2007. "Sorokin, Vladimir. Děň opričnika" [Czech: "Vladimir Sorokin. *Day of the Oprichnik*"]. *iLiteratura.cz* January 15. http://www.iliteratura.cz/Clanek/20467/ sorokin-vladimir-den-opricnika, accessed January 7, 2019.

Marsh, Rosalind. 2007. *Literature, History and Identity in Post-Soviet Russia, 1991–2006*. Oxford: Lang.

Marusenkov, Maksim P. 2012. *Absurdopediia russkoi zhizni Vladimira Sorokina: zaum', grotesk i absurd* [Russian: *Vladimir Sorokin's Absurdopedia of Russian Life: Transrational Language, Grotesque, and Absurd*]. St. Petersburg: Aleteiia.

Menzel, Birgit. 2007. "The Occult Revival in Russia Today and Its Impact on Literature." *The Harriman Review* 16.1: 1–14. http://rhga.ru/science/center/ezo/publications/The_ Occult_Revival.pdf, accessed January 7, 2019.

<Monastyrskii, Andrei> A.M. 1985. "O proze Sorokina" [Russian: "On Sorokin's Prose"]. *A–Ia: literaturnoe izdanie / A–Ya: Literary Issue* 1: 74–6.

_____ (ed.). 1999. *Slovar' terminov moskovskoi kontseptual'noi shkoly* [Russian: *Glossary of the Moscow Conceptualist School*]. Moscow: Ad Marginem.

Morelli, Eleonora. 2006. "The Deconstruction of Representation in Vladimir Sorokin's Short Stories." *Transcultural Studies* 2: 261–77.

Morozova, Katia; Iarovaia, Nastia. 2013. "Al'ternativnaia karta Rossii i Evropy po *Tellurii* Sorokina" [Russian: "An Alternative Map of Russia and Western Europe according to Sorokin's *Telluria*"]. http://www.lookatme.ru/mag/how-to/books/197235-sorokin-map, accessed January 7, 2019.

Morson, Gary S. 1981. *The Boundaries of Genre: Dostoevsky's* Diary of a Writer *and the Traditions of Literary Utopia*. Austin (TX): University of Texas Press.

Mortensen, Stehn Aztlan. 2017. "Russlands uforutsigbare fortid" [Norwegian: "Russia's Erratic Past"]. *Vagant* December 30. http://www.vagant.no/vladimir-sorokins-spadommer-om-russlands-uforutsigbare-fortid/, accessed January 7, 2019.

Murašov, Jurij. 2016. *Das unheimliche Auge der Schrift: Mediologische Analysen zu Literatur, Film und Kunst in Russland* [German: *The Uncanny Eye of Writing: Mediological Analyses of Literature, Film, and Art in Russia*]. Munich: Fink.

Murav, Harriet. 2003. "Sorokin's Lawsuits and the Boundaries of the National Body." *Compar(a)ison* 1: 73–80.

Narinskaia, Anna. 2017. "Kniga o vkusnoi i dukhovnoi pishche: o novom romane Vladimira Sorokina *Manaraga*, vykhodiashchim [sic] v izdatel'stve Corpus 10 marta" [Russian: "The Book of Tasty and Spiritual Food: About Vladimir Sorokin's New Novel *Manaraga* which Will Be Released by Corpus Publishers on March 10"]. *Novaia gazeta* March 6. https://www.novayagazeta.ru/articles/2017/03/06/71708-kniga-o-vkusnoy-i-duhovnoy-pische, accessed January 7, 2019.

Naumann, Kristina. 2017. *Russische Satire im 21. Jahrhundert als Zeitkommentar: Vladimir G. Sorokins* Sacharnyj Kreml' *und Oleg Kašins* Roissja vperde [German: *Russian Satire in the Twenty-First Century as Commentary on the Times: Vladimir G. Sorokin's* Sugar Kremlin *and Oleg Kashin's* Fardwer, Rasha]. PhD dissertation. University of Kiel.

Naval'nyi, Aleksei; Prokhorova, Irina; Krylov, Konstantin. 2013. "Novyi Sorokin: Naval'nyi, Prokhorova i Krylov chitaiut *Telluriiu*" [Russian: "The New Sorokin: Naval'nyi, Prokhorova, and Krylov Read *Telluria*"]. *Afisha* October 17. https://daily.afisha.ru/archive/vozduh/books/navalnyy-prohorova-i-krylov-chitayut-telluriyu/, accessed January 7, 2019.

Nazarenko, Tatiana. 2003. "Vladimir Sorokin. *Lëd.*" *World Literature Today* 77.2: 133–4.

Nedel', Arkadii. 1998. "Doska transgressii Vladimira Sorokina: sorokinotipy" [Russian: "Sorokin's Tableau of Transgressions: The Sorokinotypes"]. *Mitin Zhurnal* 56: 247–87.

Nemzer, Andrei. 2003. *Zamechatel'noe desiatiletie russkoi literatury* [Russian: *A Splendid Decade of Russian Literature*]. Moscow: Zakaharov.

———. 2006. "Eshche dva 'nichego'" [Russian: "Two more Nothings"]. *Vremia novostei* September 29. http://www.vremya.ru/print/162026.html, accessed January 7, 2019.

Nikolenko, Ol'ga; Kopach, Elena. 2006. *Sovremennaia russkaia antiutopiia: traditsii i novatorstvo* [Russian: *The Contemporary Russian Dystopia: Traditions and Innovation*]. Poltava: Tekhservis.

Noordenbos, Boris. 2016. *Post-Soviet Literature and the Search for a Russian Identity*. New York: Palgrave Macmillan.

Nove, Alec. 1989. *Glasnost in Action: Cultural Renaissance in Russia*. Winchester (MA) et al.: Unwin Hyman.

Novokhatskii, Dmitrii V. 2009. *Romannaia trilogiia Vladimira Sorokina Lëd, Put' Bro, 23 000: problematika i zhanrovo-kompozitsionnye osobennosti* [Russian: *Vladimir Sorokin's Trilogy of*

Novels Ice, Bro's Path, and 23,000: The Subject and the Peculiarities of Genre and Composition]. PhD dissertation. Crimean University for the Humanities, Yalta.

Obermayr, Brigitte. 1999. "Die Liebe zum Willen zur Wahrheit: Der Höhepunkt als Exzeß der Macht in *Tridcataja ljubov' Mariny*" [German: "Love to the Will to Truth: The Climax as Excess of Power in *Marina's Thirtieth Love*"]. In Dagmar Burkhart (ed.). *Poetik der Metadiskursivität: Zum postmodernen Prosa-, Film- und Dramenwerk von Vladimir Sorokin*, 81–93. Munich: Sagner.

———. 2005. "Man f… nur mit dem Herzen gut: Pornografien der Liebe bei Vladimir Sorokin" [German: "You F… Well only with Your Heart: Pornographies of Love in Vladimir Sorokin"]. In Jörg Metelmann (ed.). *Porno-Pop: Sex in der Oberflächenwelt*, 105–23. Würzburg: Königshausen & Neumann.

———. 2006. "Verfemte Teile eines Werkes: Sorokin zwischen Sub- und Pop(ulär)kultur" [German: "Ostracized Parts of an Oeuvre: Sorokin between Subculture and Pop(ular) Culture"]. In Rainer Grübel, Gun-Britt Kohler (eds.). *Gabe und Opfer in der russischen Literatur und Kultur der Moderne*, 519–52. Oldenburg: BIS-Verlag der Carl-von-Ossietzky-Universität.

———. 2013. "Choosing a Different Example Would Mean Telling a Different Story: On Judgement in *Day of the Oprichnik*." In Tine Roesen, Dirk Uffelmann (eds.). *Vladimir Sorokin's Languages*, 245–65. Bergen: University of Bergen. Also online: http://boap.uib.no/books/sb/catalog/book/9, accessed January 7, 2019.

Ohme, Andreas. 2003. "Iconic Representation of Space and Time in Vladimir Sorokin's Novel *The Queue*." In Wolfgang G. Müller, Olga Fisher (eds.). *From Sign to Signing: Iconicity in Language and Literature*. Vol. 3, 153–65. Amsterdam: John Benjamins.

Orens, Geoff. 2007. "Sorokin, Vladimir." In Jennifer Curry, David Ramm, Mari Rich, Albert Rolls (eds.). *World Authors 2000–2005*, 702–5. New York, Dublin: H.W. Wilson.

Oushakine, Serguei A. 2001. "The Terrifying Mimicry of Samizdat." *Public Culture* 13.2: 191–214.

Paulsen, Martin. 2009. *Hegemonic Language and Literature: Russian Metadiscourse on Language in the 1990s*. PhD dissertation. University of Bergen.

———. 2013. "The Latin Alphabet in Sorokin's Works." In Tine Roesen, Dirk Uffelmann (eds.). *Vladimir Sorokin's Languages*, 193–208. Bergen: University of Bergen. Also online: http://boap.uib.no/books/sb/catalog/book/9, accessed January 7, 2019.

Pavlenko, Alexei. 2009. "Sorokin's Soteriology." *Slavic and East European Journal* 53.2: 261–77.

Petrovskaia, Elena. 2000. "Golubaia vata" [Russian: "Blue Cotton Wool"]. *Novoe literaturnoe obozrenie* 41: 414–7.

Pietraś, Elżbieta. 2007. "Moskiewski konceptualizm—między awangardą a postmodernizmem" [Polish: "Moscow Conceptualism—between Avant-Garde and Postmodernism"]. *Acta Neophilologica* 9: 131–42. Olsztyn: Wydawnictwo Uniwersytetu Warmińsko-Mazurskiego.

Pogorelaia, Elena 2012. "Marche funebre na okraine Kitaia" [Russian: "Funeral March on the Chinese Border"]. *Voprosy literatury* 1: 54–71.

Polonsky, Rachel. 2012. "Violent, Ecstatic Russians." *The New York Review of Books* March 22: 28–30.

Poluboiarinova, Larisa N. 2004. "Leopol´d fon Zakher-Mazokh i Vladimir Sorokin" [Russian: "Leopold von Sacher-Masoch and Vladimir Sorokin"]. *Vestnik Sankt-Peterburgskogo universiteta. Seriia 9. Filologiia. Vostokovedenie. Zhurnalistika* 3–4: 3–11.

Porter, Jillian. 2017. "Introduction to the Forum 'The Queue in Soviet and Post-Soviet Literature and Culture.'" *Slavic and East European Journal* 61.3: 490–4.

Porter, Robert. 1994. *Russia's Alternative Prose*. Oxford, Providence (RI): Berg.

Poyntner, Erich. 2005. *Der Zerfall der Texte: Zur Struktur des Hässlichen, Bösen und Schlechten in der russischen Literatur des 20. Jahrhunderts* [German: *The Disintegration of Texts: On the Structure of the Nasty, Evil, and Bad in Twentieth-Century Russian Literature*]. Frankfurt/Main et al.: Lang.

Pozdniakov, Konstantin S. 2003. *Gipertekstual´naia priroda prozy Vladimira Sorokina* [Russian: *The Hypertextual Nature of Vladimir Sorokin's Prose*]. PhD dissertation. Samara State University.

Prigov, Dmitrii A. 2003. *Sobranie stikhov. t. IV. No. 660–845* [Russian: *Collected Poems. Vol. 4. No. 600–845*]. Vienna: Gesellschaft zur Förderung Slawistischer Studien.

"Prostranstvo." 2012. "Prostranstvo V. Sorokina" [Russian: "Vladimir Sorokin's Space"]. *Vestnik Permskogo universiteta: rossiiskaia i zarubezhnaia filologiia* 1: 194–237.

Qualin, Anthony. 2015. "Rituel, violence et perversion: la drôle de cuisine de Vladimir Sorokine" [French: "Ritual, Violence, and Perversion: The Comical Nature of Vladimir Sorokin's Cuisine"]. Trans. Rodolphe Baudin. *La Revue Russe* 44: 175–84.

Räsänen, Salla. 2005. *Osobennosti natsional´noi okhoty na pisatelia: literaturnaia bor´ba 2002 goda vokrug romana Vladimira Sorokina "Goluboe salo"* [Russian: *The Peculiarities of the National Hunt for a Writer: The 2002 Literary Controversy about Vladimir Sorokin's Novel "Blue Lard"*]. Diploma thesis Helsinki University.

Remizova, Mariia. 1995. "Roman umer, da zdravstvuet Sorokin?" [Russian: "The Novel Is Dead, Long Live Sorokin?"]. *Literaturnaia gazeta* February 15: 4.

Ritter, Martina. 2008. *Alltag im Umbruch: Zur Dynamik von Öffentlichkeit und Privatheit im neuen Russland* [German: *Everyday Life in Transition: On the Dynamics of Public and Private Spheres in the New Russia*]. Hamburg: Krämer.

Roesen, Tine. 2013. "Drive of the Oprichnik: On Collectivity and Individuality in *Day of the Oprichnik*." In Tine Roesen, Dirk Uffelmann (eds.). *Vladimir Sorokin's Languages*, 266–81. Bergen: University of Bergen. Also online: http://boap.uib.no/books/sb/catalog/book/9, accessed January 7, 2019.

Roesen, Tine; Uffelmann, Dirk (eds.). 2013. *Vladimir Sorokin's Languages*. Bergen: University of Bergen. Also online: http://boap.uib.no/books/sb/catalog/book/9, accessed January 7, 2019.

Roll, Serafima. 1998. "Conclusion: Alternative Tendencies in Contemporary Russian Literature." In Serafima Roll (ed.). *Contextualizing Transition: Interviews with Contemporary Russian Writers and Critics*, 145–75. New York et al.: Lang.

Romanova, Elena; Ivantsov, Egor. 2004. "Spasenie, ili Apokalipsis (eskhatologiia liubvi v romane V. Sorokina *Lëd*)" [Russian: "Redemption, or Apocalypse (the Eschatology of Love in Vladimir Sorokin's Novel *Ice*"]. https://www.srkn.ru/criticism/romanova.shtml, accessed January 7, 2019.

Rubinshtein, Lev. 1995. *Vse dal'she i dal'she: iz "Bol'shoi kartoteki" (1975–1993)* [Russian: *Farther and Farther: From the "Big File Index" (1975–1993)*]. Moscow: Obscuri Viri.

Rutten, Ellen. 2006. "Vladimir Sorokin: postmodernist zoekt tranen?" [Dutch: "Vladimir Sorokin: A Postmodernist Seeking Tears?"]. *Tijdschrift voor Slavische Literatuur* 45: 54–8.

———. 2010. *Unattainable Bride Russia: Gendering Nation, State, and Intelligentsia in Russian Intellectual Culture*. Evanston (IL): Northwestern University Press.

———. 2017. *Sincerity after Communism: A Cultural History*. New Haven (CT): Yale University Press.

Rybakov, Anatolii. 1998a. *Children of the Arbat*. Trans. Harold Shukman. Boston (MA), Toronto: Little, Brown & Company.

———. 1988b. *Deti Arbata* [Russian: *Children of the Arbat*]. Tallinn: Eesti Raamat.

Ryklin, Mikhail. 1992. *Terrorologiki* [Russian: *Logics of Terror*]. Tartu, Moscow: Eidos.

———. 1998. "Medium i avtor: o tekstakh Vladimira Sorokina" [Russian: "Medium and Author: About Vladimir Sorokin's Texts"]. In Vladimir Sorokin. *Sobranie sochinenii v dvukh tomakh*. Vol. 2, 737–51. Moscow: Ad Marginem.

———. 2001a. "Nemets na zakaz" [Russian: "Comissioned German"]. In *Prostranstva likovaniia: totalitarizm i razlichie*, 225–42. Moscow: Logos.

———. 2001b. "Borshch posle ustrits" [Russian: "Borscht after Oysters"]. In *Prostranstva likovaniia: totalitarizm i razlichie*, 243–53. Moscow: Logos.

———. 2003. "Kto podzhëg Reikhstag?" [Russian: "Who Set Fire to the Reichstag?"]. In *Vremia diagnoza*, 181–6. Moscow: Logos.

Ryzhova, Polina. 2013. "Gosudarstvo eto zria" [Russian: "Forget the State"]. *Gazeta.ru* October 17. http://www.srkn.ru/criticism/gosudarstvo-eto-zrya.html, accessed January 7, 2019.

Sasse, Sylvia. 1999. "Gift im Ohr: Beichte—Geständnis—Bekenntnis in Vladimir Sorokins Texten" [German: "Poison in the Ear: Penance—Confession—Avowal in Vladimir Sorokin's Texts"]. In Dagmar Burkhart (ed.). *Poetik der Metadiskursivität: Zum postmodernen Prosa-, Film- und Dramenwerk von Vladimir Sorokin*, 127–37. Munich: Sagner.

———. 2003. *Texte in Aktion: Sprech- und Sprachakte im Moskauer Konzeptualismus* [German: *Texts in Action: Speech and Language Acts in Moscow Conceptualism*]. Munich: Fink.

Sasse, Sylvia; Schramm, Caroline. 1997. "Totalitäre Literatur und subversive Affirmation" [German: "Totalitarian Literature and Subversive Affirmation"]. *Die Welt der Slaven* 42.2: 306–27.

Schmid, Ulrich. 2015. *Technologien der Seele: Vom Verfertigen der Wahrheit in der russischen Gegenwartskultur* [German: *Technologies of the Soul: On the Production of Truth in Russian Contemporary Culture*]. Frankfurt/Main: Suhrkamp.

Scholz, Nora. 2010. "Die Schönheit des Erwachens: Zum ursprünglichen Licht in Vladimir Sorokins *Put' Bro*" [German: "The Beauty of Awakening: On Primordial Light in Vladimir Sorokin's *Bro's Path*"]. *Wiener Slawistischer Almanach* 66: 325–36.

Shatalov, Aleksandr. 1999. "Vladimir Sorokin v poiskakh utrachennogo vremeni" [Russian: "Vladimir Sorokin in Search of Lost Time"]. *Druzhba narodov* 10: 204–7.

Shevtsov, Vasilii. 2004. "Put´ moralista" [Russian: "The Path of a Moralist"]. *Topos* September 28. http://www.topos.ru/article/2810, accessed January 7, 2019.

————. 2005a. "Slovesnyi teatr: mozhno li verit´ Vladimiru Sorokinu?" [Russian: "Word Theater: Can We Believe Vladimir Sorokin?"]. *Nezavisimaia Gazeta Ex Libris* March 24: 6.

————. 2005b. "*Lëd* tronulsia? Korotkii otvet Vladimiru Sorokinu" [Russian: "Has the Ice Broken? A Short Answer to Vladimir Sorokin"]. *Nezavisimaia Gazeta Ex Libris* PRIL 14: 5.

Shlapentokh, Vladimir. 1989. *Public and Private Life of the Soviet People: Changing Values in Post-Stalin Russia*. New York et al.: Oxford University Press.

Skakov, Nariman. 2013. "Word / Discourse in *Roman*." In Tine Roesen, Dirk Uffelmann (eds.). *Vladimir Sorokin's Languages*, 48–67. Bergen: University of Bergen. Also online: http://boap.uib.no/books/sb/catalog/book/9, accessed January 7, 2019.

Skillen, Daphne. 2017. *Freedom of Speech in Russia: Politics and Media from Gorbachev to Putin*. London: Routledge.

Skoropanova, Irina S. 1999. *Russkaia postmodernistskaia literatura* [Russian: *Russian Postmodernist Literature*]. Moscow: Flinta.

————. 2002. *Russkaia postmodernistskaia literatura: novaia filosofiia, novyi iazyk* [Russian: *Russian Postmodernist Literature: New Philosophy and New Language*]. 2nd edition. St. Petersburg: Nevskii prostor.

Smirnov, Igor´ P. 1994a. *Psikhodiakhronologika: psikhoistoriia russkoi literatury ot romantizma do nashikh dnei* [Russian: *Psychodiachronologic: The Psycho-History of Russian Literature from Romanticism to Today*]. Moscow: Novoe literaturnoe obozrenie.

————. 1994b. "'O druz´iakh … pozharishchakh …'" [Russian: "'On Friends … and Scorched Ruins …'"]. *Novoe literaturnoe obozrenie* 7: 285–9.

————. 1995. "Oskorbliaiushchaia nevinnost´: O proze Vladimira Sorokina i samopoznanii" [Russian: "Offensive Innocence: On the Prose of Vladimir Sorokin and Self-Cognition"]. *Mesto pechati* 7: 125–47.

————. 1999. "Der der Welt sichtbare und unsichtbare Humor Sorokins" [German: "Sorokin's Humor that Is Visible and Invisible to the World"]. In Dagmar Burkhart (ed.). *Poetik der Metadiskursivität: Zum postmodernen Prosa-, Film- und Dramenwerk von Vladimir Sorokin*, 65–73. Munich: Sagner.

————. 2004a. "Novyi Sorokin?" [Russian: "A New Sorokin?"]. In Renate Hansen-Kokoruš, Angela Richter (eds.). *Mundus narratus: Festschrift für Dagmar Burkhart zum 65. Geburtstag*, 177–82. Frankfurt/Main et al.: Lang.

————. 2004b. "Vladimir Sorokin. Put´ Bro" [Russian: "Vladimir Sorokin. *Bro's Path*"]. *Kriticheskaia massa* 4. http://magazines.russ.ru/km/2004/4/smi34-pr.html, accessed January 7, 2019.

————. 2018. "Oskorbliaiushchaia nevinnost´" [Russian: "Offensive Innocence," reprint of Smirnov 1995 with a postscript, pp. 62–3]. Evgenii Dobrenko, Il´ia Kalinin, Mark Lipovetskii (eds.). *"Eto prosto bukvy na bumage …" Vladimir Sorokin: posle literatury*, 51–63. Moscow: Novoe literaturnoe obozrenie.

Smirnova, Marina V. 2012. "Dve Mariny (po romanu V. Sorokina *Tridtsataia liubov′ Mariny*)" [Russian: "The Two Marinas (on Vladimir Sorokin's Novel *Marina's Thirtieth Love*)"]. *Vestnik Permskogo universiteta: Rossiiskaia i zarubezhnaia filolofiia* 1 (17): 227–31.

Smith, Terry. 2012. "One and Three Ideas: Conceptualism Before, During, and After Conceptual Art." In Boris Groys (ed.). *Moscow Symposium: Conceptualism Revisited*, 42–72. Berlin: Sternberg Press.

Sokolov, Boris. 2005. *Moia kniga o Vladimire Sorokine* [Russian: *My Book on Vladimir Sorokin*]. Moscow: AIRO-XXI, Probel-2000.

———. 2006. "Staraia novaia Rus′" [Russian: "Old New Russia"]. *APN* November 1. http://www.apn.ru/publications/article10805.htm, accessed January 7, 2019.

———. 2015. "Novaia geopolitika Vladimira Sorokina" [Russian: "Vladimir Sorokin's New Geopolitics"]. *Zbornik Matice Srpske za Slavistiku* 87: 251–64.

———. 2017. "Epitafiia knige" [Russian: "An Epitaph for the Book"]. *Den′* 38/39 (March 2017). https://www.srkn.ru/criticism/epitafiya-knige.html, accessed January 7, 2019.

Stelleman, Jenny. 2016. "Essen und Nationalität in Sorokins *Hochzeitsreise*" [German: "Food and Nationality in Sorokin's *The Postnuptial Journey*"]. *Pegasus Oost-Europese Studies* 26: 519–35.

Stewart, Neil. 2006. "'Ästhetik des Widerlichen' und 'Folterkammer des Wortes': Die russische Konzeptkunst von Vladimir Sorokin" [German: "'Aesthetics of Disgust' and 'Torture Chamber of the Word'"]. In Jochen Fritz, Neil Stewart (eds.). *Das schlechte Gewissen der Moderne: Kulturtheorie und Gewaltdarstellung in Literatur und Film nach 1968*, 231–72. Cologne et al.: Böhlau.

Strätling, Susanne. 2000. "Hypermnemonik: Puškin-Bilder bei Dovlatov, Bitov und Sorokin" [German: "Hypermnemonics: Images of Pushkin in Dovlatov, Bitov, and Sorokin"]. *Wiener Slawistischer Almanach* 45: 151–74.

Stryjakowska, Anna. 2016. "Transgresyjny wymiar miłości cielesnej w powieści *Goluboe salo* Władimira Sorokina" [Polish: "The Transgressive Dimension of Carnal Love in the Novel *Blue Lard* by Vladimir Sorokin"]. *Świat tekstów: Rocznik Słupski* 14: 105–16.

———. 2017a. "Dramat *Hochzeitsreise* Władimira Sorokina na tle polityki pamięci Federacji Rosyjskiej" [Polish: "Vladimir Sorokin's Play *Hochzeitsreise* against the Backdrop of the Memory Politics of the Russian Federation"]. In Dominika Gortych, Łukasz Skoczylas (eds.). *Implanty pamięci społecznej: teoria i przykłady*, 95–103. Poznań: Wydawnictwo Rys.

<Stryjakowska> Stryjakovska, Anna. 2017b. "Kanonicheskii potentsial tvorchestva Vladimira Sorokina" [Russian: "The Canonical Potential of Vladimir Sorokin's Oeuvre"]. In <Katarzyna Jastrzembska> Katazhyna Jastshembskaia, Magdalena <Ochniak> Okhniak, <Ewelina Piliarczyk> Evelina Piliarchik (eds.). *Problemy kanonichnosti russkoi literatury: teoriia, evoliutsiia, perevod*, 163–73. Cracow: scriptum.

Surkov, Pavel. 2017. "Novyi roman Vladimira Sorokina: Gori, Vavilon!" [Russian: "Vladimir Sorokin's New Novel: Burn, Babylon!"]. *Sobesednik* May 21. https://sobesednik.ru/kultura-i-tv/20170321-novyy-roman-vladimira-sorokina-gori-vavilon, accessed January 7, 2019.

Swick, Tom. 1988. "Vladimir Sorokin, The Queue." *The New York Times* October 2: Book Reviews 26.

Talvet, Juri. 2003. "Vladimir Sorokin. Norma, Book Review." http://www.srkn.ru/criticism/talvet.shtml, accessed January 7, 2019.

Tamruchi, Natalia. 1995. *Moscow Conceptualism: 1970–1990*. Roseville: Craftsman House.

Tchouboukov-Pianca, Florence. 1995. *Die Konzeptualisierung der Graphomanie in der russischsprachigen postmodernen Literatur* [German: *The Conceptualization of Graphomania in Russian-Language Postmodern Literature*]. Munich: Sagner.

<Siniavskii, Andrei> Tertz, Abram. 1960. *On Socialist Realism*. Trans. George Dennis. New York: Pantheon.

———. <Terts, Abram>. 1967. *Fantasticheskie povesti. Sud idet. Liubimov. Chto takoe sotsialisticheskii realizm* [Russian: *Fantastic Short Novels. The Trial Begins. Liubimov. What Is Socialist Realism?*], 401–46. Washington, D.C.: Inter-Language Literary Associates.

<Tolstoi, Lev N.> Tolstoï, Lyof [sic] N. 1899. *Master and Man. The Kreutzer Sonata. Dramas.* No trans. New York: Thomas Y. Crowell & Co.

———. 1954. "Khoziain i rabotnik" [Russian: "Master and Servant"]. *Polnoe sobranie sochinenii*, vol. 29, 3–46. Moscow: Gosudarstvennoe izdatel´stvo khudozhestvennoi literatury.

Tretner, Andreas. 2007. "Komjagas Klöten: *Der Tag des Opritschniks* aus der Nahsicht des Übersetzers" [German: "Komiaga's Bollocks: *Day of the Oprichnik* from the Close Perspective of the Translator"]. *kultura* 2: 12–4.

Trotman, Theodore O. 2017. *Mythopoetics of Post-Soviet Literary Fiction: Viktor Pelevin and Vladimir Sorokin*. PhD dissertation. University of Chicago.

Tupitsyn, Viktor. 1998. *Kommunal´nyi (post)modernizm: russkoe iskusstvo vtoroi poloviny XX veka* [Russian: *Communal (Post-)Modernism: The Russian Art of the Second Half of the Twentieth Century*]. Moscow: Ad Marginem.

Uffelmann, Dirk. 2000. "Dagmar Burkhart (Hg.), Poetik der Metadiskursivität. Zum postmodernen Prosa-, Film- und Dramenwerk von Vladimir Sorokin, München 1999" [German: "Dagmar Burkhart (ed.). *Poetics of Metadiscursivity: On Vladimir Sorokin's Postmodern Prose, Filmic, and Dramatic Oeuvre*, Munich 1999"]. *Wiener Slawistischer Almanach* 45: 279–82.

———. 2003. "Marinä Himmelfahrt und Liquidierung: Erniedrigung und Erhöhung in Sorokins Roman *Tridcataja ljubov´ Mariny*" [German: "Marina's Ascension and Extinction: Humiliation and Elevation in Sorokin's Novel *Marina's Thirtieth Love*"]. *Wiener Slawistischer Almanach* 51: 289–333.

———. 2006. "Lëd tronulsia [The Ice Has Broken]: The Overlapping Periods in Vladimir Sorokin's Work from the Materialization of Metaphors to Fantastic Substantialism." In Ingunn Lunde, Tine Roesen (eds.). *Landslide of the Norm: Language Culture in Post-Soviet Russia*, 100–25. Bergen: University of Bergen. Also online: http://boap.uib.no/books/sb/catalog/view/3/5/113-1, accessed January 7, 2019.

———. 2009. "The Compliance with and Imposition of Social and Linguistic Norms in Sorokin's *Norma* and *Den´ oprichnika*." In Ingunn Lunde, Martin Paulsen (eds.). *From Poets to Padonki: Linguistic Authority and Norm Negotiation in Modern Russian Culture*, 143–67. Bergen: University of Bergen. Also online: http://boap.uib.no/books/sb/catalog/view/8/7/134-1, accessed January 7, 2019.

_____. 2010. *Der erniedrigte Christus—Metaphern und Metonymien in der russischen Kultur und Literatur* [German: *The Humiliated Christ: Metaphors and Metonymies in Russian Culture and Literature*]. Cologne: Böhlau.

_____. 2012a. "Spiel und Ernst in der intertextuellen Sinnkonstitution von Vladimir Sorokins *Metel' [Der Schneesturm]*" [German: "Play and Austerity in the Intertextual Construction of Meaning in Vladimir Sorokin's *The Blizzard*"]. *Poetica* 44.3/4: 421–41.

_____. 2012b. "Efterord" [Danish: "Afterword"]. Trans. Tine Roesen. In Vladimir Sorokin: *Snestormen*, 155–59. Copenhagen: Vandkunsten.

_____. 2013a. "Sorokins Schmalz oder Die Küche des Konzeptualismus" [German: "Sorokin's Lard Or The Cuisine of Conceptualism"]. In Norbert Franz (ed.). *Russische Küche und kulturelle Identität*, 229–52. Potsdam: Universitätsverlag Potsdam.

_____. 2013b. "The Chinese Future of Russian Literature: 'Bad Writing' in Sorokin's Oeuvre." In Tine Roesen, Dirk Uffelmann (eds.). *Vladimir Sorokin's Languages*, 170–93. Bergen: University of Bergen. Also online: http://boap.uib.no/books/sb/catalog/view/9/8/168-1, accessed January 7, 2019.

_____. 2017. "Eurasia in the Retrofuture: Dugin's 'tellurokratiia,' Sorokin's *Telluriia*, and the Benefits of Literary Analysis for Political Theory." *Die Welt der Slaven* 62.2: 360–84.

Umbrashko, Dmitrii B. 2004. *Roman V. G. Sorokina* Goluboe salo *kak gipertekst* [Russian: *Vladimir Sorokin's Novel* Blue Lard *as a Hypertext*]. PhD dissertation. Novosibirsk State Pedagogical University.

Uznayvse! 2018. "Vladimir Sorokin, biografiia, novosti, foto" [Russian: "Vladimir Sorokin, Biography, News, and Photos"]. *Uznayvse*. https://uznayvse.ru/znamenitosti/biografi-ya-vladimir-sorokin.html, accessed January 7, 2019.

Vail´, Petr. 1994. "Sorokin's Sacrilege." Trans. Catherine A. Fitzpatrick. *Grand Street Magazine* 48: 254–5.

_____. 1995. "Konservator Sorokin v kontse veka" [Russian: "The Conservative Sorokin at the End of the Century"]. *Literaturnaia Gazeta* February 1: 4.

Van Baak, Joost. 2009. "Sorokin's *Roman*: A Postmodernist Attempts the Destruction of the Domus." In Joost van Baak. *The House in Russian Literature: A Mythopoetic Exploration*, 459–70. Amsterdam, New York: Rodopi.

Vassilieva, Ekaterina. 2014. *Das Motiv des Straflagers in der russischen Literatur der Postmoderne: Dovlatov, Sorokin, Makanin* [German: *The Motif of the Concentration Camp in Postmodern Russian Literature: Dovlatov, Sorokin, and Makanin*]. Munich et al.: Sagner.

Vishevsky, Anatoly. 1998. "The Other among Us: Homosexuality in Recent Russian Literature." *Slavic and East European Journal* 42.4: 723–9.

Vishnevskaia, Iuliia. 1985. "Giperrealizm povsednevnoi zhizni" [Russian: "The Hyperrealism of Everyday Life"]. *Sintaksis* 14: 175–8.

Vitukhnovskaia, Alina. 2007. "Strashnaia kniga: retsenziia na knigu Vladimira Sorokina *Den´ oprichnika*" [Russian: "Terrifying Book: Review of Vladimir Sorokin's *Day of the Oprichnik*"]. *Nazlobu* May 4. http://www.nazlobu.ru/publications/article1693.htm, accessed March 31, 2009.

"Vladimir Sorokin." 2006. "Vladimir Sorokin." *Tijdschrift voor Slavische Literatuur* 45: 1–63.

Vladiv-Glover, Slobodanka. 1999a. "Heterogeneity and the Russian Post-Avant-Garde: The Excremental Poetics of Vladimir Sorokin." In Mikhail Epstein, Alexander Genis, Slobodanka Vladiv-Glover (eds.). *Russian Postmodernism: New Perspectives on Post-Soviet Culture,* 269–98. Oxford, New York: Berghahn.

———. 1999b. "Vladimir Sorokin's Post-Avant-Garde Prose and Kant's Analytic of the Sublime." In Dagmar Burkhart (ed.). *Poetik der Metadiskursivität: Zum postmodernen Prosa-, Film- und Dramenwerk von Vladimir Sorokin,* 21–35. Munich: Sagner.

Vojvodić, Jasmina. 2012. *Tri tipa ruskog postmodernizma* [Croatian: *Three Types of Russian Postmodernism*]. Zagreb: Disput.

Wawrzyńczak, Aleksander. 2007. "Zbrodnia na literaturze: Powieść *Roman* Władimira Sorokina" [Polish: "Crime against Literature: The Novel *A Novel* by Vladimir Sorokin"]. In Anna Gildner, Magdalena Ochniak, Halina Waszkielewicz (eds.). *Postmodernizm rosyjski i jego antycypacje,* 185–98. Cracow: Collegium Columbinum.

Wehr, Norbert. 2000. "Sorokin ist Sorokin ist Sorokin ist …" [German: "Sorokin Is Sorokin Is Sorokin Is …"]. *Schreibheft.* www.schreibheft.de/fileadmin/website/daten/pdf/Norbert_Wehr__Sorokin_ist_Sorokin_ist_Sorokin_ist_….pdf, accessed January 7, 2019.

Weststeijn, Willem G. 1995. "De roman van het einde en het einde van de roman: *Roman* en *Norma* van Vladimir Sorokin" [Dutch: "The Novel of the End and the End of the Novel: *A Novel* and *The Norm* by Vladimir Sorokin"]. *Armada: Tijdschrift voor wereldliteratuur* 1.1: 37–46.

Wiedling, Thomas. 1999. "Essen bei Vladimir Sorokin" [German: "Food in Vladimir Sorokin"]. In Dagmar Burkhart (ed.). *Poetik der Metadiskursivität: Zum postmodernen Prosa-, Film- und Dramenwerk von Vladimir Sorokin,* 151–60. Munich: Sagner.

Witte, Georg. 1989. *Appell—Spiel—Ritual: Textpraktiken in der russischen Literatur der sechziger bis achtziger Jahre* [German: *Appeal—Play—Ritual: Text Practices in Russian Literature, 1960s to 1980s*]. Wiesbaden: Harrassowitz.

Wołodźko-Butkiewicz, Alicja. 2003. "Grabarz literatury rosyjskiej? (spory wokół Władimira Sorokina)" [Polish: "Gravedigger of Russian Literature? (The Debates about Vladimir Sorokin)"]. *Przegląd Rusycystyczny* 3: 71–84.

———. 2011. "Symbolika zamieci w literaturze rosyjskiej—od Puszkina do Sorokina" [Polish: "The Symbol of the Blizzard in Russian Literature—from Pushkin to Sorokin"]. *Przegląd Humanistyczny* 4: 3–13.

Wood, Tony. 2011. "Howling Soviet Monsters." *London Review of Books* June 30: 32–3.

Yurchak, Alexei. 2006. *Everything Was Forever, Until It Was No More: The Last Soviet Generation.* Princeton (NJ): Princeton University Press.

Zakhar'in, Dmitrii 1999. "*Onania* im Spiegel der russischen Postmoderne" [German: "*Onania* in the Mirror of Russian Postmodernism"]. In Dagmar Burkhart (ed.). *Poetik der Metadiskursivität: Zum postmodernen Prosa-, Film- und Dramenwerk von Vladimir Sorokin,* 167–77. Munich: Sagner.

Zdravomyslova, Elena. 2003. "The Café Saigon *Tusovka*: One Segment of the Informal-Public Sphere of Late-Soviet Society." In Robin Humphrey, Robert Miller, Elena Zdravomyslova (eds.). *Biographical Research in Eastern Europe: Altered Lives and Broken Biographies*, 141–77. Aldershot, Burlington (VT): Ashgate.

Zdravomyslova, Elena; Voronkov, Viktor. 2002. "The Informal Public in Soviet Society: Double Morality at Work." *Social Research* 69.1: 49–69.

Zolotonosov, Mikhail. 1999. "Vladimir Sorokin. Goluboe salo: roman" [Russian: "Vladimir Sorokin. *Blue Lard: A Novel*"]. *Novaia russkaia kniga* 1: 18–9.

_____. 2008. "Mistifikatsiia Vladimira Sorokina" [Russian: "Vladimir Sorokin's Mystification"]. *Openspace* June 11. www.openspace.ru/literature/events/details/1482, accessed August 27, 2018.

Zygar, Mikhail V. 2016. *All the Kremlin's Men: Inside the Court of Vladimir Putin*. New York: Public Affairs.

24smi. 2017. "Vladimir Sorokin." *24smi*. http://24smi.org/celebrity/5129-vladimir-sorokin.html, accessed January 7, 2019.

Index

9 781644 692851